REMINISCENCES

OF

SWAMI BRAHMANANDA

The Mind-born Son of Sri Ramakrishna

An English translation of
Brahmananda Leelakatha
written in Bengali by
Brahmachari Akshayachaitanya

Translated by

Swami Bhaskarananda

Published by
The President
Sri Ramakrishna Math
Mylapore, Chennai-4

I-2M 3C-12-2006
ISBN 81-7823-422-X

Printed in India at
Sri Ramakrishna Math Printing Press
Mylapore, Chennai-4

DEDICATION

Humbly dedicated to
Sri Ramakrishna,
the personification of religious harmony,
whose mind-born son was
Swami Brahmananda

PUBLISHER'S NOTE

To reminisce is to simply recall. But when one reminisces about a holy person, about a spiritual giant of Swami Brahmananda's stature, it becomes an act of meditation. It, then, is a part of one's *sadhana*. The Hindu scriptures term it as *leela chintana* or contemplation on the Divine Play of a holy personality. Swami Brahmananda, a direct disciple of Sri Ramakrishna and the first President of the Ramakrishna Order, has left behind a rich legacy of how to live a spiritually vibrant life. His lofty state of mind, practical wisdom and a deep love and sympathy for all those who came in touch with him, is a legend in the Ramakrishna tradition.

This book is a translation from Bengali. *Brahmananda Leelakatha*, as the original book is titled, was written by Brahmachari Akshaya-chaitanya, a disciple of Holy Mother Sri Sarada Devi.

Swami Bhaskarananda, the translator of the present volume, has taken great pains to provide a faithful and clear translation, with copious explanatory notes and a glossary. He has also added a short biographical sketch of Swami Brahmananda which has enhanced its value. The translator is the Minister-in-charge of Vedanta Society of Western Washington, Seattle, USA.

This book fulfills a long-felt need and we hope, it will serve as a manual of practical spirituality. Nothing could be of greater help in the contemporary world where the need for such books is keenly felt but is rarely met.

Swami Brahmananda Jayanti
20.1.2007.

— *Sri Ramakrishna Math*
Chennai

PREFACE

The year 1963 was a very important year for the Rama-krishna Order. During that year the birth-centenaries of both Swami Vivekananda and Swami Brahmananda were celebrated in the branches of the Order, as well in as many other places all over the world. I was then a trainee (brahma-chari) at the Probationers' Training Centre at the headquar-ters of the Ramakrishna Order in Belur Math. Many books and articles on the lives of these two great swamis were written and published that year. One of them was the book *Brahmananda Leelakatha* written in Bengali on the extraor-dinary, saintly life of Swami Brahmananda by Brahmachari Akshayachaitanya, a disciple of the Holy Mother Sri Sarada Devi. Every trainee at the Probationers' Training Centre was given a copy of that book by Swami Nirvanananda, who later became the Vice-President of the Order.

Thus I got a copy of the book and was charmed and in-spired by reading it. Nearly twelve years later, in 1974, I was sent to the Vedanta Centre in Seattle, USA, as an as-sistant to Swami Vividishananda. When I came to Seattle I brought the book along with me. Whenever I read it, I felt that it would be wonderful if I could translate this in-spiring book into English for the benefit of those who did not know Bengali. But I could not do it without written permission from its publisher. I mentioned this to Swami Swahananda, head of the Vedanta Society of Southern Cal-ifornia in Hollywood. During a visit to India nearly a year ago, Swami Swahananda very kindly obtained that permis-sion from the publisher.

At first I thought of publishing the book in the United States. Accordingly I used the language and spelling suitable for American readers. But Swami Chetanananda, head of the Vedanta Society of St. Louis, suggested that the book should be published in India, because there would be a much larger number of readers there. That's why I rewrote the book to suit the Indian readership. The rewritten version of the book follows the British way of spelling. At the same time, I provided copious explanatory notes and a glossary for easy understanding by both Indian and Western readers.

In the publication of this book the following persons have helped immensely and I acknowledge their loving assistance with deep gratitude.

• The Secretary, Sarada Mandir, Khardah, for permission to translate the book *Brahmananda Leelakatha* written in Bengali by the late Brahmachari Akshayachaitanya.

• Swami Gautamananda, President, Sri Ramakrishna Math, Mylapore, Chennai, India, for offering to publish the book through their publication department.

• Devra A. Freedman for her help in proofreading and editing.

• Mrs. Mira Guerquin for painting the beautiful illustration of Swami Brahmananda for the front cover.

• Charles Mathias for creating a line drawing of Swami Brahmananda.

• Charles S. Wirth and Allen R. Freedman for providing assistance with the typesetting and printing of the manuscript.

I shall consider my labour well rewarded if the book proves to be helpful to the readers.

Swami Bhaskarananda
June 2006

List of Illustrations

TABLE OF CONTENTS

A Short Biography of
Swami Brahmananda

by Swami Bhaskarananda

Sri Ramakrishna divided the devotees of God into two groups—*ishwarakotis* and *jivakotis*. Divine incarnations like Sri Chaitanya and their close companions (apostles) are ishwarakotis. They are not born compelled by the force of prarabdha karma. They are born free. Unflinching faith in God is natural for them. Nothing in the world can ever tarnish them. The ishwarakotis alone can experience *mahabhava*, the kind of high spiritual ecstasy that was experienced by spiritually exalted souls like Sri Chaitanya and Prahlada. Their natural-born love of God makes them oblivious even of their own bodies. Ishwarakotis are also called *nitya-muktas* (ever free) and *adhikarika purushas*. Jivakotis are spiritual aspirants who through intense spiritual practice become spiritually illumined in this life. After their death, they never return to earth for the good of humanity. On the other hand, out of compassion ishwarakotis reincarnate on earth to spiritually uplift humanity.

Sri Ramakrishna said that among his disciples, six were ishwarakotis—highly exalted spiritual souls born to assist Sri Ramakrishna in propagating his spiritual message to humanity. Those disciples were Swami Vivekananda, Swami Brahmananda, Swami Yogananda, Swami Premananda, Swami Niranjanananda and Purna Chandra Ghosh.

Sri Ramakrishna declared Swami Vivekananda to be of the highest spiritual calibre among his ishwarakoti disciples. But Swami Brahmananda also held a very high and special position among them. Sri Ramakrishna looked upon him as his "mind-born son" or manasa-putra.

Swami Brahmananda's premonastic name was Rakhal. A few days before he came to see Sri Ramakrishna at the Dakshineswar Temple, Sri Ramakrishna had a spiritual vision. He described his vision as follows: "The Divine Mother appeared before me and placing a boy on my lap said, 'This is your son.' Hearing that I shuddered out of panic and said, 'What are you saying? How is it ever possible for me to have a son?' Then She smiled and said, 'He is not your son in the worldly sense. He is your all-renouncing manasa-putra (mind-born son).' Hearing that I felt relieved. A few days later Rakhal came to see me. As soon as I saw him I recognized him to be the boy I had seen in my vision."

A few days later Sri Ramakrishna had another spiritual vision about Rakhal. In that vision he saw a large hundred-petalled lotus floating on the river Ganga. A boy resembling Rakhal was holding young Sri Krishna's hand and dancing on that lotus. Immediately after that vision, Rakhal came to see Sri Ramakrishna. This is how Sri Ramakrishna knew that Rakhal had been a companion of Sri Krishna in his previous incarnation.

Rakhal's full name was Rakhal Chandra Ghosh. He was born in an aristocratic family on January 21, 1863, in Shikra-Kulin-Gram, a village in the northern part of the 24-Parganas district of Bengal. His father, Ananda Mohan Ghosh, (also known as Haran Chandra Ghosh) was a very prosperous zamindar (landlord). Rakhal's mother died when he was five. His father remarried and Rakhal's stepmother, Hemangini, lovingly brought him up.

While a student in elementary school, Rakhal was very

much liked by his classmates and teachers for his gentle and loving nature. He excelled in his studies and was very good at sports, particularly wrestling. He was naturally endowed with the quality of leadership and easily became the leader of the students in his class. Even at that young age he displayed an interest in gardening inherited from his father, which he retained throughout his life.

As he grew up, his natural devotion for God gradually manifested. He sometimes made clay images of Mother Kali, and with his friends playfully worshipped Her. This worship was one of his favorite games.

In addition to all this, he had keen interest in music and was very fond of singing devotional songs. Just by hearing the songs on Sri Krishna or Mother Kali sung by others, he learned to sing them well. He learned to sing many songs on Mother Kali composed by the saint Ramprasad and also some songs from Krishna-lila. He would sometimes go with his friends to a *darga* (tomb) of a Muslim saint one mile from his home, and together they would sing the songs on Mother Kali there. While singing he would become completely absorbed in it out of devotion. He would become oblivious of the world around him.

In 1875, when he was twelve years old, his father took him to his grandparents' (stepmother's parents') home on Varanasi Ghosh Street in the Kansaripara neighbourhood of Calcutta to get an English education. He was to stay there and study in a nearby school called The Training Academy. Around this time he met Narendranath Dutta, the future Swami Vivekananda. Narendra lived in the contiguous neighbourhood called Simulia. Narendra was only nine days older than Rakhal, but was three or four classes ahead of him in school.

Narendra studied in another school named the Metropolitan Institution. Within a short time they became fast friends.

As they grew older Rakhal was influenced by Narendra to often attend the meetings of the reformist Brahmo Samaj church. The Brahmo Samaj encouraged only the adoration and worship of Saguna Nirakara Brahman (God without form but endowed with attributes). It did not believe in the worship of God in images. Anyone willing to become a member of the Brahmo Samaj had to take a vow to worship only the formless Saguna Brahman. Narendra took that vow and Rakhal followed his example.

There was a wrestling club on Mashjidbari Street owned by one Ambikacharan Guha. Narendra and Rakhal regularly went there for physical exercise. Developing a healthy and strong body through exercising regularly, practicing celibacy, and regularly attending the prayer meetings of the Brahmo Samaj became the main points of interest to Rakhal. To him studying in school became of secondary importance.

Mahendranath Dutta, Narendra's younger brother, also came to know Rakhal quite well. According to his description:

> In our younger days we noticed that Rakhal was generally fond of fun, frolic and pranks. But occasionally he would become very quiet and indrawn. He would then seem to be oblivious of what was happening around him. After a while, he would become normal again. While thinking of anything intently, he would often blink his eyes rapidly. We used to think that he was not that smart, that's why he blinked his eyes when he was unable to understand what had been said to him. We really thought that he was somewhat dim-witted and wouldn't be able to accomplish much in his life. As we were young boys we couldn't understand what was going on inside his mind. We only judged him superficially. At that time we didn't understand

that Rakhal was an adept in meditation from his very birth. It was his nature to be absorbed in meditation; that's what made him so different from us.

As Rakhal's interest in his studies declined, his father became worried. In all possible ways he tried to persuade him to be more attentive to his studies, but nothing succeeded. His relatives thought that if Rakhal, who was only eighteen years old at that time, could be persuaded to marry he would develop a keener sense of responsibility and become more enthusiastic about his studies. Marriage at a relatively young age was not uncommon in those days, particularly in rich families of Bengal. Accordingly, in 1881 Rakhal was married to a girl named Bishweshari, who was the daughter of the late Dr. Bhuban Mohan Mitra of Konnagar. She was only eleven years old at that time.

Bishweshwari's eldest brother and guardian, Manomohan Mitra, was a devotee of Sri Ramakrishna. Her mother was also very much devoted to him. Mahendranath Dutta has written in his book *Ajatashatru Srimat Swami Brahmananda Maharajer Anudhyan* that Manomohan Mitra bought a house in the Simulia neighbourhood of Calcutta and started living there. It has not been mentioned in the book in which year he changed his residence from Konnagar to Calcutta. Swami Gambhirananda writes in his book *Sri Ramakrishna Bhakta-malika* that after his marriage, Rakhal was brought by Manomohan to Sri Ramakrishna at the Dakshineswar Kali Temple one day on their way back to Calcutta from Konnagar. Manomohan wanted his younger sister's husband to be blessed by Sri Ramakrishna. And this visit to Sri Ramakrishna was the turning point in Rakhal's life.

This is the first time Sri Ramakrishna saw his manasa-putra in real life after his above-mentioned spiritual visions. Sri Ramakrishna did not tell them anything about his visions. He only said to Manomohan about Rakhal, "He has great spiritual potential." Then he lovingly asked Rakhal, "What's your name?"

He replied, "My name is Rakhal Chandra Ghosh."

Hearing that Sri Ramakrishna went into spiritual ecstasy and exclaimed, "Yes, indeed you are Rakhal—the cowherd playmate of Sri Krishna in Vrindaban!" Then regaining his normal state of mind, he lovingly said to Rakhal, "Please come and see me again."

Rakhal was overwhelmed by Sri Ramakrishna's spiritual presence and captivated by his love. He felt great attraction toward him, and at the earliest opportunity wanted to come and visit him again. Shortly after the first visit, he came one day to see Sri Ramakrishna after school. As soon as he arrived, Sri Ramakrishna asked him, "Why have you delayed so much in coming to see me?" Rakhal didn't reply. His mind was then transported to a high level of spiritual consciousness. In that mental state he felt that Sri Ramakrishna was his loving mother and he was his eternal child. Even though Rakhal was then a young man, Sri Ramakrishna's spiritual eyes saw him as a little boy. Thus a wonderful spiritual relationship developed between Rakhal and Sri Ramakrishna.

Thereafter Rakhal visited Sri Ramakrishna quite frequently, sometimes staying with him for a few days at the Dakshineswar Kali Temple. In the words of Sri Ramakrishna as mentioned in *Sri Sri Ramakrishna Lilaprasanga:*

Rakhal at that time was in such a spiritual mood that he behaved like a three or four year old boy. He looked upon me as his mother. Every now and then he would come running to me and sit on my lap… He wanted to stay with me and wouldn't like to go home. Lest his father be displeased and not allow him to come to see me I would somehow persuade Rakhal to go home.

His father was a zamindar and had a lot of money. But he was quite miserly. At first he tried hard not to allow his son to come and visit me. Then he noticed that many wealthy and highly educated men would come to see me. Seeing that he wouldn't object anymore to his son's coming here. Sometimes looking for his son he visited here as well. Then for the sake of Rakhal I made him well pleased through hospitality.

No objection was ever raised by Rakhal's in-laws' family about his coming here, because Manomohan's mother, wife and sisters used to come and visit me. Sometime after Rakhal's coming here, Manomohan's mother brought Rakhal's young wife to see me. Wondering if Rakhal's love and devotion for God would be affected by his wife's company I asked her to come close to me. Then I examined her thoroughly from head to foot and determined that she was a devi-shakti—a girl endowed with divine propensities. Thus I came to know that she wouldn't ever be an obstacle to her husband's spiritual life. Being satisfied thus, I sent her to the Nahabat (where the Holy Mother Sri Sarada Devi lived) with the request that she (the Holy Mother) greet her daughter-in-law (Rakhal's wife) by giving her the traditional gift of money.

It is hard to describe how Rakhal would become overwhelmed with the spiritual attitude of a child in my presence. Anyone who saw that attitude of Rakhal became struck with wonder. I would also enter into an ecstatic spiritual mood then and treat him like a child. I would feed him *khir* (doughy condensed milk) and cream, and also played with him. Sometimes I would carry him on my shoulders. He felt no embarrassment when I did that. But I said that when he became older and would start living with his wife he would lose his childlike spiritual attitude.

In this connection let me quote the following paragraphs from the *Sri Sri Ramakrishna Kathamrita:*

> The Master (Sri Ramakrishna) is seated on the small couch in his room. Immersed in spiritual ecstasy, he is looking at Rakhal and gradually becoming overpowered by an intense feeling of motherly affection toward him. Due to this emotion the Master has goose bumps all over his body. Is he, like Yashoda, now seeing Rakhal as his Gopala? Within a short while the Master enters into a deep Samadhi.

> Being overwhelmed by a motherly feeling the Master gazes at Rakhal and lovingly uttering the word 'Govinda' a few times, enters into Samadhi.

Similar incidents took place frequently. As far as we know, for nearly three years Sri Ramakrishna played the role of a mother to Rakhal.

Sri Ramakrishna at the very first sight could know the past, present and future of a person. In one place in the *Sri Sri Ramakrishna Kathamrita* we find Sri Ramakrishna asking Mahendranath Gupta (also known as Master Mahashay), "Do I know your past, present and future?" Mahendra replies, "Yes sir, you do."

When he saw Rakhal for the first time he knew by his penetrating insight all about him. He knew that he had been born to assist him in his spiritual ministry by playing a very special role.

Sri Ramakrishna also knew that the idea of Sakara Brahman (God endowed with form) was more suitable for Rakhal's mental make-up and not Nirakara Brahman (formless

God). Inspired by the example of Sri Ramakrishna, Rakhal felt more comfortable adoring and worshipping God in images. He also started saluting the different gods and goddesses (devas and devis) of traditional Hinduism, defying the rules of the Brahmo Samaj.

A few months after Rakhal's meeting with Sri Ramakrishna, Narendra also started visiting him at Dakshineswar. When Narendra saw Rakhal saluting the images of deities he reprimanded him, calling him a hypocrite, because he had broken the vow taken at the Brahmo Samaj. This embarrassed the sensitive and softhearted Rakhal so much that he was hesitant to face Narendra after that.

Sri Ramakrishna came to know this and calling Narendra aside said to him, "Don't blame Rakhal anymore for worshipping God in images. When he sees you he almost freezes out of embarrassment. What can he do! He has now gained faith in God with form. Some have to go through this stage before becoming ready for accepting God without form." Sri Ramakrishna by that time had also come to know that unlike Rakhal, Narendra was temperamentally fit for accepting the formless aspect of God.

To Sri Ramakrishna, Rakhal was his mind-born son—the veritable manifestation of Lord Narayana in human form. That's why he treated him differently from the other devotees. The other devotees would sit on the floor in front of Sri Ramakrishna, but Rakhal would sit next to Sri Ramakrishna on his cot. He would sleep on a camp cot in Sri Ramakrishna's room, while the other devotees would sleep on mats spread out on the floor. Rakhal was fond of khichuri (a dish made of rice and lentils). The Holy Mother Sarada Devi used to cook this special dish for him, while for others she would prepare rice or chapatis.

Due to his motherly attitude toward Rakhal, Sri Ramakrishna felt hurt when others scolded Rakhal or asked him
to do chores. Sri Ramakrishna would say to them, "Rakhal is
just a baby, don't find fault with him, or scold him!" He would
also tell others not to ask Rakhal to do any household chores
saying, "He is very gentle and soft-hearted. He is just a young
child. Don't ask him to do all those chores."

While visiting the temple at Dakshineswar, Rakhal got the
opportunity to see various aspects of Sri Ramakrishna's divine
personality. Rakhal was deeply impressed and inspired by seeing his intense love of the Divine Mother Kali and other deities. Aside from that, Sri Ramakrishna would always tell those
who would come to him that the purpose of human life was
God-realization. Seeing and hearing him, gradually Rakhal's
interest in studies declined further and he developed a keen
desire to renounce worldly life and its pleasures and engage
himself in spiritual practice.

Around this time he started staying with Sri Ramakrishna
at Dakshineswar and would not like to go home.

Nevertheless, Sri Ramakrishna obviously wanted Rakhal
to go through a little bit of worldly experience in order that
in the future, when Rakhal would have to play the role of a
guru, he would be able to understand the problems of worldly
people better and sympathize with them. That's why he allowed Rakhal to sometimes go home and spend time with
his wife. In *Sri Sri Ramakrishna Kathamrita* (4/13) we see
Sri Ramakrishna saying: "Now Rakhal has acquired the ability to discriminate between what's real and what's unreal. He
has come to realize what's jnana (true knowledge) and what's

ajnana (ignorance). Now I tell him, 'Go home. Sometimes you may come here and stay for a day or two.'"

As a result, a son was born to Rakhal. The son was given the name Satyacharan.

In this connection Swami Turiyananda, another great saintly disciple of Sri Ramakrishna, said, "Swami Brahmananda is an acharya—he belongs to the group of world-teachers. Unless one has all kinds of experiences, one cannot be an acharya. That's why he had to marry. Otherwise, how would he be able to give proper spiritual guidance to all kinds of people?"

After the birth of his son, a spirit of renunciation completely overwhelmed Rakhal. We find here a great similarity between Sidhartha—the future Buddha—and Rakhal. Prince Siddhartha renounced the world shortly after his son, Rahul, was born. When Sri Ramakrishna was terminally ill at the Cossipore garden house, Rakhal renounced his family for good, and along with some of his brother disciples began serving his guru, Sri Ramakrishna, with all his heart and soul. Side by side he engaged in intense spiritual practice under his guidance.

At that time Sri Ramakrishna was helping his disciples achieve the highest levels in spiritual life according to their individual spiritual capacities and temperaments. His mind-born son Rakhal was no exception.

After the passing away of Sri Ramakrishna on August 16, 1886, some of his disciples, including Rakhal, renounced the world and became sannyasins. They formed the nucleus of the future Ramakrishna Order. Thus Rakhal became Swami Brahmananda.

I would like to mention here that once Sri Ramakrishna

commented about Rakhal, "Rakhal has the intelligence of a king; he can rule a kingdom." That's why Narendra and other monastic brothers gave him the nickname "Raja" or "Maharaj."

Swami Brahmananda continued his intense spiritual practices even after the passing away of Sri Ramakrishna. While speaking of the Swami's intense spiritual practices during that period, Swami Subodhananda, another great saintly disciple of Sri Ramakrishna, said, "I was then with Maharaj for a few days. The intensity of his spiritual practice was such that he would forget even to eat or sleep! He was doing japa (chanting of the holy name of God) or dhyana (meditation) all the time. I couldn't help asking him one day, 'Why are you doing such intense spiritual practice? The Master (Sri Ramakrishna) has given you everything that's to be attained in spiritual life; why then are you going through such intense spiritual practice?'

"Hearing this, Maharaj became very grave. Then he said to me, 'Do I not have to understand the worth of the great spiritual wealth that he has given me? My spiritual practice is just to understand and appreciate that gift!'"

Once when Swami Brahmananda was in Vrindaban and performing spiritual austerities there, he met Sri Vijaykrishna Goswami, a renowned leader of the Brahmo Samaj and a great admirer of Sri Ramakrishna. Sri Vijaykrishna said to Swami Brahmananda, "The Master (Sri Ramakrishna) has given you everything. There is no reason why you should go through such intense spiritual practice."

Swami Brahmananda said, "I am only trying to gain total control over whatever spiritual visions and experiences I've had by the Master's grace."

It was Sri Ramakrishna who said, "As long as I live I learn." Swami Adbhutananda, a saint and a brother monk of Swami Brahmananda, once said to a devotee, "There is no end to sadhana (spiritual practice)."

The devotee responded, "Revered sir, doesn't sadhana end when one experiences the goal of spiritual life?"

Swami Adbhutananda replied, "No. First the spiritual aspirant has to do sadhana to experience the noumenon (nitya). Then he has to engage himself in another kind of sadhana to come down to this world of phenomena (leela). Thereafter he will be ferrying back and forth between leela and nitya—the noumenon and the phenomenon."

Swami Brahmananda also made a statement relevant to this idea. It is believed that one attains the highest goal of spiritual life through nirvikalpa samadhi—a state where the mind melts away in Nirguna Brahman (the ultimate divine Reality). That should be considered the end of one's sadhana. But Swami Brahmananda said, "Spiritual life starts after nirvikalpa samadhi." So it is no wonder why Swami Brahmananda continued doing his intense spiritual practices even after inheriting all the spiritual wealth from Sri Ramakrishna.

Sri Ramakrishna used to call a knower of God a *jnani*. But there is a knower of God who belongs to a superior class. Sri Ramakrishna would call that knower a *vijnani*. The vijnanis know and experience God more intimately than the jnanis. A vijnani knows that the divine absolute or noumenon (nitya) and the world of phenomena (leela) are only two aspects of the same ultimate divine Reality. Judging by this, Swami Brahmananda was a vijnani—a supreme knower of Brahman.

A son often inherits the characteristics of his father. Swami

Brahmananda, as Sri Ramakrishna's mind-born son, inherited some of Sri Ramakrishna's traits—both spiritual as well as physical. Reportedly, when seen from behind, Swami Brahmananda looked like Sri Ramakrishna.

Sri Ramakrishna was very witty and humourous. He had once prayed to the Divine Mother, " Mother, please don't make me a dry sadhu (monk). Please grant me a sense of humour that I'll exercise with due restraint." Humour can often be used to hurt people. Sri Ramakrishna never used humour to hurt or ridicule people. His humour gave people innocent joy as well as spiritual inspiration. Swami Brahmananda was also endowed with a similar sense of humour.

Sri Ramakrishna knew that it would not be possible for others to fathom the depth of his spirituality. The following conversation between him and Mahendranath Gupta, as recorded in *Sri Sri Ramakrishna Kathamrita,* clearly proves this point.

Sri Ramakrishna: "Well, do you find me to be like anyone else?"

Mahendra: "No, sir."

Sri Ramakrishna: "Am I like any other paramahamsa?"[1]

Mahendra: "No, sir."

Sri Ramakrishna (smiling): "Have you heard of the 'achine tree'"[2]

Mahendra: "No, sir."

Sri Ramakrishna: "There is a tree by that name. But even when seen, nobody can recognize it."

---

1. A paramahamsa is a saint who can separate the Divine Reality from this world.
2. It literally means a tree which is not recognizable.

Mahendra: "Likewise, it is not possible to recognize you. The more a man understands you, the more uplifted will he be."

In another place in the same book, Mahendra says to Sri Ramakrishna, "Outwardly you appear to be simple, but you're very deep. It's hard to understand you!"

Sri Ramakrishna was a past master in disguises. Using disguises he tried to hide from others that he was a divine incarnation. Once he said, "I am like a king travelling incognito in his kingdom. As soon as the subjects come to recognize the king, he has to return to his palace." That's what actually happened in his life. When many started recognizing him to be a divine incarnation, he departed from this world. One of his disguises was his childlike simplicity. His mind-born son, Swami Brahmananda, also was highly skilled in hiding his great spirituality. Like Sri Ramakrishna, he also used the disguise of childlike simplicity.

As stated earlier, Swami Brahmananda was an ishwarakoti; he was born free. He did not really need any spiritual practice for his own spiritual enlightenment. His spiritual practice was only to set an example to others. His mind had a natural tendency to commune with God all the time. But, to play the role of a spiritual teacher as ordained by Sri Ramakrishna, with great effort he had to bring his mind down to the worldly level. This he did by sometimes indulging in playful activities such as playing cards, going fishing, playing pranks, etc. The reminiscences about him recorded in this book will acquaint the readers with all these aspects of his somewhat enigmatic spiritual personality.

Swami Vivekananda once described Sri Ramakrishna as "love personified."

Like Sri Ramakrishna, Swami Brahmananda also was very loving and compassionate.

Sri Ramakrishna had innumerable spiritual moods. Swami Brahmananda also displayed many different spiritual moods.

Rakhal's (Swami Brahmananda's) life after his guru's passing away can be briefly summarized as follows:

He stayed at the home of Balaram Bose in Calcutta until an old, run down, haunted double-storied house was rented in the first part of October 1886, in Baranagore, to be used as a monastery. The monastery was started through the efforts of Narendra (Swami Vivekananda) and the financial help of some householder devotees of Sri Ramakrishna. Inspired by Narendra, several young men including Rakhal began living in that monastery. This monastery came to be known as "Baranagore Math."

There they engaged themselves in intense spiritual practice. The only food they could afford was just plain boiled rice, sometimes accompanied by a soup of telakucha leaves. They spent almost the entire day and night in meditation, japa, scriptural study, and singing of devotional songs.

During that period Rakhal's father came to take his son home. But Rakhal said to him, "Why do you take the trouble of coming here? I am quite happy here. Please bless me in order that you forget me and I also can forget you!"

In January 1887, he formally took sannyasa (the final vows of monastic life) along with some of his brother disciples.

In 1888 he visited Puri accompanied by the Holy Mother Sri Sarada Devi and stayed there for about two months.

At the end of 1889 he went on a pilgrimage and returned to Calcutta in the first part of 1894. By that time the monastery had been shifted from Baranagore to Alambazar. During his pilgrimage he visited Vrindaban, Varanasi, Omkarnath, Dandakaranya, Bombay, Dwaraka, Sudama-Puri, Junagarh, Girnar Hill, Ahmedabad, Pushkar, Ajmir, Hardwar, Kankhal, Meerat, Jwalamukhi, Kangra Vaijnath, Pathankot, Gujranwalla, Lahore, Montgomery, Multan, Sadhuvela, Karachi, Mount Abu and Jaipur. Of all these places he was particularly fond of Vrindaban.

On May 1, 1897, Swami Vivekananda founded the Ramakrishna Mission and Swami Brahmananda was placed in charge of the Calcutta branch of the Mission.

In 1898 he was given the responsibility of supervising the construction of the buildings of Belur Math. The task was completed with the help of Swami Vijnanananda, who had been a professional engineer in his premonastic days.

In 1901 the Ramakrishna Math was registered as a trust and Swami Vivekananda installed Swami Brahmananda as president of both the Ramakrishna Mission and the Ramakrishna Math. This position he held for almost twenty-one years until his passing away on April 10, 1922.

As President, he always sought guidance from Swami Vivekananda. But on July 4, 1902, Swami Vivekananda suddenly passed away in samadhi in Belur Math. That day Swami Brahmananda was at Balaram Bose's house in Calcutta. After getting that heart-breaking news, he immediately returned to Belur Math and embracing the body of his dearest friend and brother monk, exclaimed with tears in his eyes, "All these days it was as though I was protected by the mighty Himalayas.

Now that protection is gone!"

In the absence of Swami Vivekananda's towering personality, Swami Brahmananda initially went through some difficulties in running the Order. But he soon succeeded in overcoming them by his great spiritual strength and selfless love. In addition to this, Swami Vivekananda had implicit faith in the judgment of Swami Brahmananda. Therefore we are sure that Swami Vivekananda knew that the Order would be in safe hands during Swami Brahmananda's leadership. How much Swami Vivekananda trusted Swami Brahmananda will be very clear from the following quotation from his letter written to Sister Nivedita on February 12, 1902:

> My dear Margo,
>
> ... I recommend you none—not one—except Brahmananda. That 'old man's' (i.e. Sri Ramakrishna's) judgment never failed—mine always do. If you have to ask any advice or to get anybody to do your business Brahmananda is the only one I recommend, none else, none else. With this my conscience is clear...[3]

But after the passing away of Swami Vivekananda, some of his admirers temporarily created a commotion in the Order saying, "We shall act only according to the mandate of Swamiji (Swami Vivekananda)." Obviously, they were reluctant to accept Swami Brahmananda's leadership. Thus Swami Brahmananda initially faced difficulties in running the Order.

Around this time Swami Turiyananda, who had been working in the United States, returned to India by ship. While on the ship, he was extremely shocked to hear the sad news of the passing away of Swami Vivekananda. The news upset him so

---

3. Source: Swami Nirlepananda..

much that he made up his mind never to return to America, and immediately tossed into the sea his expensive watch and some other belongings that he had acquired as gifts in America. Almost immediately after his return to Belur Math, he decided to go to Vrindaban and live there like a traditional monk, living on madhukari (begging for food as traditional monks are expected to do) and leading a life of contemplation. But Swami Brahmananda did not allow him to go there alone. He also accompanied him.

After some days Swami Brahmananda returned to Belur Math from Vrindaban with great self-confidence and renewed spiritual vigour. Upon his return, referring to the commotion created by those confused admirers of Swamiji, he commented to some monks, "Thakur (Sri Ramakrishna) told me that all of them will become completely subdued." This is what actually happened. Those disgruntled devotees were transformed by the overwhelming spirituality of Swami Brahmananda. They submitted to him and wholeheartedly accepted him as the new leader of the Ramakrishna Order.

Attracted by his love and spirituality, many devotees started coming to the Math. Like Sri Ramakrishna, he had the ability to know the inner nature of people. Thus he could guide them in their spiritual lives according to their temperaments. A good number of idealist young men came and joined the Order as monks.

During his presidency Swami Brahmananda did a lot of travelling inside India. He visited, among other places, Bhubaneswar, Madurai, Rameswaram, Madras, Bangalore, Kanyakumari, Perembudur, Srirangam, Trichinapalli, Kanchipuram, Tirupati, Trivandram, Allahabad, Kankhal, Ayodhya, Gauhati, Kamakhya, Dacca and Mymensingh. He visited some of these places more than once.

While he was visiting Dacca, some devotees and admirers got the opportunity to discuss various problems with him relevant to the existing Hindu society and religion. During such a discussion Swami Brahmananda expressed some opinions. A few of them are recorded below:[4]

1. Hinduism is based on the Vedas; therefore it is the Sanatana Dharma (perennial religion). The Ramakrishna Mission will preach only this Sanatana Dharma. The Mission will stay away from all kinds of dogmatism and fanaticism.

2. Only all-renouncing sannyasins are fit to be acharyas and teachers of religion. We do not support the system of hereditary gurus.

3. Efforts have to be made to bring back those who have left their ancestral Hindu religion for various reasons. To do it, however, may take some time.

4. In this age women will gain a lot of freedom. As a result, mixing between men and women will become somewhat unrestricted. This will cause some degradation in society. But we have accommodation for rectification of that defect. The moral degradation that caused the decline of Buddhism in India will not happen this time.

Swami Brahmananda's method of administration was unique. He would never interfere with the work being done by those who were of proven reliability. He trusted them completely. For example, Swami Premananda was the manager of the Belur monastery and Swami Saradananda was the Secretary of the Ramakrishna Math and the Ramakrishna Mis-

_____

4. Source: Atul Chandra Chaudhury..

sion. Swami Brahmananda gave his support to them whole-heartedly and felt completely satisfied with their performance. Swami Saradananda once commented, "It was a great joy to work under Maharaj."

Once some disharmony and conflict among the monastic workers and the volunteer workers of the Ramakrishna Mission Sevashrama in Varanasi disrupted the smooth running of this important hospital centre. Swami Saradananda went to Varanasi to resolve the problem. After a thorough inquiry he felt that a certain set of rules had to be introduced to resolve the crisis. After consultation with Swami Turiyananda (who was then at the Varanasi Sevashrama), he suggested that a managing committee made up of monks and volunteers be formed. The Sevashrama would function under the guidance of the managing committee. But some felt that it was better to work under the guidance of an individual rather than a committee. However, they agreed to the formation of the managing committee on condition that Swami Brahmananda would approve of it first. Swami Brahmananda wrote to the dissenters, "Know that whatever Swami Saradananda has decided is my decision as well."

But after a year it was discovered that the instructions of Swami Saradananda had not been carried out, and the conflict and disharmony in the Varanasi Sevashrama still continued as before. Therefore, on January 20, 1921, Swami Saradananda went to Varanasi accompanied by Swami Brahmananda. Many other monks and devotees also accompanied them.

While in Varanasi, Swami Brahmananda did not discuss the problem at all. Instead, just his presence alone created a blissful spiritual atmosphere in the Sevashrama. Time passed in spiritual discussion, meditation and devotional singing. Influenced by that atmosphere, the minds of the dissenting workers, both monastic and lay, were lifted to a higher level. The problem was resolved without any kind of persuasion or controversy, and the previous suggestions given by Swami Saradananda were accepted and carried out by everyone. After the resolution of this crisis, Swami Saradananda said to Swami Brahmananda, "You should have been a king instead of a monk! You solved the problem so effortlessly! Yet, even with our combined effort, myself and Swami Turiyananda failed to resolve it."

Swami Brahmananda's mind had a natural tendency to remain absorbed in Brahman. Only through effort could he bring his mind down to perform worldly duties. That's why, even though he was the President, it was hard for him to always agree to participate in the meetings of the Trustees of the Order. The other office-bearers, therefore, had to somehow bring his mind down from its high spiritual plane to participate in solving the important, yet mundane, problems of the Order. However, as and when he could be persuaded to be present in the meetings of the Trustees, he would display his extraordinary ability to make the right decisions in solving all kinds of problems. Charmed by his deep understanding and knowledge regarding all aspects of the Order, the Trustees would unanimously accept his decisions and act accordingly.

During his presidency the Ramakrishna Order saw much growth in its number of branches and the number of young men who joined the Order as monks.

Sri Ramakrishna once said, "When Rakhal will come to know his true spiritual identity—who he really is—he will give up his body." Another time, in his absence, Sri Ramakrishna told his other disciples that Rakhal would pass away while having the vision of Sri Krishna dancing on a lotus. However,

Sri Ramakrishna asked them not to tell this to Rakhal.

On March 24, 1922, Swami Brahmananda was staying at the Balaram Mandir in Calcutta. There he had a sudden attack of cholera. With homoeopathic treatment he recovered within a few days, but shortly thereafter he developed diabetes. He was first treated by allopathic doctors and then by ayurvedic physicians. But his condition worsened day by day.

On Saturday, April 8th, 1922, he called the monks and the devotees who were present to his bedside, and one by one blessed them all. He said to them, "Have no fear; Brahman alone is real, the world is illusory." Then gradually he entered into a state of deep spiritual ecstasy. In that state he kept on repeating, "Krishna has come. Can't you all see Him? He is here! ... Make me wear my anklets; I shall dance with Krishna holding His hands! I'm the cowherd of Braja (Vrindaban)! Ah, how beautiful is my Krishna! He is standing on a lotus and asking me to go to Him. My play of this life is over!" After saying this he became silent. In this manner Sunday passed. On Monday, April 10th at 8:45 p.m., Swami Brahmananda, the mind-born child of Sri Ramakrishna, entered into mahasamadhi after finishing his divine play in this world. He was then a little over 59 years old.

Sri Ramakrishna (1836–1886)

CHAPTER I

SWAMI BRAHMANANDA—HIS LIFE SPOKE MORE ELOQUENTLY THAN HIS WORDS

Reminiscences of Dr. Ratikanta Mazumdar: "It was the year 1906. I was then working for the Indian railways and was stationed at Puri. I saw four, dignified-looking sannyasins strolling back and forth on the platform of the Puri railway station. Curious, I asked one of them why they were walking back and forth on the platform.

"He replied that they had come to receive Swami Abhedananda, who was to arrive there by the Madras Mail. I informed them that the Madras Mail was running late that day by one hour. I then invited them to come and wait inside a saloon car, which was at the railway station. After they were all seated, I came to know that the sannyasi with whom I had been talking was Swami Brahmananda. The other three were Swamis Shivananda, Akhandananda and Premananda.

"After talking to them for a while I asked, 'You all seem to be advaitins, why then do you respect the wooden image of Jagannath?'

"Swami Brahmananda replied, 'We know Lord Jagannath to be no other than Satchidananda Brahman!'

"His words immediately penetrated my heart. Having been associated with the Brahmo Samaj, my thinking had been greatly influenced by Brahmo teachings, such as God cannot have any images, and God is formless. No amount of reasoning or argument had been able to dislodge my views in the past. But just by hearing Swami Brahmananda's words once,

1

I got a new light. My mind then had a wonderful glimpse of Lord Jagannath in His unparalleled, spiritual splendour. I remained speechless. I had no desire to question or argue any more. Such was the impact of the words of a knower of Brahman on my mind!

"Swami Brahmananda then inquired of my family life. I said that my wife had died and that I was only 39 years old. He was pleased to hear that I had no desire to marry again. He then gave me some spiritual advice and later sent me a copy of *Sri Sri Ramakrishna Kathamrita*."

◊◊◊◊◊

Reminiscences of Swami Shyamananda: "The place was Belur Math and the time was late evening. Swami Brahmananda was then suffering badly from a high fever. He was restless. To get some relief, he would sometimes lie in bed for a short while and then go out to the veranda and sit in an easy chair. His sevaks (attendants) would either fan him with hand fans or softly stroke his feet and head in order to give him some relief. Hearing the loud ticking of the clock Swami Brahmananda asked, "What's the time now?"

"His attendants replied, 'It's two o'clock in the morning.'

" 'I've been giving you all a lot of trouble, haven't I?' asked Swami Brahmananda.

"I was one of the attendants there. I said, 'Not at all Maharaj! It's our great fortune that we are able to give you this little service.'

"Swami Brahmananda said, 'Look, I can give you everything that I have, but I can't give you God! The Master (Sri Ramakrishna) was capable of giving us everything. There was nothing

2

that he couldn't give. But he used to wake us up at night and ask us to meditate. He used to say: "If you spend the day in eating and the night in sleeping, then when will you realize God?"'

"The following incidents happened in 1910. Swami Brahmananda used to get up from bed every morning around three o'clock. After preparing the hubble-bubble for him to smoke, I would sit in front of him on the floor.

"He would then ask me to chant a hymn in adoration of Sri Krishna.[1] I would chant it to a melody that he had taught me. He would listen to the hymn while smoking the hubble-bubble. As he listened, his mind would become indrawn and he would lose outer consciousness. The pipe of his hubble-bubble would then drop from his mouth. But if I stopped chanting, he would come out of that spiritual state and say, 'Go on! Continue. Please don't stop!' Then I would go on chanting without stopping. On some days while listening to the chanting, he would enter into such a deep spiritual state that it would appear as though he had stopped breathing. Sometimes at that time Swami Premananda would quietly enter the room, and touching his forehead to the ground, salute Swami Brahmananda.

"Swami Brahmananda used to tell us, 'Become intoxicated by chanting the holy name of God. Your spiritual practice—whether that is meditation or japa (chanting of the holy name of God) or anything else—should be a relationship between only you and God. Don't give any importance to what other

---

1. Hari Haraye namah Krishna Mādhavāya namah
   Yadavāya Mādhavāya Keshavāya namah
   Gopāla Govinda Rāma Sri Madhushudana
   Giridhāri Gopinātha Madanamohana.

people may think or say about your spiritual practice. Don't think, *am I doing my spiritual practice right?* Just be totally intoxicated. Be completely immersed in your spiritual practice!'

"Either in the afternoon or after the Aratrikam,[2] Swami Brahmananda would arrange singing sessions with the monks of the Math (Belur monastery). He would ask us to sing the songs that were sung in Sri Ramakrishna's presence when he was alive. The Swami would tell us which songs to sing, and we would sing them one after another. Krishna Babu of Entally Archanalaya would come and sing songs composed by Mr. Devendranath Mazumdar during those sessions. Swami Brahmananda liked to hear those songs very much.

"Swami Brahmananda was charmed to hear Nama-Ramayana or Ramanama-Sankirtanam when he visited Bangalore in South India. He collected those songs and brought them along with him to Puri in May 1909. He added some extra hymns to the songs, and adding new melodies, arranged for them to be sung first at the Sashiniketan, and then at the Sri Mandir.

"Nirad Maharaj (Swami Ambikananda) had accompanied him on his trip to South India. It is Nirad Maharaj who added the melodies to the songs and taught others to sing them. Later, in 1911, many copies of the Nama-Ramayana were printed and distributed to the devotees. And the singing of the Nama-Ramayana, along with the worship of Lord Mahavira, was introduced in all the Sri Ramakrishna Ashramas."

◊◊◊◊◊

Reminiscences of Swami Varadananda: "What I am going

---

2.   Aratrikam is vespers in Hindu temples or shrines.

to tell you about happened around 1912 or 1913. As wished by Swami Brahmananda, arrangements were made for the singing of Ramanama Sankirtanam in both the Ashramas of the Ramakrishna Order in Varanasi. It was sung on the ekadasi[3] days at the Ramakrishna Mission Sevashrama, and during the new or full moon of every month at the Sri Ramakrishna Advaita Ashrama. During the singing, a seat for Lord Mahavira and a copy of the book on the Sankirtanam would be placed there.

"Once we, the monks from both the Ashramas, went to Shankatmochan by several ekkas.[4] On the veranda of the temple Nirad Maharaj, Bishwaranjan Maharaj and myself were seated facing the image of Lord Mahavira. Other singers were seated on both sides of us. The Sankirtanam went on in full swing.

"We saw a very fair-complexioned gentleman with a long beard and long hair come and sit facing the east, near the doorstep of Lord Mahavira's temple. He sat opposite to Swami Brahmananda, almost face to face with him. The gentleman's body was covered with a thick, white chuddar (wrapper). As soon as the singing was over, he left. I noticed him many times while he was seated there. After he left, Swami Brahmananda said, 'Lord Mahavira himself appeared before us today. That fair complexioned, elderly gentleman who was seated here listening to the singing was Lord Mahavira.'

"Hearing that, immediately some of us ran out to find Lord Mahavira. But we found no one outside except some black-faced monkeys (hanumans) on the trees.

---

3. The eleventh day of the lunar fortnight.
4. A two-wheeled carriage drawn by a horse.

"As directed by Swami Brahmananda, our monks in Varanasi learned to sing Kalikirtan[5] as a group under the guidance of Nirad Maharaj. One morning when we were singing Kalikirtan, Swami Brahmananda was with us. He suddenly went into spiritual ecstasy. He started dancing in front of the entrance to the door of Thakur's shrine, and went on fanning him with a chamara. That day I also saw him telling his beads using his rosary. That's the only time in my life I saw him using his rosary. I saw him count the beads at a very slow pace for only about twelve times.

"Once we sang Kalikirtan at the temple of Mother Annapurna in Varanasi. Hariprasanna Maharaj (Swami Vijnanananda) was present with us that day. The famous, elderly pakhoaj player, Madan Mishra, accompanied us on his pakhoaj[6] as we sang a few songs. Mr. Mishra was a musician at the royal court of the Maharaja of Mayurbhanj. Shiv Puri, the abbot of the Annapurna temple, was so charmed by Swami Brahmananda's great spiritual presence that he invited him to have the prasad of Mother Annapurna with all of us.

"Shiv Puri first gave us a guided tour of Mother Annapurna's storeroom (bhandar) at the temple. After this, Swami Brahmananda and we were made to sit in the room of Golden Annapurna. Shiv Puri brought some cardamoms on an oval silver platter. He then offered them to Swami Brahmananda one by one, after removing their shells. This was the temple's traditional gesture of welcome to an honoured guest. Thereafter, we all were given Mother Annapurna's prasad in the room of Golden Annapurna."

◊ ◊ ◊ ◊ ◊

5. Devotional singing in adoration of the Divine Mother Kali.
6. The pakhoaj is a kind of drum played with two hands.

Reminiscences of Swami Mukteswarananda: "Swami Brahmananda encouraged us very much to engage in spiritual practice and study of the scriptures. Till the end of his life, he rose at three o'clock in the morning and then sat for meditation. He frequently said, 'Do spiritual practice.' He also frequently told us, 'At the initial stage of your devotional life you must do a lot of meditation and japa. You all have left behind your home and families; yet what are you doing here now? Become immersed in chanting the holy name of God. Pray to God, saying, *please bless us with devotion and divine knowledge.* If you don't do all these things now, you'll regret it later!'

"I still recall those wonderful days when Belur Math was as though engulfed by a storm of japa, meditation and study of the scriptures. At that time Swami Brahmananda would give us individual encouragement to do a lot of japa and meditation. During that period there weren't that many sadhus and brahmacharis at Belur Math. This doesn't mean, however, that not many other people came to the Math. Most of those great disciples of Sri Ramakrishna were still there. Many school and college students used to come. The number of devotees—both men and women—who used to visit Belur Math was fairly large. Feeding and entertaining the visitors continued day and night. Baburam Maharaj (Swami Premananda) wouldn't allow any visitor to leave without taking prasad. Had I not seen him, I would never have been able to realize how much joy and satisfaction could be derived from feeding people.

"Around this period a sort of competition was going on in Belur Math among the monks about how much japa and meditation each one could do. We, the monks, also had to do a lot of laborious work. We had to do a lot of spade work in the vegetable gardens. Forming a human chain, we had to bring water in buckets to the monastery from the river Ganga. We had to cut grass; and help in the work of the kitchen by cutting vegetables, etc. Baburam Maharaj would give us severe scoldings if he saw us idling or chitchatting with others. At the same time, Swami Brahmananda watched over us to make sure that we were doing our spiritual practices as instructed by him, along with our other activities at the monastery.

"It was December of 1914. One day Swami Brahmananda said to Bi—, 'From tomorrow you wake me up at three o'clock in the morning. I would like to see how long you can meditate sitting next to me!' Many of us were present there when Swami Brahmananda said this to Bi—.

"Sachin (Swami Chinmayananda) was sort of a leader among us junior monks. We all discussed it between ourselves and decided to get up from bed at three o'clock in the morning and meditate as Bi— had been asked to do.

"I find it hard to describe the joy that we experienced in those days. We all would sit facing the Ganga upstairs on the veranda next to Swami Brahmananda's room. We would take our seats even before he would come out of his room to sit for meditation. After rinsing his hands and mouth with water, he would come out of his room and see which monks had come for meditation. Then he would bless us and sit for meditation.

"Day after day, as though overpowered by a strange, spiritual fervour, we kept on doing our meditation and experiencing intense joy. At that time we really felt that we would be able to experience God, because day and night we had no talk between us other than about spiritual life—about renunciation, devotion and how to acquire the knowledge of God. We became overwhelmed with the hope of attaining the highest

CHAPTER I

spiritual experience, and that generated a lot of enthusiasm in us. Sometimes we were not even aware of how the days were passing. During that period one or two of us had some genuine spiritual experiences.

"It was not yet dawn. A deep silence pervaded everywhere. The entire creation appeared to be absorbed in the meditation on Brahman. Swami Brahmananda said to us, 'Please sing this song: *Look, there exists the abode of bliss—exceedingly beautiful, effulgent, and beyond the ocean of worldly existence!*'[7]

"We sang mostly Brahma-sangeet after our meditation hours. When we sang the line 'O we know not how many saints and sages are absorbed in the deepest meditation in that abode of bliss!' with great enthusiasm, we felt inspired by the deep, spiritual mood of Swami Brahmananda. Our voices reverberated all around, saturating the whole atmosphere, and we were transported to a domain of exceeding bliss.

"I hear that particular song being sung even today, but I don't experience that heart-enthralling bliss that we experienced when we sang it together in the presence of Swami Brahmananda. Whenever we sang the song 'Meditate on His feet resting on the lotus seat of thy heart. Behold the unparalleled beauty of His countenance with thy eyes soaked in love!,' I saw, to speak the truth, the 'lotus seat' of my heart quite empty! But when I looked out and saw Swami Brahmananda's face, I was amazed to see the wonderful transformation that had come to it. His face shone with a kind of divine light. His gaze was indrawn and steady, and his eyelids didn't blink! Most probably at that time he was seeing the presence of his dearest Lord in his inmost heart. And in wonder I couldn't

7. "Aije dekhā jāi ānandadhām, apurvashobhana, bhavajaladhir pāre jyotirmay"—a Brahma sangeet (song about Brahman) in Bengali.

9

take my eyes off his peaceful and grave countenance.

"Singing continued from daybreak till 7:30 in the morning. On some days it continued even longer. On those days when the singing became quite lively, Swami Brahmananda would choose one song after another and ask us to sing them. During one such day, as we were singing with great joy and enthusiasm, Swami Premananda's voice suddenly broke the spell of our music. He said, 'Don't you realize that it has already become very late? A lot of work has to be done, but you're still singing! Get up and start doing your duties.' Then many of us stopped singing, and somewhat reluctantly went downstairs.

"Swami Brahmananda then said to Swami Premananda, 'Baburam Da, have these boys left their homes to come here to work as day labourers and porters? Please reduce the volume of their duties. If they are not allowed to taste the joy of love of God, how will they find joy in doing the Lord's work? If one doesn't get that joy, work will be only the cause of bondage for them. Of course, we have to watch that they don't indulge in idleness in the name of doing spiritual practice!'

"Then Swami Brahmananda said to us, 'Singing or chanting the holy name superficially without any genuine spiritual feeling won't help. You should all become absorbed in it. You should be completely submerged in the ocean of the holy name. The more you chant His name, the more joy will you experience. Along with joy will also come faith. All your doubts and disbelief will flee away.'

"Another incident. It was a Saturday, and it being the birthday of Swamiji (Swami Vivekananda), Nirad Maharaj performed the worship of the Divine Mother Kali throughout the entire night.

CHAPTER I

"Ramlal Dada was at that time staying in Belur Math. Swami Brahmananda's behaviour with him was very interesting. Whenever he came and stayed at Belur Math, Swami Brahmananda would always joke and have fun with him. They enjoyed each other's company very much. At the same time, Swami Brahmananda was fully aware that Ramlal Dada belonged to the family of his guru, and therefore deserved great respect and the best of hospitality.

"There were two beds in Swami Brahmananda's room—one was an ordinary bed on which he slept at night. The other bed had springs under its mattress and was quite comfortable. Swami Brahmananda usually rested in the daytime lying in the bed fitted with springs. He also meditated sitting on it both in the morning and in the evening. Sitting on that same bed he met with the sadhus and devotees. Swami Brahmananda frequently allowed Ramlal Dada to sleep in this bed when he visited.

"On the Sunday morning after Saturday's Kali Puja, both Ramlal Dada and Swami Brahmananda were seated on one of the beds. We brought two plates of Mother Kali's prasad for them. Swami Brahmananda said, 'Bring two stools and put the plates of prasad on them.' Then he said to Ramlal Dada, 'Brother, let's have Mother's prasad today in grand European style! We shall use the stools as our dining tables!' While eating the prasad, Swami Brahmananda chitchatted and joked with Ramlal Dada.

"Then Nirad Maharaj brought a little charanamrita (holy bath water) of Mother Kali. Swami Brahmananda took a little and gave the rest to Ramlal Dada. As soon as Swami Brahmananda drank the charanamrita, he had a sudden change of mood. We noticed that he had become inebriated with spiri-

11

tual emotion. He said to Nirad, 'Please sing that song about the Divine Mother that starts with the words: *Here comes the Mother walking like someone intoxicated. With Her disheveled hair She walks fast while battling the demons.*'[8]

"Nirad Maharaj, Bhavani and myself began singing the song with great feeling and fervour. Swami Brahmananda, overwhelmed with spiritual emotion and shedding profuse tears of divine love (premashru), muttered, 'Mother! Mother!' Never before had I witnessed such a spiritual mood in Swami Brahmananda. I had heard about samadhi, but didn't know what it was. Seeing his condition, I began thinking that perhaps this was samadhi! Seeing his deep spiritual mood, we all were almost stupefied. He still had half of the consecrated luchi in his mouth. His eyelids were half closed, and his body was shaking with intense spiritual emotion.

"I don't have the proper words to describe his condition. At that time our minds were also lifted to a higher plane, and we all felt as though we were floating in an ocean of bliss that we had never experienced before. After a long time Swami Brahmananda's mind gradually came down to the awareness of this world, and he asked me to chant a hymn in adoration of the Divine Mother."

◊◊◊◊◊

Pleased with the devotion of Mr. Jiten Datta of Mymensing, Swamis Brahmananda and Premananda and their attendant monks stayed at Mr. Datta's home for five days. At that time a spiritual wave seemed to engulf the town of Mymensing. Every morning Nirad Maharaj would sing devotional songs

---

8. The Bengali song starts with the following words: "Dhaliye dhaliye ke āshe, galitachikura āshaba ābeshe, etc."

in his sweet, melodious voice. Listening to that music, Swamis Brahmananda and Premananda would enter into deep meditation. Many people would come to the house at that time. Some would sit inside, while others had to stand outside. In wonder they would observe those two great souls immersed in meditation.

The second day after the arrival of the two swamis in Mymensing, a meeting was held at the local Durgabari in the afternoon. Baburam Maharaj gave some spiritual teachings by telling some stories. Everybody wished that Swami Brahmananda would say something. But he showed great reluctance to give a talk, nor did he allow anyone else to give talks. Instead, he asked all to sing Nama-Ramayana together. For some reason, he didn't want to encourage any external publicity there.

Incidentally, a holy man from one of the western provinces of India was visiting Mymensing at that time. He expressed his desire to spiritually liberate Bengal saying, "Come! O Bengalees, all of you come! I'll give you spiritual salvation!"

When this news reached the ears of Swami Brahmananda he said, "He is asking *all* the Bengalees to come to him, but what level of spirituality has he himself attained? At the most the first, second or the third level, not anything higher than that!"

While in Mymensingh, Swami Brahmananda was invited by a member of the local branch of the Brahmo Samaj to participate in their Maghotsava festival. That Brahmo gentleman said to the swami, "As a young man you attended many of our prayer meetings in Calcutta. Please come and see our festival here." He accepted the invitation, and with Baburam Maharaj and a few others, went to the Brahmo Samaj temple in the evening. After arriving at the temple, He asked Brahmachari Binod to sing some devotional songs. Binod sang the song, "O Blissful Mother, please make us spiritually intoxicated, etc." [9] The temple became packed to capacity. Swami Brahmananda took his leave from the temple after about an hour. And as soon as he left, the temple became almost empty.

In a school named the Mahakali Pathshala in Mymensing, there was a public library named after Sri Ramakrishna. Later the library was moved from the Pathshala to the drawing room in Jiten Babu's home. But because of lack of adequate space for the books there, it became necessary to construct a building for the library. There was a gentleman named Matilal Biswas who was originally from Barisal, but who was now living and working in Mymensingh as a low paid schoolteacher. He took the initiative to buy a plot of land south of the railway station. He then inspired some young men to come and help him. He and the young men constructed, with their own labour, a fairly large building of corrugated iron sheets. As Swami Brahmananda was an exalted monastic brother of the great Swami Vivekananda, they requested him to come and inaugurate the new library building. The Swami happily agreed, and went there with some devotees and monks.

In a room inside the building, beautifully decorated pictures of Sri Ramakrishna and Swami Vivekananda had been placed on an altar. Articles needed for worship had also been kept in that room. Glancing at the altar, Swami Brahmananda joyfully said to Swami Premananda, "Have you noticed? Thakur (Sri Ramakrishna) is sitting there! I'll do the arati." Hearing this

---

9. It is a Bengali song starting with the words:"Mātiye dey mā ānandamayi, akey bāre mete jāi!"

14

everybody became extremely happy. Spending a lot of money and with their own labour of love, they had constructed the library building within a very short time. Their joy knew no bounds, because their long cherished desire to have a larger library building had at last been fulfilled!

Swami Brahmananda began the worship with meditation. Then he offered flowers at the feet of Sri Ramakrishna. While seated to conduct arati, he rang the hand bell and waved the panchapradipa (ceremonial oil lamp) to conduct arati. As soon as the bell began ringing, its sweet sound created a spiritual atmosphere inside the room. Swami Premananda started dancing in spiritual ecstasy with his arms raised. Moved by his spiritual emotion, others also felt an urge to stand up and dance. Even though they remained seated, their arms involuntarily went up in gestures of dancing!

At the end of the arati, Swami Brahmananda and others went to the large hall inside the building. With his permission, Swami Premananda gave a discourse there on Swami Vivekananda's *Karma Yoga*.

◊ ◊ ◊ ◊ ◊

It was 1916. Our Bangalore Ashrama was having its annual Durga Puja. Swami Brahmananda said to us, "If each of you can chant the name of Mother Durga one hundred thousand times during the three days of the puja, you will get the effect of performing Durga Puja." Hearing his words, with great enthusiasm the monks started doing japa in between their daily chores.

After returning from his trip to South India, Swami Brahmananda stayed at the Shashiniketan in the town of Puri. One day he said to Hari Maharaj, 'Ishwar chants Sanskrit hymns nicely, but he doesn't know Sanskrit that well. He can't understand the meaning of the hymns correctly. Will you please help him to understand the meaning of the hymns?' While visiting the Madras Math, Swami Brahmananda had asked Ishwar to chant some selected Sanskrit hymns every day. Sometimes he also asked him to chant them for the devotees.

A few days later in Puri, Swami Brahmananda said to Hari Maharaj, "You are here now. Wouldn't it be nice if we could arrange for a class to study the *Shrimad Bhagavatam* here?"

Hari Maharaj was pleased to hear this. He asked, "Who will be the reader?"

Swami Brahmananda replied, "Let Ishwar be the reader."

The classes were held in the afternoons. Swami Brahmananda would sit in the class and listen. About ten people usually attended. Sometimes devotees from outside also came and attended. Hari Maharaj would explain the difficult portions of the text. The classes continued for a while until he fell ill and was unable to conduct them.

Swami Brahmananda went from Puri to Calcutta in 1917. There he stayed at the Udbodhan Ashrama. Around that period Bhavanicharan (Swami Varadananda) was appointed his sevak. From that time onwards, he stayed with Swami Brahmananda for about four years, serving him, and giving him much joy by singing devotional songs and chanting religious hymns. Swami Brahmananda liked to listen to the chants every morning at seven o'clock. After that he went out for a walk.

The   hymns   *Gurupranāma,*   *Vedasārashiva-stotram,*

16

Kālishatanāma-stotram, *Tripurāsundari-stotram* and *Jagaddhātri-stotram* were chanted daily. On certain days Swami Brahmananda asked Bhavani to chant either *Madhusudana-stotram* or *Gopāla-stotram.* Once in a great while, the *Prapannagitā* and *Shānti-stotram* were also chanted. Earlier, in 1913 and 1914, when the Swami was in Varanasi, Hrishikesh (Swami Prashantananda) chanted the hymns on the Panchadevata every morning because Swami Brahmananda had asked him to memorize them.

While staying in the Balaram Mandir, Swami Brahmananda once arranged for classes on the *Shrimad Bhāgavatam.* Swami Vasudevananda read aloud the main Sanskrit text, its Bengali translation and the commentary. For a long time these classes continued. At the end of each class there was devotional singing. Swami Brahmananda attended the classes regularly. Many others, including ladies, also attended. They sat on the veranda. In one particular chapter of the *Shrimad Bhāgavatam* there is criticism of the nature of women. Swami Brahmananda asked Swami Vasudevananda to skip that chapter.

There used to be devotional singing every morning in Swami Brahmananda's room when he stayed at the Balaram Mandir. Mahamaya, the daughter of Ramkrishna Basu, said, "Swami Brahmananda used to ask all of us to come and listen to the devotional singing. My mother used to come, as did my auntie if she was visiting us at the time. The sadhus would sing songs such as: 'Anupama mahimāpurna Brahma karare dhyān.' (Meditate on Brahman endowed with incomparable glory!) Swami Brahmananda would sit on the small couch in his room with his eyes closed, listening intently to the singing. He would make a fist with his left hand, and maintain the beat by striking his fist with the forefinger and middle finger of his right hand. We would gaze at his peaceful face and listen to the beautiful music."

Once Gokuldas Dey asked Swami Brahmananda, "Maharaj, what should be the duty of human beings?"

Swami Brahmananda replied by sweetly chanting a line from a song starting with the words "O my mind, chant the holy name of God incessantly!"[10]

Whenever the playwright Aparesh Mukhopadhyay wrote a new play, he came to Swami Brahmananda and read it out to him for his approval or opinion. As wished by the Swami, Aparesh Babu[11] added a portion of the *Nama-Ramayana* to his play *Ramanuja*. The Swami was so eager for the *Nama-Ramayana's* inclusion in the play that he wired Swami Ambi-kananda in Murshidabad, asking him to come to Calcutta and teach the actors of the theatre how to sing it.

Acting on the wish of Swami Brahmananda, Aparesh Babu included a hymn on Lord Shiva, starting with the line "Na-gendraharaya Trilochanaya," in another play. As suggested by the Swami, the devotional song starting with the words "Abhayar abhayapada kara mana sar," (O my mind, treat as most vital the Divine Mother's feet that dispel all kinds of fear.) was also included in one of his plays.

Swami Brahmananda had great interest in propagating the scriptures. At his inspiration, Atalbehari Mitra, the Deputy Magistrate of Puri, published a collection of scriptures named *Shrutisara-sangraha*. The *Bhagavadgita, Sri Sri Chandi,* and thirty-two Upanishads were included in that collection. Copies of the book were freely distributed to people. Kiran

---

10. The line in original Bengali is: "Sādhanbhajan mon karo tnār nirantar."
11. The word *Bābu* is an equivalent of the word *Mr.*

CHAPTER I

Chandra Datta of Baghbazar, Calcutta, also published a book named *Sri Sri Ramakrishna Upadesh (The Teachings of Sri Ramakrishna)*, and freely distributed several thousand copies of it.

SWAMI BRAHMANANDA

CHAPTER II
Swami Brahmananda's Role as Sadguru

For several years Dr. Kanjilal had been trying to be invested with purnabhisheka[12] of the Tantrika tradition by Swami Brahmananda. But he kept stalling saying, "Not now, you'll get it later."

Having been refused so many times, Dr. Kanjilal became desperate. He said to Swami Brahmananda, "You must invest me with purnabhisheka this time. You must not say 'No'!"

Hearing this, the Swami became very grave and said to Dr. Kanjilal, "Do you think I'll invest you until I know that it is good for you? Is God a snake and you a snake charmer that whenever you chant a mantra, God will immediately come to you? No spiritual practice, austerity or renunciation can enable a person to experience God. Only one whom God chooses experiences Him."

Swami Brahmananda eventually blessed Dr. Kanjilal with purnabhisheka.

◊ ◊ ◊ ◊ ◊

Another incident. Swami Brahmananda was at that time staying in Calcutta. Three or four brahmacharis came to him from Belur Math to get permission to take sannyasa. Out of them Swami Brahmananda didn't permit U—. Then U— complained that some monks junior to him had already been permitted to have sannyasa. Hearing that complaint, the Swami told him, "It is I who will invest you with sannyasa. If I know that you are not ready, should I give you sannyasa?"

---

12. Purnabhisheka is a kind of sannyasa.

21

Saying that he became very grave. With great feeling he then muttered to himself, "People come to me and want diksha, sannyasa, and brahmacharya! But no one says, 'I want God!' Let them come and say that they want to experience God, and request my help in getting God-vision, then I can show them if I'm capable of helping them or not!"

U— was later given sannyasa by Swami Brahmananda.

◊ ◊ ◊ ◊ ◊

This happened when Swami Brahmananda was visiting the Bangalore Ashrama. One night he wanted to have a drink of water. When Ishwar brought him a glass of water, he stared at Ishwar intently. He didn't appear to notice the glass of water at all. Aside from that, he looked extremely grave. Slowly he said to Ishwar, "Do you want to be a God-realized soul? Do you want God?"

A strange fear suddenly seized Ishwar, and his hand holding the glass of water started shaking. Trembling, he replied in a hushed voice, "Yes, Maharaj!"

A little later Swami Brahmananda came out of that grave mood. He smiled at Ishwar and said to him, "Remind me tomorrow." But, alas, he couldn't muster enough courage to remind the Swami again!

◊ ◊ ◊ ◊ ◊

While they were in Belur Math, Bha— and Charu (Swami Bhajanananda) would remain awake at night and do a lot of japa. After Swami Brahmananda's return to Belur Math, Bha— went to salute him. The Swami then said to him, "You must be doing a lot of japa. I can sense it just by looking at a person's face. Your kulakundalini has become awakened, but is not yet finding its way to ascend. Please ask me later. I'll then tell you what you should do."

Later he taught Bha— how to do ajapa,[13] and gave other spiritual instructions as well.

◊ ◊ ◊ ◊ ◊

Another incident. Gokuldas Dey was sitting inside Swami Brahmananda's room facing the Swami and thinking, "Sri Ramakrishna is the most gracious one. Sri Ramakrishna is personified compassion. Sri Ramakrishna is personified love. Sri Ramakrishna is personified prana (cosmic energy). Sri Ramakrishna is personified dhyanam (meditation). Sri Ramakrishna is personified jagat (the creation). Sri Ramakrishna is personified samsara (the transmigratory world of living beings)."

As these thoughts arose in Gokuldas Dey's mind one by one, exactly at that same moment, Swami Brahmananda would articulate that particular thought aloud. After uttering, "Sri Ramakrishna is personified samsara," he said to Gokuldas Dey, "Meditate on Sri Ramakrishna this way." It was obvious that every idea that came to Gokuldas Dey's mind had been generated by Swami Brahmananda's powerful thoughts.

◊ ◊ ◊ ◊ ◊

Another similar incident. Swami Brahmananda's attendant Ishwar was sitting absentmindedly on the veranda of the Bangalore Ashrama. Suddenly the Swami came out of his room and said to him, "Tell me honestly what you were thinking just now! Don't hide anything from me." Ishwar then recollected his past thoughts and related them to him. Then the Swami returned to his room, and came out again a few min-

13. Effortless chanting of the holy name by the mind.

utes later, and drew Ishwar's attention by shaking his finger in front of his face and said, "Tell me what you were thinking now!" When Ishwar told him what he had been thinking about, Swami Brahmananda smiled a little and said, "Go and prepare a smoke for me." Obviously, he wanted to check whether his holy thoughts were being transmitted to Ishwar's mind.

◊ ◊ ◊ ◊ ◊

While in Puri, Swami Brahmananda was asked by Ratikanta Mazumdar how to get rid of the restlessness of his mind. The Swami asked him if he had had spiritual initiation. Mr. Mazumdar informed that a Vaishnava sadhu had given him two holy names to chant many years earlier. Hearing those two mantras the Swami said, "Please continue to chant them. You don't need any spiritual initiation." Then he instructed him to do mental worship of the deities first, and then to chant the mantras. He also instructed him how to pray to God, saying, "O Lord, Thou art present in the sun and the moon. Thou art present in the stars. Thou art present everywhere. I am devoid of any spiritual qualities. Out of Thy compassion please show Thyself to me."

◊ ◊ ◊ ◊ ◊

It is well known in the Ramakrishna Order that Swami Brahmananda wouldn't readily agree to give spiritual initiation to anyone. If approached by someone for initiation, he would become very grave. After a person had associated with him for a considerable period of time, he might agree to initiate that person. In some cases, before giving initiation, he would ask the devotee to chant a holy name of God of his or her choice for many days. In case of a few monks of the Ramakrishna Order, he even gave them initiation long after they had had their sannyasa. He observed literally the scriptural injunction "Na kurvita vahun shishyan" (Thou shalt not make many disciples.). His behaviour clearly indicates that there is much greater risk in giving spiritual initiation than in granting sannyasa.

◊◊◊◊◊

While in Varanasi in 1921, on Sri Ramakrishna's birthday, Swami Brahmananda invested fifteen monks with brahmacharya and twenty-two monks with sannyasa. Someone (most probably Shukul Maharaj) asked him, "You have given sannyasa to all these monks, but are they all fit for sannyasa?"

He replied, "If you ask about their fitness I have to admit that none of them is really fit. But my mind is now overwhelmed with a feeling of compassion and sympathy. How can I stand in the way of those who want to have sannyasa—the highest ideal of human life? I just offer them at the feet of Thakur, the rest is between them and him."

◊◊◊◊◊

It is heard that Swami Brahmananda would not initiate anybody until he got the vision of the Ishta (chosen deity) of the devotee who had prayed for initiation. Most probably this is the reason some candidates were given diksha as soon as they approached him, while others didn't get it even after waiting for six years. In regard to a certain devotee, the Swami had a vision of an unknown chosen deity. He did not know the mantra associated with this deity and had to find it from the *Tantrasara*. We also know that he gave initiation to some who hadn't even asked for it.

◊◊◊◊◊

One summer afternoon in Mymensing, Binodbehari Deb was standing on the bank of the pond next to his house. Suddenly a gust of hot wind hit his right eye, and he was almost blinded. For about twenty days after that incident he covered that eye with a bandage. It couldn't stand the bright light of the sun. Then he had a dream. In it he saw Swami Brahmananda seated in front of him. There were some puja articles around. The Swami sprinkled some water on him and gave him a mantra.

Mr. Deb had already been initiated by the Holy Mother Sri Sarada Devi. So he became quite confused. He went to see her in Koalpara and told her his dream. She said, "What you have had in your dream is also initiation. From now on you should chant both mantras."

Then Mr. Deb went to Swami Brahmananda in Calcutta, and talked to him about his dream. The Swami remained quiet for a little while, and then he said cheerfully, "Yes, you have been initiated. Go and buy a fruit from the bazaar and give it to me."

◊ ◊ ◊ ◊ ◊

It is no wonder that Swami Brahmananda knew the past, present and future of his disciples, because he could see in and through anyone at first sight. Before giving initiation to a particular, unmarried young man, he said to him, "Once you committed a great sin." Then mentioning that sinful act the Swami added, "Don't do it ever again!"

◊ ◊ ◊ ◊ ◊

Swami Brahmananda was fond of another young man because of his devotion to God. When the young man approached him for spiritual initiation, the Swami said, "Your

CHAPTER II

guru is in Varanasi." As instructed by Swami Brahmananda, the young man went to Totadri Math of the sect of Sri Ramanuja in Varanasi. There he took initiation from a guru of that sect and later became a sannyasin.[14]

◊◊◊◊◊

Reminiscences of a devotee who prefers to remain anonymous:[15] "I went to Jayrambati for the first time in January 1916. The day after my arrival the Holy Mother initiated me. Just before my initiation, she hinted that I had been connected with a historical incident in my previous incarnation. When I was about to ask her for further details of that incident, she said, 'Ask Rakhal and others.'

"I left Jayrambati that day and arrived in Calcutta via Tarakeswar the next day. One day later I went to Belur Math. As asked by Swami Premananda, I spent the night at the Math. The next morning around eight o'clock, I went to salute Swami Brahmananda. As soon as he set eyes on me, he addressed me by my name from my previous incarnation, and mentioned some incidents that tallied with what the Holy Mother had said about my past incarnation.

"Two or three weeks later Swami Brahmananda went for a visit to Dacca. There I had more opportunity to talk to him. He asked me, 'What do you want?'

"I replied, 'I want to spend this life working like a donkey.'

---

14. One who has renounced the world and taken the last vows of monastic life.

15. When Brahmachari Akshayachaitanya recorded these reminiscences, the gentleman whose reminiscences are recorded here was reluctant to give his name. His wish was that his reminiscences would be published only after his death. For this reason the author didn't mention his name.

27

He said, 'Your prayer is granted!'"

◊◊◊◊◊

Swami Brahmananda would accept the entire responsibility of the disciple at the time of giving initiation. He would open the path of liberation from the cycle of repeated births and deaths (samsara). He once said to Pulinbehari Mitra, "What do you say Pulin? Don't we have to cross this ocean of worldliness?" Then he laughed and said, "We'll do that effortlessly—through fun and frolic and exuberant joy!"

◊◊◊◊◊

We have heard that some devotees had spiritual realizations at the time of their initiation from Swami Brahmananda. Swami Yatiswarananda felt a spiritual power coming to him from his guru. At the touch of his guru's hand, he felt that the entire world was soaked in an all-pervading divine consciousness.

◊◊◊◊◊

Pareshnath Sengupta wrote: "One day, as soon as I entered the room of Swami Brahmananda in the Balaram Mandir, he glanced at me with great affection and asked, 'What brings you here?' I then saluted him and sat on the floor. A little later he said to me, 'Ma bhaih! Ma bhaih! (Don't be scared!) Hold on to God with a spirit of complete resignation! For a year or two forget yourself, and get completely immersed in prayer and meditation. Everything will become favourable. Don't worry about what *you* should do. You are His instrument. Why should you think about what you will do? When you think that way all troubles come. Be satisfied with what you have got. O how great, how wonderfully beautiful He is! He is the very essence of all the beauty in the world! Be absorbed in His bliss, and then you'll never be able to forget Him! Do japa incessantly!'

"Then he stroked my body with great affection and said, 'Now you may go.' That entire day I was full of sublime joy, and felt as though my chosen deity had become manifest in the lotus of my heart. My guru's chant, 'Valarka-mandala-bhasang,' went on resounding in my ears all the time."

◊◊◊◊◊

Swami Gaurishananda wrote: "One day at eight o'clock in the morning, Swami Brahmananda was walking in Belur Math on the bank of the river Ganga. When he saw me he asked me to come over to him. Then he asked, 'Nepal, how are you?' When I told him that my health was all right he said, 'I didn't inquire about your physical health. I wanted to know if your mind was all right.' Then he checked my chest and back, touching them gently with his hand, and said, 'Yes, your mind is all right. Always keep it this way.' His divine touch filled my heart with joy that entire day."

◊◊◊◊◊

It is reported that in 1916 Swami Brahmananda went to see the play *Ramanuja* at the Minerva Theatre in Calcutta. The play had a scene that showed Sri Ramanuja showering his love and compassion on all, even the lowliest of the lowly. Swami Brahmananda was moved to tears by that touching scene. Many think that it was from that time onwards that he became quite liberal in giving initiation to devotees. But this notion is not quite correct. He always was picky and choosy about giving initiation. Toward the end of his life, only once did he give initiation to five or six devotees at Belur Math on a single day. And even on that day one candidate did not get it, in spite of the fact that he had already joined the Order as a monk.

In his entire life only once was there an exception to his strictness about giving initiation. In December 1916, he went on a visit to Kanyakumari and stayed there in a dharmashala[16] for nine days. One day Tulsi Maharaj brought a group of ten devotees to Swami Brahmananda for diksha and he initiated all of them, one by one. While in Bangalore, before coming to Kanyakumari, he also initiated about fifty devotees, but not on the same day.[17]

Just as he was very strict about giving initiation, he was also very reluctant to give religious discourses in public. He would never give spiritual instruction to anyone unless he was sure that the person was fit for spiritual life. However, when he would notice that someone had developed genuine spiritual yearning through frequent association with him, he would not mind giving that person instruction.

◊ ◊ ◊ ◊ ◊

Swami Brahmananda knew by heart many lines from Chandidas's poems and would sometimes quote them. Ishwar asked Swami Brahmananda, "At first Chandidas was a Shakta and worshipped the Divine Mother. Did he become a Vaishnava later?"

Swami Brahmananda replied, "He was after all a saint. Besides, is the Divine Mother different from Krishna?"

◊ ◊ ◊ ◊ ◊

A class on Vedanta philosophy would be held in a certain

---

16. A dharmashala is a rest house for pilgrims.
17. Source: Swami Bhumananda.

room at the Udbodhan Ashrama. While Swami Brahmananda was staying there, Khudumani brought him a smoke and said, "All this philosophy will never enter my head. Different philosophers have tried to prove the greatness of one or the other philosophical views that they held, and claimed that their individual views alone were true. Now, if one of them be true, how can all others be true?"

Swami Brahmananda replied, "According to the different levels of spiritual experiences of the spiritual aspirants, the dvaita (dualistic), vishistadvaita (qualified nondualistic), and advaita (non-dualistic) positions are experienced by them to be true. After the non-dualistic experience, one can experience that both the non-dual noumenon and the phenomenon belong to the same Divine Reality. In this manner the phenomenal world is also experienced to be real. But, let me tell you one thing. After samadhi—after becoming completely dissolved in divine consciousness—true spiritual life starts."

◊ ◊ ◊ ◊ ◊

Pareshnath Sengupta wrote: "This happened in 1921 at the Madras Math. When Ishwar Maharaj, Bankim Ghorai, and myself returned from a walk, we saw that Swami Brahmananda's room was full of people. From the adjacent room we could hear him talking.

"He was saying, 'God's lila[18] is going on all the time. After attaining spiritual illumination, aspirants experience this lila. It is experienced one step lower than at the advaita level. Of course, the acme of spiritual experience is the advaita experience. The events that are happening in this world, whatever we are experiencing—all of them remain existing in finer form.

18. Lila is the divine play on the phenomenal plane.

31

The subtle world of lila is becoming the gross world, and again the gross world is becoming the subtle world of God's lila. This is what is happening. That's why God's lila is eternal. It is without beginning and end. After experiencing God's lila at the maturity of sattva guna, the spiritual aspirant acquires a sense of total fulfilment.'"

◊◊◊◊◊

As told by Swami Jagadananda, Swami Brahmananda once said, "No matter what high and lofty ideas you may form through your imagination and intellectual reasoning, once you directly experience God you'll realize that all those ideas were nothing."

◊◊◊◊◊

Swami Govindananda once asked Swami Brahmananda, "How can one have the vision of God?"

Swami Brahmananda replied, "If one can become completely helpless like a beggar on the street, then by God's grace one may have God-vision."[19]

◊◊◊◊◊

At the time of this incident, Professor Nikhil Maitra had come to Bangalore for a change, and was staying very close to the Ashrama. Swami Brahmananda was at the Bangalore Ashrama at that time. He met the professor and his servant Ramsingh a few times and got to know them. Ramsingh was

---

19. Swami Brahmananda used to quote every now and then this couplet composed by Sri Chaitanya: "Trinādapi sunichen taroriba sahishnunā. Amāninā mānaden kirtaniya sadā harih." [Being humbler than a blade of grass and more enduring than a tree, and without the craving for honour, and yet with the eagerness to honour all others, one should chant the holy name of God all the time.]

from the Garwal region in the Himalayas, and was a tall and handsome young man. Seeing the behaviour of Swami Brahmananda with him, the attendants of Swami Brahmananda could sense that the swami was fond of the young man.

Every now and then, whenever he got some free time after doing his duties at Nikhil Maitra's home, Ramsingh would come to the Ashrama to see Swami Brahmananda. If it were not possible to see him, he would immediately go back.

The morning after the worship of Mother Kali, as Swami Brahmananda was having the Mother's prasad inside his room, Tulsi Maharaj came and informed that Ramsingh had come to see him. It was reported that the young man was extremely eager to see the Swami immediately. Thereupon the Swami said, "All right, bring him to my room." He came and saluted him, prostrating before him. Then he knelt down in front of the Swami like Lord Rama's devotee Mahavira. Swami Brahmananda put his two hands on Ramsingh's head and said, "Ramsingh, from now on you'll belong to Sri Ramakrishna!" He looked at Ramsingh with his wonderful, compassionate eyes and uncontrollable tears rolled down Ramsingh's cheeks. As wished by the Swami, the leftover prasad was given to Ramsingh to eat.[20]

◇ ◇ ◇ ◇ ◇

The renowned author Debendranath Basu was a contemporary of Sri Ramakrishna. Swami Brahmananda would occasionally talk about God with him for a long time. Deben Babu had the same kind of devotion for the Swami that he used to have for Sri Ramakrishna.

◇ ◇ ◇ ◇ ◇

20. Source: Swami Mukteswarananda.

33

Yogin Ma and Golap Ma would often come together to see Swami Brahmananda. When they would come, he would talk with them on spiritual topics for a long time. While meditating, Yogin Ma would have spiritual visions. She would come and tell Swami Brahmananda about them. Yogin Ma's mind would be at rest only when he would confirm them to be genuine spiritual experiences.

One day he was standing with his back to Yogin Ma. Yogin Ma looked at him and saw Sri Ramakrishna instead! Swami Brahmananda was younger than Yogin Ma, yet she used to salute him, touching his feet with her forehead.

◊ ◊ ◊ ◊ ◊

Pundit Kshirod Prasad Vidyavinod wrote the following in his autobiography: "In 1920 I met Swami Brahmananda in the Bhubaneswar Ashrama. Then I told him, 'I could have seen Sri Ramakrishna. It is my misfortune that I missed the opportunity. I was a student then. Having heard about him, one day I wanted to go and see him in Dakshineswar. I started for Dakshineswar, but when I reached Alambazar, I remembered that he could read the thoughts of people and sometimes would talk about them. I was a young man then, and I had all kinds of thoughts in my mind, some of which I would keep carefully hidden. If he talked about them in front of others, I would be extremely embarrassed. This thought scared me and I turned back. That's why I didn't get to see him!'

"Swami Brahmananda said, 'Since you went as far as Alambazar to see him, it was as good as having seen him.'

"'No, Maharaj,' I insisted, 'I haven't seen him.'

"Then I started shedding tears, remembering my great misfortune. He said again, 'I'm telling you that you actually saw him!' Just then I quickly glanced over at him and saw that it was not him, but it was Sri Ramakrishna who was sitting there!"

SWAMI PREMANANDA
(ALSO KNOWN AS BABURAM MAHARAJ)

CHAPTER III

SWAMI BRAHMANANDA—PROTECTOR OF THOSE TO WHOM HE GAVE SHELTER

How much care Swami Brahmananda took of those to whom he had given spiritual shelter has been beautifully expressed in the autobiography of one of his attendants. His is the story of an artless, sentimental, headstrong, short-tempered, healthy and handsome young man who had encountered adverse circumstances at every step of his life. Eventually he found shelter at the feet of Swami Brahmananda, and all his fears vanished forever. His story is both interesting and inspiring.

He said, "When I first came to Belur Math in February 1914, the monks had just finished eating their lunch. I had not eaten anything since the previous evening, and had come to Belur Math via Howrah, walking on foot all the way from Sealdah railway station. I saw Baburam Maharaj standing on the veranda of the Math and saluted him, folding my hands. Looking at my face once, he called someone named Ashok and asked, 'Do we have any food left?' He informed that there was enough food for only the brahmin cook. I heard later that the food saved for the cook was given to me, and the cook had only a snack lunch to eat.

"After taking lunch, I had the following conversation with Baburam Maharaj. He asked me, 'From where have you come?'

"I replied, 'From Bagura.'

"He asked me, 'Are you a native of Bagura?'

"I replied, 'No, sir, I'm a native of Pabna.'

37

"He asked me, 'What's your education?'

"I replied, 'I didn't get to go to college.'

"He then said, 'We don't allow uneducated people to join our monastery. Those who join here have either B.A. or M.A. degrees. Come when you get your B.A degree.'

"I said, 'Sir, I can't do that! I've come here to stay.' He became very displeased with me when I asked, 'How many college degrees did Paramahangsa-Dev (Sri Ramakrishna) have?'

"His face reddened. After remaining quiet for a while he asked me, 'What will you do here? Will you be able to do spade work? Will you be able to cut hay for the cows in our dairy?'

"I replied, 'Yes, sir, I'll be able to do all that.' Then he showed me the visitors' room and said, 'Go and rest there.' He entered the visitors' room along with me and asked, 'Have you been involved with the anarchists? Did you make bombs? In that case I should inform you that the police often come here.'

"I replied, 'No, sir!'

"In spite of that he told me, 'You have to leave after resting.'

"In the late afternoon I was reading the copy of Ashwini Kumar Datta's *Bhakti Yoga* that I had with me. Baburam Maharaj came and said, 'Pack up your clothes and leave!'

"But I told him rather firmly, 'I am not going to leave. I don't care if the police come here or not. I have come here to stay.' He then left me without saying anything and I went on staying at the Math.

"On the fourth day of my stay Baburam Maharaj came to

me and asked, 'Will you be able to work in our shrine store-room?' I nodded my head in assent.

"From then on I worked in the shrine storeroom, and wouldn't talk much with anybody. I came to like Baburam Maharaj, but only for a while. Thereafter, I didn't like him that much. Nirad Maharaj would ask me to go to him, and sometimes asked me to prepare the hubble-bubble for him. He would also talk to me about Swami Brahmananda. I liked that very much. He used to say, 'Swami Brahmananda is God Himself.'

"Swami Kaivalyananda (Yogi Maharaj) used to talk to me about the Holy Mother and say, 'She is the Divine Mother Herself.' Hearing that I became confused. I had heard that God and the Divine Mother were the same. But I couldn't understand how there could be many Gods. I therefore decided that I must not stay at Belur Math.

"The Holy Mother Sri Sarada Devi came to visit the Math on Sri Ramakrishna's birthday, but no one had told me about her coming. I came to know about her visit as she was about to leave the Math by a horse-drawn carriage. Seeing her from a distance, I started calling out to her, 'Mother! Mother!' and ran after the carriage.

"When I caught up with her, she said, 'Come, my child!' Touching her feet I saluted her, and she blessed me, putting her hand on my head. Thereafter, on the auspicious day of the Akshaya Tritiya, she gave me initiation at the Udbodhan Ashrama in Calcutta. Still I could not shake off my desire to leave the Math.

"When I had been at the Math for ten months, Baburam Maharaj went to Varanasi to bring Swami Brahmananda back to the Math. Before leaving for Varanasi, he told the junior monks at the monastery, 'I know that you all love me, but once you see him you won't like me any more.'

"They said, 'That can't be true, Maharaj.'

"Baburam Maharaj replied, 'What I am saying is true. He is the mental child of Sri Ramakrishna. Sri Ramakrishna is working now through this Bala-Gopala.'[21] Hearing all this, I decided that I would wait a little and leave the Math as soon as I have seen Swami Brahmananda. One of the monks said to me, 'Not everyone can stay at Belur Math. Here they can ask you to leave at a moment's notice. And it appears to me that you will surely be asked to leave!'

"Swami Brahmananda had just come to the Math. As his health was not all right, he was given his patient's diet earlier, at ten o'clock in the morning. Then he sat on the veranda facing the Ganga and was having a smoke.[22] At first sight I liked him very much. I sat opposite to him on a bench, and just kept on looking at his face. He looked at me every now and then, smiling a little. He asked me, 'How long have you been here?'

"I replied, 'Ten months.'

"Then he beckoned to me to come to him. After I went, he took one of my arms, and laying it on his other hand, tried to measure its weight. Then he asked, 'Have you ever been a monk?'

"I replied, 'No, I haven't. Before coming here, I only saw naga (naked) sadhus. After coming here, I've seen babu (gentlemen) sadhus.' He didn't mind my comments.

---

21. Bala-Gopala means "Child Krishna" or "Baby Krishna."
22. No narcotics and liquor are allowed in the Ramakrishna Order; only smoking of tobacco is allowed, but not encouraged.

"He said, 'Think a little deeply, closing your eyes. Do it.' I had heard that he was childlike. So I didn't close my eyes. Even before meeting him, I had seen his picture and heard stories about him, and had come to like him. As I stayed on at Belur Math, my fondness for him went on increasing, and I had no more wish to leave the Math.

"One day, after participating in group singing in Swami Brahmananda's room, I saluted him. Then I began arranging for the daily worship in the shrine. Baburam Maharaj suddenly came to the shrine and said, 'Come with me, I'll take you to Swami Brahmananda.' Then he dragged me upstairs to the Swami's room and said, 'Go and salute him!' Swami Brahmananda was sitting on his cot. Baburam Maharaj said to him, 'This fellow is very hot-tempered. He quarrels with me a lot, and fights with the boys at the monastery. Please put your hand on his head and bless him so that his head becomes cool.'

"Swami Brahmananda examined both sides of his hand and said, 'My hand isn't all right, I can't do it today. Why don't you yourself take care of this?'

"Thereupon Baburam Maharaj grabbed me by the neck, and forcibly put my head on Swami Brahmananda's feet. As soon as that happened, he became very still, and slowly stroked my head with his very soft hand. Baburam Maharaj then said, 'It's not the fault of the boys. It's I who make them lose their tempers by scolding them frequently. I've become old. Then again I have to supervise the activities of the monastery. That also makes me lose my temper. Would you please stroke my head as well?' Saying this he put his head on the lap of Swami Brahmananda. Without protesting, he stroked Baburam Maharaj's head with his hand. There were four or five sadhus and brahm-

41

acharis in his room. He stroked the heads of all of them.

"Baburam Maharaj then started calling aloud from the window of his own room, 'Come, come! Swami Brahmananda has become the wish-fulfilling tree (Kalpataru) today!' Hearing that call, whoever was there, including our two servants—Sona and Kena—came running and were quietly blessed by Swami Brahmananda. The cross-eyed and crippled Dr. Bipin of Konnagar had just come out of the latrine and was rinsing his hands. He was late in coming. So Baburam Maharaj ran down the stairs and dragged him up to Swami Brahmananda. By that time he had risen from his seat. When the doctor came to him he said in Hindi, 'Jo āyā thhā so chalā gayā!' (That which came is gone now!) He did not bless the doctor.

"It was Sunday. The birthday of Sri Ramakrishna was being held at Belur Math. The courtyard was full of people. Everybody was waiting for the Kali Kirtan[23] to start shortly. After the worship of Sri Ramakrishna, Baburam Maharaj came down from the upstairs shrine and told me, 'Don't allow anyone to sit and eat today in our dining room. Sometimes women unknowingly enter the shrine room. Make sure that no one sits and eats anything there.'

"On the celebration days at the Math, food would be offered to the deity before noon. After the food-offering in the shrine of Sri Ramakrishna, Mahapurush Maharaj (Swami Shivananda) and Khoka Maharaj (Swami Subodhananda) came to the dining room and said to the cook, 'Serve us our meal.' They asked me to prepare two seats for them.

23. A special kind of devotional singing in Bengal in adoration of the Divine Mother Kali.

"Then I told them very politely that Baburam Maharaj had asked me not to allow anyone to sit and eat in the dining room that day. Hearing that Mahapurush Maharaj said, 'Where else shall we go? Make our seats here.' I did as ordered by him. Mahapurush Maharaj was a very small eater. After he finished eating, he stood up and said to me, 'Sit down and eat prasad from my plate.' I didn't want to eat; I told him again what Baburam Maharaj had ordered me to do. Hearing that Mahapurush Maharaj said, 'Just forget what he said. When again will you eat? Later on you won't have any chance to eat. I'm telling you, sit and eat!'

"As ordered, I sat down to eat. But as soon as I was about to put the first morsel of food into my mouth, Baburam Maharaj suddenly appeared. Grabbing me by the ear, he pulled me up and took me out to the porch. Still holding my ear, he started telling everybody there, 'Look, he has come to become a monk! He is greedy; he didn't get anything to eat at home. That's why he has taken shelter here! If I see him doing it again, I'll drive him away!'

"That same day, as I was sitting on a stool in front of the shrine storeroom, Sudhangsu Datta (at that time he was a young boy) came and said, "Ishwar Maharaj, hurry up, please go upstairs. Some girls are sitting in the shrine of Sri Ramakrishna and eating prasad.' I went up with Sudhangsu and told the girls, 'Why have you entered the shrine? And why are you eating prasad here?'

"Seeing that I was very displeased, a young widow in the group said excitedly, 'It's our pleasure to sit and eat here. Who are you to question it?'

"I was then quite young; there was no trace of beard or

43

moustache on my face yet! I angrily said, 'Please get out of this room!'

"Then that girl responded, 'Do you know who we are?'

"I replied, 'Yes, I know very well who you are!' In fact, I didn't even think that they were from any respectable family.[24] Being displeased at my rude behaviour, they stopped eating and very excitedly left the shrine. While leaving, they threatened me with grave consequences.

"I cleaned up the mess in the shrine, and went downstairs to do my duties in the storeroom. I had become somewhat proud thinking that by carrying out the orders of Baburam Maharaj, I had been able to at last give the right kind of service to Sri Ramakrishna. About two hours passed after that incident. In the courtyard Kali Kirtan was going on in full swing. Suddenly Swami Bhumananda came and said to me, 'Come, Swami Brahmananda is calling you.'

"I said, 'I'll be there right after finishing this work.'

"Swami Bhumananda pulled me by the hand and said, 'Come right now! Do you know what you've done?' He pushed me into the room at the southwest corner of the building and left. I could see several direct disciples of Sri Ramakrishna sitting there with Ramlal Chattopadhyay. It appeared as though

24. Krishnamayi Devi, the eldest daughter of Ramlal Chattopadhyay, informed Brahmachari Akshayachaitanya that a girl named Ramani was in that group. She used to be a prostitute. Those who had accompanied her had heard that once the Divine Mother had appeared to Sri Ramakrishna in the form of Ramani. That's why they respected her. Even though Ramani had by that time given up her questionable profession, she still dressed as gaudily as before. She still used two very large earrings—the kind of ornament women of respectable families would not use.

I had entered into a cave filled with Himalayan gravity. Swami Saradananda said to me angrily, 'Do you know what you've done? You've put all of us to shame!' Mahapurush Maharaj and all the others acquiesced in what Swami Saradananda had said.

"With great pain in his voice, Swami Brahmananda very slowly articulated, 'You have insulted the family of our Ishta.'

"Ramlal Chattopadhyay said almost in tears, 'My daughters left the Math weeping. Even though I tried hard to make them understand, they wouldn't stay.' Hearing that, I realized for the first time the offence I had committed.

"Sharat Maharaj (Swami Saradananda) said to me, 'You have to leave the Math immediately!'

"Mahapurush Maharaj said, 'Yes. You have to leave right now. You have committed an unforgivable offence.'

"Swami Brahmananda stood up and said, 'Now you must go to Dakshineswar to ask for their forgiveness. If they forgive you, you can come back to the Math. Otherwise, you have to leave from there itself.'

"Then Swami Brahmananda took me upstairs to his room. There he said to Amulya Maharaj, 'Please fill a basket with all kinds of prasad. Ishwar will take it by boat to Dakshineswar.' Then he said to me, 'You will carry this prasad to Lakshmi Didi[25] and tell her what offence you committed. Take these five rupees that I am giving you. Salute her after offering this money to her. And request the girl whom you scolded to forgive you. If she forgives you, bring a letter from them stating that you have been forgiven. Also you must wait on them

25. She was the niece of Sri Ramakrishna.

while they eat this prasad. Please also tell them that they are all invited to come next Thursday and have prasad at lunch time at the Math.'

"Ramlal Chattopadhyay accompanied me to Dakshineswar. He was still angry. While in the boat he told me, 'My daughter will never forgive you! You must leave the Math.' My mind was filled with great pain and remorse. I felt as if I had committed a fathomless offence! I made up my mind that if I were not forgiven, I would give up my life by plunging into the river.

"When I arrived at Dakshineswar, Lakshmi Devi received me very cordially saying, 'Come, my child!' Then I saluted her and told her everything. When that girl saw me, she moved away from me. When I asked for her forgiveness, she said that she would never forgive me. Lakshmi Devi rebuked her saying, 'Did you introduce yourselves to him and say who you were? He is just a young boy. How could he know who you all were! Besides, you also said many things out of anger!' Lakshmi Devi took quite some time to pacify her, and bring her back to where I was. I saluted the girl, and tearfully asked her again to forgive me. Lakshmi Devi said to her, 'Look, the boy is crying. Don't you have any compassion in your heart?'

"Then she said, 'I have forgiven him.'

"Then I served them prasad on leaf plates, and waited on them until they finished eating. Lakshmi Devi placed all kinds of prasad on a leaf plate, and asked me to come and eat. Like feeding a child, she began feeding me with her own hand and said, "My child, I once fed Thakur with my own hands. With the same hands I am feeding you now.' When I requested her to eat she said, 'Let me rinse my hands first with water; then I shall eat. I wouldn't have minded eating with my hand smeared with your leftover food. But it might have done some spiritual harm to you, because I belong to the family of your Ishta.'

"She didn't allow me to return that day. She made me stay with her; and until the late hours of the night she told me many stories about Sri Ramakrishna. In great joy I spent a wonderful time with her. On the following morning, she handed me a letter to be given to Swami Brahmananda and I left for Belur Math.

"On Thursday when they all came to Belur Math to have lunch, Swami Brahmananda took me with them to the shrine. After everyone had saluted the deity in the shrine, he asked Lakshmi Devi, 'Lakshmi Di, have you forgiven this boy? He is very foolish. He doesn't understand anything.'

"She replied, 'Yes, I have forgiven him. Then again, he didn't do anything that bad!' Swami Brahmananda asked me to salute her.

"In the afternoon, when they were about to go back to Dakshineswar, he took me along with him near their boat. Lakshmi Devi was standing on the staircase to the boat. Touching her feet with his hand, he saluted her and said, 'Lakshmi Di, please bless this boy.'

"She put her hands on my head and said, 'May you have great love and devotion for God!'

"While at the Math, I occasionally suffered from malaria. Baburam Maharaj had this notion that those who become frequently ill, in spite of staying in Belur Math, are not fit to serve Sri Ramakrishna. He didn't want them to stay at the Math. Once I had just recovered from my illness, and was still

47

very weak. After several days I was able to have a regular meal. Baburam Maharaj came to me and said, 'You can't stay at the Math. You have to go home.'

"Without protesting, I prepared to leave. Just as I reached the gate of the Math, Sachin came and said, 'You are leaving because Baburam Maharaj asked you to leave. But Swami Brahmananda is the President of the Order. It's your duty to tell him that you are leaving.'

"Sachin put his arms around me, and dragged me to Swami Brahmananda. He was sitting downstairs in a room of the monastery building. After I saluted him, he asked me, 'How are you? Can you prepare a smoke for me?' After I brought him the smoke, he asked me again, 'Why do you look so sickly?'

"I replied, 'For quite sometime I have been suffering from malaria, and Baburam Maharaj has asked me to leave the Math today.'

"He then called Amulya Maharaj and said, 'Write to Kothar today that one of our brahmacharis is going there. Let them arrange to receive him.' He then told me, 'You don't have to go anywhere right now. You stay here.' With his blessings, from that day on I had no more attacks of malarial fever. Gradually I recovered from my weakness as well. I didn't have to go to Kothar.

"My younger brother was going to have his sacred thread ceremony (upanayanam) in Purulia, but my father was very ill at the time. My uncle came with someone else to Belur Math to take me home to be present during the ceremony. I had no wish to go home, but Baburam Maharaj kept on goading me to go. He had given his word to my uncles that he would send me home for the ceremony. One day, when Baburam Maharaj was asking me to go home, and I was telling him that I wouldn't go, Swami Brahmananda came down from his room. I told him, 'Baburam Maharaj is asking me to go home to attend my brother's upanayanam ceremony, but I don't have the slightest wish to leave Belur Math and go there.'

"Swami Brahmananda said, 'You are right. How can a sadhu have a father or grandmother? *We* are your father and grandmother!' (This means that sadhus are not expected to have any family ties.) Then he paused for a moment and said, 'All right, as your father has sent for you to attend your brother's sacred thread ceremony, go there only for a short while. But don't eat the food connected with the upanayanam ceremony. Ask your mother to cook havishya[26] for you.'

"As I was starting for Purulia he told me, 'You are going to Purulia. What gift are you going to bring me from there?' I didn't know what suitable items for gifts were available in Purulia. But Swami Brahmananda on his own said, 'I have heard that good walking canes are available there. Bring one for me.' When I returned from Purulia, I brought with me a walking cane for him and malpoas made of khir that had been prepared by my mother. He enjoyed eating the malpoas.[27]

"Sometime later I and Virupaksha (Swami Videhananda) were sent to work in the Bangalore Ashrama in South India. In August 1916, Swami Brahmananda came from Calcutta to Bangalore for a visit via Madras. He brought with him Swamis Bhumananda and Gopalananda as his additional sevaks. In the Bangalore Ashrama Swami Brahmananda sometimes

---

26. Havishya is a meal consisting of cooked rice, ghee, boiled vegetables, and milk. Such a meal is considered to be conducive to spiritual life.

27. Malpoa is a kind of sweetmeat made of thickened, doughy milk first deep-fried in butter and then soaked in sweet syrup.

asked me also to do some simple things for him, while he asked one of his senior sevaks Bi— to work outdoors, such as digging in the vegetable garden.

"Bi— realized that Swami Brahmananda had already made up his mind to get rid of him. One day Bi— said to me, 'Let me tell you one thing.' Then he quoted a popular saying, 'The love of the great ones is as unstable as a dam made of sand. This moment they may give you wonderful things, but the next moment they may throw you in jail!'

"After Swami Brahmananda went from Bangalore to Madras, he stopped allowing Bi— to serve him anymore. He asked Bi— to go to Kanchi and perform spiritual austerities there. But when Swami Brahmananda visited South India the third time, he said to Mahapurush Maharaj, 'Bi— served me just like my mother. But he would try to monopolize me, and wouldn't allow anyone else to come close to me. At the same time, behind my back, whatever things he had to do for me he would have them done by others. But now that he has gone through a lot of austerities, I'll bring him back to me.' However, Bi— did not become that close to Swami Brahmananda again, although the Swami had the same love and affection for him.

"Earlier, when Swami Brahmananda was in Belur Math, Bi— used to serve him in the daytime. Khudumani served him at night. Khudumani once said that one night he had to give Swami Brahmananda a dhoti to wear, but when he searched through the swami's clothes in the clothes rack, he only found dhoties that were tattered and torn! At last, at the bottom of the rack, he found a dhoti that was intact. Swami Brahmananda then said, 'They (some of his attendants) want to control my everything. They want me to do what they want!'

"In 1913 or 1914, while Swami Brahmananda was in Varanasi, Hrishikesh (Swami Prashantananda) was staying with him. But Bi— didn't like that at all. Bi— would ask Hrishikesh to make the hubble-bubble ready for Swami Brahmananda to smoke. Then he himself would carry it to the Swami. One day in the late evening, Swami Brahmananda asked Bi— to prepare his food in the kitchen, and asked Hrishikesh to come and massage his feet. (Bi— used to do that.) Standing, Hrishikesh began massaging the Swami, who said to him, 'Come and sit on my bed.' But according to tradition, out of respect a junior monk is never supposed to sit on a senior monk's bed. So Hrishikesh hesitated. But Swami Brahmananda endearingly asked him again to sit. Bi— happened to see Hrishikesh sitting on Swami Brahmananda's bed. Later he scolded Hrishikesh for that.

"While I was in Bangalore I had the following conversation with Swami Brahmananda:

"He asked me, 'Who is your best friend?'

"I replied, 'I'm not too friendly with anyone.'

"He asked, 'Why? Can't you get along with Virupaksha? Don't you have any love for him?'

"I replied, 'No. Maharaj, I can't get along with him. I don't love anybody!'

"Then he said, 'That's all right. If you love anybody you're sure to get pain. Just see, I love Amulya (one of his sevaks) so much, but he has gone away to Mysore leaving me here. He told me

51

that he would return after a day. But three days have passed and he hasn't come back. See how worried I am about him!'[28]

"The Swami in charge of the Bangalore Ashrama didn't like me. So reluctantly I had to go to Madras Math while Swami Brahmananda was still visiting Bangalore. I had a keen desire to visit Kanyakumari with him, but it was not fulfilled. Swami Brahmananda told me, 'Now you go to Madras. When I go there I'll take you with me to visit some other place.' He kept his promise. He allowed me to accompany him when he later visited Trichinapalli, Kanchi and Tirupati.

"After he came to Madras from Bangalore, Swami Brahmananda allowed me to give him some personal service. But daily I had plenty of regular duties to perform at the Madras Math. It would take me a long time to finish my duties in the shrine. There were many details to be taken care of in the service of the deity. Swami Brahmananda would summon me every now and then to give him various kinds of personal service, such as to prepare a smoke for him or to give him water to drink. I was also asked to wait on him when he would eat his meals or to massage him a little. As a result, often I couldn't be punctual at our meal times. The abbot of the Ashrama complained about me to Swami Brahmananda saying, 'Ishwar is not attentive to his duties. We eat lunch at 1 pm. But he is never punctual. This very much inconveniences the cook who serves the meals.'

"Swami Brahmananda heard the complaints, but said nothing. Instead, he asked me to do many more things for him, causing even greater delay. As a result, I would finish taking my lunch as late as at three o'clock in the afternoon.

---

28. About love Swami Brahmananda once said, "You can only love *one* person." He put special emphasis on the word *one*. Another day he said, "If the person whom I love is able to know that I love him, that's no love."

"The responsibility of taking care of all the needs of Swami Brahmananda rested with a particular sevak. Swami Brahmananda consented to everything that the sevak decided to do. It was also noticed that he supported this sevak when the sevak complained about any arrangement made by someone else. Acting upon the complaint, Swami Brahmananda would cancel the arrangement. This gradually inflated the false ego of the sevak.[29]

"The abbot of Madras Math complained to this sevak about my negligence in work. The sevak had already developed a great dislike for me seeing that Swami Brahmananda was partial to me.

"After hearing the complaint from the abbot, the sevak decided to take some drastic action towards me. He called me and said, 'From tomorrow you must go punctually to have your meals.'

"I responded, 'Swami Brahmananda asks me to wait on him when he has his meals in his room. That's why I am unpunctual.'

"He said, 'I am always present when he has his meals. Whatever he needs to have done, I'll do. You don't have to be there.'

"I thought that I would follow the orders of the sevak. But a day later, Swami Brahmananda again called me and from then

---

29. Some of the sevaks who served the Holy Mother or Swami Brahmananda became pretty egotistical; for this, they had to suffer a lot. To explain this, Swami Saradananda said, "While serving these great souls, the sevaks come in contact with their tremendous spiritual power. But they can't digest the benefit they get from such contact. They abuse it." Hari Maharaj used to say, "Unless one is a spiritually illumined soul, one can neither really serve nor digest personal service given by others."

on started giving me so many jobs to do every day that I was even later for meals than before.

"Swami Brahmananda was then staying on the second floor of a house rented by the Madras Math. He used to eat his meals in his room on that floor. One day after serving him, as I was climbing down the stairs, I saw the sevak standing at the base of the staircase. He gave me a severe scolding and said, 'I told you to go and eat your meals punctually, but you paid no heed to my words. What have you been doing all this time?'

"It was already quite late in the afternoon, and I hadn't had time even to take my shower. I was also very hungry. His words hurt me, and his scolding made me lose my temper. The exchange of words that we then had between us is neither worth repeating nor worth hearing. Swami Brahmananda heard our entire altercation from upstairs.

"While taking his lunch the next day, Swami Brahmananda sent for me. I went to him and started fanning him with a hand fan with fear as well as a feeling of disgust. Then the sevak came and began reading out the incoming mail to him. Normally Swami Brahmananda interjected comments in between the reading of the letters. But that day he remained completely silent.

"He used to have two or three chapaties along with his meals. That day he himself called Barju, the Ashrama cook, to come and give him an extra chapati. After a few calls Barju came running and said, 'I am going to bake one immediately and bring it to you.'

"The sevak gave Barju a severe scolding. Swami Brahmananda then said to the sevak, 'Do you also want to control what I eat? Do I have to eat according to your wish? I've tolerated you a lot, but I won't do it anymore! You have been trying to use me as your puppet.' Saying this, he went on narrating in great detail when and how in the past the sevak had behaved badly with him as well as with others, and how and when he had complained to him about others, etc. I was simply astounded to see this wonderful display of his memory power. Finally he said, 'From now on you won't be serving me anymore! All these days I have been watching to see how much more egotistical you can become!' Then he became quiet.

"The sevak shed tears and prayed for forgiveness, but Swami Brahmananda remained totally unmoved. Swami Sharvananda also requested him on behalf of the sevak, but it yielded no effect.[30]

"I had the following conversation with Swami Brahmananda when arrangements were being made for his trip to Puri from Madras: "Swami Brahmananda asked, 'Will you stay with me?'

"I replied, 'Maharaj I'm afraid of serving you!'

"He asked, 'Why should you be afraid?'

"I said, 'You used to love Bi— so much. He also served you so well. Yet, you got rid of him! You made another person also leave. Whenever I saw you scolding Bi—, I would become awfully nervous.'

---

30. After this incident the sevak did many other things as wished by Swami Brahmananda. But he never got the opportunity to give personal service to his guru during the last few years of his guru's life. But Swami Brahmananda, while on his deathbed, sent for the sevak and talked to him very lovingly. He then allowed the sevak to give him personal service, such as serving him his meals during the last few days of his life.

"He said, 'Do I scold much? It was necessary for them to stay away from me for a while. Do I not love them? Taking advantage of my love for them, they were entangling me in Maya. Bi— couldn't tolerate anyone else coming close to me or serving me. That's why it became necessary for them to be asked to stay away.'

"I said, 'Maharaj, I must tell you that I won't be able to stand that much scolding from you. Nor should you ever ask me to go away!'

"Then in a very affectionate voice he said, 'I won't ever ask you to leave, nor will I scold you!'

"While in Madras, Swami Brahmananda asked me to read some Sanskrit hymns every day. But I lost interest in reading them after about a year and a half.

"One day he asked, 'Do you read the hymns every day as I instructed you to do?'

"I replied, 'No.'

"He asked me again, 'Why don't you do it?'

"I said, 'I don't find it interesting.'

"He said, 'If you don't do what I ask you to do, why are you staying here?'

"I replied, 'You love me and I also like you, that's why I'm staying here. The day I'll realize you don't love me anymore, I shall leave this place.'

"After this conversation he went to Dakshineswar in his disciple Shyamsundar's car. He took Swami Vasudevananda along with him to chant Sanskrit hymns. He was fond of listening to the chanting of hymns inside the Dakshineswar Kali Temple.

"I felt very hurt because he hadn't taken me along with him. So I went to visit the home of one of his disciples. On my way back, as I was about to enter Ramkanta Bose Street, I suddenly noticed that Swami Brahmananda's car was just behind me! From the moving car he called loudly to me, 'Where did you go?' I didn't answer.

"As soon as he returned from Dakshineswar he sent for me. Still hurt and angry, I said to Bhavani who had come to give me Swami Brahmananda's message, 'I won't go to him, I'm very angry now!'

"From his room he heard what I had said. He said to Bhavani very sweetly, 'All right, let him come later.'

"As Swami Brahmananda was having a smoke after his dinner, I entered his room and shut the door behind me. He was leisurely sitting with the pipe of his hubble-bubble in his hand. He was not smoking. One of his hands, resting on his knee, was held in the abhaya mudra (traditional hand sign to dispel fear in the hearts of others). And it appeared that his eyes were dripping love and compassion. I sat on the floor, and putting my head close to his lap asked, 'Maharaj, are you angry with me?' He didn't say anything; he only touched my head with his soft hand. There was no indication whatsoever of even the slightest anger or displeasure on his face.

"I began crying and said tearfully, 'Maharaj, please don't abandon me! I don't have anyone else but you to call my own.'

"He said, 'Can I ever abandon you?'

"I said, 'I'll be with you as long as you are here. After that I'll leave the Ramakrishna Mission.'

"With some surprise in his voice he asked me, 'Why won't you stay in the Order? Why?'

"I replied, 'I don't like anyone else here!'[31]

"He became silent for a while. Then he said, 'Go and take your meal after showering.'

"Every day, around 2:30 in the afternoon, I used to go to Swami Brahmananda and give him a massage. Then at four o'clock I would prepare a smoke for him. A few days after the above incident as I was massaging him, he seemed to be fast asleep. While massaging him, I put my finger between his thumb and forefinger, and he grabbed it. I tried hard to pull my finger out of his grip, but no matter how much I tried I couldn't do it. At last I put my one foot against the wall for leverage, and with all my strength tried to pull my finger out. But I failed. Swami Brahmananda's body was as soft as butter, and he was still sleeping. It didn't appear that he had been ap-

---

31. Ishwar had difficulty in getting along with others. It is apparent from his behavior that he was not cut out for disciplined monastic life. Swami Premananda was an extremely loving soul. But he had to train and discipline the young monks in Belur Math, sometimes through scolding. Ishwar resented that. Eventually, he left the Order.
Once Swami Premananda said to Swami Brahmananda, "To discipline the young men who join the Order I have to scold them. For that reason they're very displeased with me."
Swami Brahmananda told him, "They're extremely fortunate that you scold them. Swami Vivekananda scolded us so severely! If these boys get even one-hundredth part of that kind of scolding from us, they will all leave the Order."

plying any strength at all! And I considered myself a wrestler; I could easily lift 572 lbs. from the floor up to my knees. As though realizing my helplessness, he suddenly chuckled a little and released my finger. His eyes were still closed and it appeared to me that he was still sleeping!

"He had told me, 'Can I ever abandon you?' By this playacting did he symbolically try to make me understand the meaning of those words? Did he want me to know that even if *I* wanted to leave, he wouldn't let me go? I also came to understand that day that unless he allowed me to go, it was not within my power to leave."

◊ ◊ ◊ ◊ ◊

One of the sevaks of Swami Brahmananda did something unethical. Another sevak complained about it to Hari Maharaj, who then brought it to the attention of Swami Brahmananda.

He sent for the sevak who had complained and said to him, "I've heard that you went and complained to Hari Maharaj. While I am here, I don't understand why you had to go and complain about such insignificant things to him. My child, if you don't feel comfortable here you may go elsewhere. People of various temperaments are living with me. Later, all kinds of people—good and bad—will come to me. You are here to serve me; you are not to judge other people. Am I not watching over them? I know that the defect of the person you've been talking about isn't that serious. Compared to the many good qualities that he has, this defect is nothing. People have good qualities as well as bad. Please remember that none of those who are with me is inferior."

Once there was a proposal by those in the Math office to

transfer a sevak of Swami Brahmananda somewhere else. When the Swami was informed about it, he became annoyed and said to them, "I can relinquish the position of your President, but I'll never abandon one to whom I've given shelter!"

CHAPTER IV

SWAMI BRAHMANANDA'S CONCERN FOR THE DEVOTEES

It was 1910. Swami Brahmananda had just returned to Belur Math from South India, bringing with him the *Nama-Ramayana*. For the first time at Belur Math, arrangements were made for singing it to the right melodies. On the evening of the performance the courtyard was filled with people. Girish Babu (Girish Chandra Ghosh) and Master Mahashaya (Mahendranath Gupta) were present.

Sitting cross-legged in the crowd, Gokul Babu was listening intently to the singing. Suddenly he felt that both his legs had gone to sleep. The courtyard was so packed with people sitting cross-legged on the ground that he had no way to stretch his legs to get the circulation going. Nor could he leave the courtyard because people were blocking the exit. Eventually, he was in great pain and discomfort. Then he saw two extremely bright eyes glancing at him. It is strange that immediately after that all his suffering and pain were gone!

It was Swami Brahmananda who had glanced at him. Gokul Babu didn't know him, because he had never met him before.

◊◊◊◊◊

Not only did Swami Brahmananda think of the after-life well being of the monks and householders whom he loved, but he tried to ensure their worldly well being as well. He anticipated that after his passing away, one of his sevaks would feel helpless and would also need money to support himself. That's why he created the opportunity for the sevak to be intimate with a person who, Swami Brahmananda knew, would take care of the sevak later. It happened as he had wished.

◊◊◊◊◊

His close association with the sadhus increased Dr. Kanjilal's desire to lead a life of renunciation. He became obsessed with the idea that after making moderate financial provision for his family, he would spend most of his time in spiritual practice. Luckily an opportunity came. The head of the Kankhal Sevashrama informed that there was a vacancy in the position of the medical officer for the Kankhal Municipality. If Dr. Kanjilal wanted, he could get that position.

Very elated at the news, the doctor went to the Holy Mother to get her permission. But she said, "First make sure that it will be good for you!" He then wrote to Swami Brahmananda in Varanasi seeking his permission. At that time Kumud Bandhu Sen was in Varanasi. Swami Brahmananda told him, "Look what Kanjilal wants to do! He has written that leaving his practice in Calcutta, he'll go to Kankhal to work for only 100 or 150 rupees a month! He has a large family to support. He also has to take care of his elderly parents. Tell him the adage that 'One who has it here also has it there; and one who doesn't have it here also doesn't have it there.' Let him try to earn well in Calcutta rather than wasting time going here and there. After returning to Calcutta, tell Sharat Maharaj that I've asked him not to allow Kanjilal to waste two or three hours at the Udbodhan Ashrama when he goes there."

After Swami Brahmananda's return to Calcutta, one day Kanjilal came and began giving the Swami a massage. Then Swami Brahmananda said, "We've helped so many people and yet the doctor is finding it hard to earn a good living. Nevertheless, he'll have a good practice later."

At this, the doctor said, "Please bless me so that I have more love and devotion to God than money."

Swami Brahmananda said, "That's all right, but how will you take care of your family without money?" Thereafter the doctor's income steadily grew.

◊ ◊ ◊ ◊ ◊

Jiten Babu brought Swami Brahmananda, Baburam Maharaj and their party to Mymensingh and served them with great love and devotion. Baburam Maharaj had great love and affection for Jiten Babu. The day after their arrival in Dacca from Mymensing, Swami Brahmananda said to Swami Premananda, "Please show your spiritual power. Make sure that Jiten experiences God in this very life!" This was of course said when Jiten Babu was not present.

◊ ◊ ◊ ◊ ◊

Satyendranath Mazumdar came to Bhubaneswar from Calcutta on a visit. After staying in Bhubaneswar for a few days, and just as he was getting ready to visit Puri, Swami Brahmananda asked him not to go there, but instead to return to Calcutta. Mr. Mazumdar said that he had come all the way from Calcutta mainly wishing to visit Puri. But Swami Brahmananda wouldn't heed to Mr. Mazumdar's words, insisting that he must return to Calcutta and not go to Puri. When Mr. Mazumdar reached the Bhubaneswar railway station, he was amazed to see that the Swami had already sent a brahmachari there to make sure that Mr. Mazumdar bought a ticket for Calcutta.

Later Mr. Mazumdar came to Belur Math one day and

asked Swami Brahmananda, "Maharaj, why didn't you allow me to go to Puri?"

He replied, "The time was most inauspicious for your visit to Puri. Had you gone there you would have died."[32]

◊ ◊ ◊ ◊ ◊

Lalit Chatterjee of Baghbazar was a very large-hearted person. Swami Brahmananda had great love and affection for him. Lalit Babu had a moustache resembling that of Kaiser Wilhelm II of Germany. That's why the Swami gave him the nickname Kaiser. Lalit Babu had the habit of drinking. Once his addiction to liquor became so bad that he left home and started staying in the Chowringhee area. He ate his meals at the Grand Hotel of Calcutta. His wife came to Swami Brahmananda one day and tearfully reported all these things to him. He gave her the assurance that he would do his best to remedy the situation.

One morning after this, Swami Brahmananda went alone to the Grand Hotel. Hiding himself from Lalit Babu, he waited for him to come and have his meal. As soon as he entered the dining hall and was about to eat, Swami Brahmananda came up to him and picked up his glass of liquor from the table. Then he offered the liquor to the Divine Mother, and holding it in front of Lalit Babu said, "Lalit, now drink! From now on drink in moderation, and whenever you drink, please offer it to the Divine Mother first.'

Seeing the Swami there, Lalit Babu was overwhelmed and stunned. After being asked a few times by Swami Brahmananda, he drank the liquor. Then he insisted on driving the Swami back to Baghbazar. After arriving, Swami Brahma-

---

32. Source: Nilkanta Chakrabarty.

nanda asked him to go home, see his wife, and then go to work. This incident had a great beneficial influence on Lalit Babu's life.[33]

Another incident. One day Lalit Babu had the following conversation with Swami Brahmananda, who said to Lalit Babu, "Try to have holy company often. One derives great benefit from the company of a genuine holy man. Don't stop being in his company even if the saint indulges in joking and other such frivolities. At any moment even a single word spoken by him may change the entire course of your life."

Lalit Babu asked, "Shall we make any spiritual progress if we don't make any effort, but just sit and talk to you?"

Swami Brahmananda replied, "Both are needed. Otherwise, everyone who does japa and meditates would have become a God-realized soul. Certainly there are benefits of having holy company. You have so many clubs to go to, yet why do you come here every day? Sri Ramakrishna used to say, 'Your hand will burn whether you knowingly or unknowingly put it into fire.' He used to say, 'You will be immortal whether someone pushes you or you yourself jump into the lake of ambrosia.' One who has been bitten by a cobra can never get rid of that venom. I saw a sadhu in the western province. He also used to say, 'Don't leave the company of a sadhu even if he indulges in fun and frolic. The beneficial impact of his holiness can never be avoided.'" (Source: Pareshnath Sen Gupta)

◊ ◊ ◊ ◊ ◊

A young man of the Baghbazar neighbourhood went astray through bad company. Yet he had devotion for Swami Brah-

---

33. The source of this incident is Swami Parameshananda.

mananda and would sometimes come to salute him. One day Swami Brahmananda on his own asked the young man to come and give some personal service. Then after taking his meal he said to the young man, "I'm not asking you to change your lifestyle. Do what you've been doing. But before you do anything, please remember me once."

That evening the young man went to his club. As he was listening to the singing, he raised his glass of liquor, about to drink. Then he remembered Swami Brahmananda's request, "Remember me once!" And the Swami's compassionate face flashed in his mind. This made him pensive. Under pressure from his friends he drank some liquor, but everything seemed insipid and tasteless. On the second day as well there was a repetition of the same experience. When he went to the club on the third day, he was overpowered by a feeling of disgust for drinking. He dashed the glass of liquor against the wall and gave up evil company forever.[34]

◇◇◇◇◇

It was 1921. Swami Brahmananda was then in Bangalore. He got a letter from Nadu in Vrindaban, informing him that he had married a young widow. Nadu was a disciple of Swami Brahmananda, and Swami Vivekananda had been quite fond of him. He used to be the head of the Ramakrishna Mission Sevashrama in Vrindaban. Getting the news of his marriage, Swami Brahmananda became worried and was seen every now and then muttering to himself, "Why did he marry? He could have avoided it!" He seemed quite worried for the next one or two days.

After his return to Belur Math, Nadu and his wife came to

---

34. Source: Brahmagopal Datta.

see him. He received Nadu as lovingly as before. Then both of them sat close to each other and talked for quite a while. He heartily blessed Nadu and asked him particularly to take care of his health. When he took leave of him, Swami Brahmananda kept looking at him intently until he disappeared from sight. Within the next one or two years Nadu died in Vrindaban of tuberculosis.

◊◊◊◊◊

This incident happened when Swami Brahmananda was staying at the Balaram Mandir in Calcutta. One day, early in the morning, the news came from the Yogodyana that Yogavinod, a monastic disciple of Ramchandra Datta, was vomiting blood. Swami Brahmananda became very worried and instructed them to call in a good doctor for his treatment. After about two hours the news came that Yogavinod had passed away. Hearing that, the Swami was grief-stricken and began pacing back and forth inside the large hall in an abstracted mood. After sometime a devotee came. He saluted him and asked, "Maharaj, are you all right?"

Swami Brahmananda replied sadly, "One of our sadhus has died today," Then he resumed pacing back and forth in the hall as before.

We have heard that once in the past Yogavinod served Swami Brahmananda as an attendant for a few days. In this incident we come to see Swami Brahmananda's nonsectarian attitude, because the relationship between Kankurgachhi Yogodyana and Belur Math was not very cordial at that time.

SWAMI TURIYANANDA
(ALSO KNOWN AS HARI MAHARAJ)

CHAPTER V

SWAMI BRAHMANANDA—A MAN OF GREAT SYMPATHY

Hari Maharaj was very ill at the Shashiniketan in Puri. The surgeon had come to perform surgery on a sore on his leg. Swami Brahmananda, who was also staying at the Shashiniketan, shuddered when he heard that Hari Maharaj was going to have surgery. Like a little boy he became extremely nervous and restless. One minute he would enter Hari Maharaj's room and the next minute he would come out and pace back and forth in the large hall. Sometimes, however, he would enter Hari Maharaj's room and stand close to his bed for a while.

The surgery was finally over. The Swami had gone through his surgery quietly and was resting peacefully in bed. Swami Brahmananda asked him, "Do you have a lot of pain, Hari Maharaj?"

Smiling, he replied, "No, I don't feel any pain. Not even as much pain as one gets from an ant-bite. But, Maharaj, I beg you to leave the room. I can see that you've been suffering much more than I." Then he placed his hand on Swami Brahmananda's hand and said, consolingly, "Please don't worry. Really, I am not in pain."

Swami Brahmananda then returned to his own room, and sitting on the smaller cot said to his sevak, "Prepare a smoke for me." There were tears of sympathy in his eyes as he said those words.

◊ ◊ ◊ ◊ ◊

At the time of this incident Swami Brahmananda was

staying at the Balaram Mandir in Calcutta. One morning at around 10 o' clock, Pra— came to see Swami Brahmananda from one of the Ramakrishna Mission Ashramas.

After his arrival he asked, "Where is Maharaj?" Then he started crying. He looked sick and his hair was disheveled. He almost looked crazed. Swami Brahmananda was seated in the hall. Pra— entered and prostrated himself in front of the Swami. He caught hold of his feet and wetting them with his tears, said, "Maharaj, so and so (naming a person) beat me so hard that I thought I was going to die. Then a brahmachari came, and pushing me down to the ground, started hitting me in the back with a brick for quite sometime." Pra—'s shirt was torn. He removed his shirt and showed Swami Brahmananda the marks of injury on his back.

Hearing all this Swami Brahmananda's eyes filled with tears. Very lovingly he began stroking Pra—'s head with his hand and said, "Stay with me here for a few days. Let me see what I can do!" He later wrote a letter to the head of that Ashrama, and in very strong language admonished him for treating Pra— so cruelly.[35] And as if to save the brahmachari as much as possible from the imminent bad effect of his misdeed, Swami Brahmananda asked him to come and stay with him. Within one year of this incident, however, Swami Brahmananda passed away. Then the brahmachari became completely insane. He later died miserably after suffering from a

35. Such ill treatment of any monastic member is unthinkable in the Ramakrishna Order. Any monk physically hurting another monk, or for that matter anyone else, will surely be expelled from the Order. But this incident happened during the earliest period of the Ramakrishna Order. Aside from that, Swami Brahmananda was personified compassion. He believed in transforming people through kindness and love. This explains his behaviour.

prolonged bout of insanity.

◇ ◇ ◇ ◇ ◇

Earlier, when Swami Brahmananda was living in Puri, he developed a friendly relationship with Atal Bihari Maitra, the deputy magistrate of Puri. Atal Babu had three wives. They did not have any children. He addressed his eldest wife as Bada-Ma. (The Bengali word "Bada-Ma" may be translated into English as the "Elder Mother" or "Senior Mother.") Every Sunday Swami Brahmananda, his sevaks, and some of his devotees were invited to dinner at Atal Babu's home.

The sevaks were happy to see Swami Brahmananda's loving behaviour towards Atal Babu, but they did not seem to like Atal Babu too much. One sevak said, "Whenever Atal Babu came to see Maharaj at the Shashiniketan in Puri, we had to prepare so many smokes for him. He had a kind of rectangular body with a short neck. When he would grin, his eyes would resemble the eyes of someone from Mongolia and his toothless face would look really scary.

"Parcels of vegetables and fruits were regularly sent for Swami Brahmananda twice or thrice a week from Calcutta. When the parcels would arrive, he would have them opened in his presence. He would always send some portion of the fruits and vegetables to Atal Babu's home. We would be surprised to see how lovingly and eagerly he would send them to Atal Babu. If the parcels arrived when Atal Babu was present at the Shashiniketan, the Swami wanted them opened in his presence. And when the parcels were opened, he would say to Atal Babu, 'See, all these nice fruits and vegetables have come from Calcutta.'

"Atal Babu would then be beyond himself with joy. With a

big smile on his face he would say, 'Maharaj, we don't even get to see such wonderful vegetables and fruits in this benighted place! All that we get here is taro roots and pumpkins. But the papayas here are excellent!'

"If he noticed in the opened parcels clusters of the famous Martyaman bananas of Bengal, he would immediately say to Swami Brahmananda, 'I love to eat these bananas! Bada-Ma also likes all these fruits very much.' Hearing this, Swami Brahmananda would laugh a lot and would arrange to send some of the bananas and fruits to Atal Babu's home. The sevaks had to carry them there. We never saw the Swami express even the slightest displeasure at his behaviour.

"The last time that he met Swami Brahmananda was in the city of Bhubaneswar. He had rented a house there and was living with Bada-Ma. The Swami, who was then in Bhubaneswar, went to see Atal Babu and his wife. We also accompanied him. We were sorry to see that Atal Babu had lost a lot of weight and had become very weak. Seeing the Swami, Atal Babu rose from his chair, and I think for the first time, saluted Swami Brahmananda, touching his feet with great respect. The Swami caught hold of his hand and made him sit close to him. Then he said to Atal Babu, 'What has happened? Your health seems to have deteriorated very much. Please take care of your health and become all right soon. The climate of Bhubaneswar will also help you to regain your health.'

"Bada-Ma saluted Swami Brahmananda with great devotion and said, 'He won't do what's good for his health. As he has problems with his digestion, the doctor has asked him not to eat a lot of fruit. But whenever he sees guavas, he has to eat them—just like a young child! He can't control himself.'

CHAPTER V

"Atal Babu said, 'Guavas, bananas, pineapples and papayas—all these fruits are fit to be offered to God! I am so fond of their smell that when I see them I can't control myself. I must eat them!'

"Swami Brahmananda said very lovingly, 'Please get well first; then you will eat them. Fruits are indeed fit for God. I also like fruits very much. But it is not proper to eat fruits when the digestion is not good. When I have stomach trouble, I don't eat them.'"

◊ ◊ ◊ ◊ ◊

The same sevak then talked about another person. He said, "When Swami Brahmananda was in Puri a letter came informing him that the attorney Paltu Kar was coming for a visit. The Swami invited him to come and stay with us. During the birthday celebration of Sri Ramakrishna I had once seen Paltu Babu in Belur Math. Baburam Maharaj hugged him cordially, but I didn't notice any cordiality that day in Paltu Babu's behaviour. I had already heard a little bit about him from Swami Brahmananda. In connection with a litigation involving Belur Math, he had to sometimes go to Paltu Kar for legal advice. On such occasions he would make the Swami sit in his office for the entire day. Paltu Kar would eat three or four meals during that period, but would never offer anything to Swami Brahmananda.

"Paltu Babu came to Puri with his wife and son-in-law. It was the year 1917. Swami Brahmananda received them very cordially and made arrangements for their stay on the second floor of the Shashiniketan. He also made sure that the guests would not feel any kind of inconvenience. He told us, 'Don't fail to take the best care of them. Serve him (Paltu Kar) very

73

well, looking upon him as a spiritual son of Thakur.'

"It was so arranged that they would all have their meals with us. Paltu Babu was very Europeanized. His lifestyle and manner of speaking were also like that of the Europeans. As long as he was our guest in Puri, Swami Brahmananda talked and behaved with him like his own brother."

◊ ◊ ◊ ◊ ◊

This incident happened in May 1917, when Swami Brahmananda was coming by train from Madras to Puri. The train stopped at midnight at the Khurdah Road station. The other train that would take him to Puri was to arrive there in the early hours of the morning. Swami Brahmananda and one of his sevaks were travelling by second class. They had reserved berths inside the coach.

Half asleep, the sevak heard Swami Brahmananda talking to someone. The Swami was asking for the news about that person's home and parents. He made many inquiries about them. Then he said, "Your father is a very good man. Have you been serving him well? I permitted you to go and live with him so that you could serve and take care of him. Now that you are living with him, know that there is no higher dharma (religious duty) for you than to serve him well. One has to serve one's parents looking upon them as God. This service will produce the same effect as that of japa and meditation. The attitude with which one gives service is the most important thing. Our scriptures teach us to worship God as our father or mother."

The sevak later heard that the person with whom Swami Brahmananda was talking was one of his initiated disciples. He also heard that the person's mother had passed away many years earlier and that his younger brother, who could have taken care of his father, had to go and work somewhere else.

◊ ◊ ◊ ◊ ◊

Gokuldas De wrote: "Swami Brahmananda's motherly heart would bleed when he would hear of the suffering of his devotees. Through words of sympathy and consolation he would try to give them some relief. When they would become ill, he would take care of them much more lovingly than a doctor would. If they planned to perform ceremonies or hold festivals in their homes, he would take care to see that they would be performed properly."

TEMPLE OF THE DIVINE MOTHER KĀLI AT DAKSHINESWAR

CHAPTER VI

SWAMI BRAHMANANDA'S COMPASSION FOR THE FALLEN AND THE DESTITUTE

Throughout the ages, God's infinite compassion for the fallen and the destitute has found expression whenever He has incarnated on earth in human form. The yearning of the heart is most intense when suffering is the most acute. Perhaps that is the reason why the Lord's compassion is showered on such yearning hearts. Saints of the stature of Swami Brahmananda also have similar compassion for the suffering souls.

Tarasundari, a famous actress of the Bengali stage, once wrote: "My mind was then very upset and restless. Nothing gave me joy, and it became impossible for me to stay quietly in one place. So I started visiting many temples and holy places. One day I went to Belur Math for a visit. Binodoni Dasi, the most famous actress of the Bengali stage, accompanied me. It was past noon when we arrived there. Having had his lunch, Swami Brahmananda was just going for his midday rest. Both of us went and saluted him. He said, 'Hello Binod; hello Tara! Come on in! But you've come so late.[36] We've all had lunch already. You should have informed earlier that you were coming! Nevertheless, please sit down.' He ordered some prasad to be given to us. Immediate arrangement was made to cook some luchis for us. That day he didn't have his usual rest. He sent for a monk and told him, 'Please show them around the Math.'

"I was an impure and fallen woman, so at first I saluted him touching his feet with some hesitation and trepidation of

---

36. He recognized them from having seen them when they had come previously to see Sri Ramakrishna.

heart, lest I do something improper. But my hesitation and diffidence disappeared completely when Swami Brahmananda asked me, 'Why don't you come to see us more often?'

"I replied, 'I hesitate to come to the Math out of fear.'

"Swami Brahmananda said, 'Why should you be afraid to come to Thakur?[37] We all are his children. Come whenever you feel like coming. My child, Thakur doesn't see what's outside; he sees what's inside you. He sees your heart. You mustn't have any hesitation to come to him.'

"We returned home in the afternoon after having tea at the Math. As we were leaving Swami Brahmananda said, 'Come here off and on. Today you had to suffer a lot. Come some other day and have lunch with us.'

"This was my first meeting with Swami Brahmananda—this was also my first spiritual tie with him.

"A few days after our visit to Belur Math, Swami Brahmananda came to our theatre to see the play *Ramanuja*. When the play was over, I came and took the dust of his feet. (I saluted him, touching his feet.) He blessed me saying, 'May you have a lot of love and devotion for God.'

"Once I went to Puri with the desire to see Lord Jagannath. On the way to Puri I stopped in the city of Bhubaneswar and stayed in a dharmashala.[38] Then I heard that Swami Brahmananda was staying at the Bhubaneswar Ramakrishna Math. So I went to see him there. O how heartily he welcomed me! With great eagerness and affection he made me sit and inquired about what I would like to eat, etc. He said, 'Alas, the

37. Thakur is an honorific Bengali word, which in this context means Sri Ramakrishna.
38. A pilgrims' shelter is called a dharmashala.

scorching sun must have made your mouth dry. You've come here for your health. You shouldn't have walked in the scorching sun! …Where do you have your meals? Starting tomorrow you must come and eat your meals with us. Tell me what kind of food you like.' Then he said lamenting, 'My child, we are penniless sadhus, sannyasins and fakirs! I wonder what good things can we procure for you here!'

"His love and cordiality completely overwhelmed me and left me speechless. Just think of who I was! Think of the low level of society to which I belonged! I was so low that I didn't deserve anything but hatred and disrespect from the world. I had no father, relatives or friends to call my own. The entire world to me was somebody else's home, and I was a stranger. No one would even talk to me or look at me without self-interest! …. But today Swami Brahmananda, the all-renouncing monk who is respected by one and all, accepted me as his own through his pure love, affection, and the unexpected attention that he gave me!

"I thought, 'Is it paternal affection? No, it must be something much higher than that!' I couldn't stop crying. It was as if all my pain and suffering began pouring out as my tears, and started falling to the ground, soaking it wet. I felt that at last I had found a place where I could find real solace and peace. I had at last found someone with genuine love and sympathy for me. To him I was not a fallen woman; I was not an untouchable; I was not a hated creature! No, I was the spiritual daughter of Swami Brahmananda! He was my father, my abode of peace, and my God!

"Swami Brahmananda told me so many things that day. I don't remember them all. But what I remember is the sole refuge of my life. He told me, 'My child, you've seen that the world is full of suffering. Don't think that we never suffered. When I first went to Thakur I was young. I used to do my spiritual practice, but wouldn't find peace. Many thoughts would arise in my mind. Sometimes I would wonder why I hadn't found peace yet! Thinking in that manner one day I felt that I wouldn't even go and see Thakur. I would quietly run away. Just then I saw him standing in front of me. He said, "What are you thinking? You've been going through a lot of suffering, isn't it?" I kept quiet. Then he gently stroked my head with his hand. Instantly all my suffering was gone! Then I felt great peace and joy.'

"Hearing Swami Brahmananda's words, suddenly these words came out of my mouth: 'Father, I am also burning inside. It's too much suffering; I can't tolerate it any more. That's why I restlessly wander here and there. Father, would you please soothe my burning heart?'

"With great affection and sympathy he said, 'My child, please pray to Thakur. There is no fear. He came only to relieve our suffering. Chant his holy name. At first you will find it a little difficult. Later Thakur will make everything all right. Don't be afraid my child; there is no cause for fear! Eventually you will have great joy, great fun.'"[39]

◊ ◊ ◊ ◊ ◊

Both Kusum and Harimati lived in Chitpore in Calcutta. Kusum was older than Harimati. They hadn't led a pure life when they were young. In later life Kusum earned a living as a singer. Both of them would frantically go here and there in search of peace. Eventually God showed them the way. They somehow came to know about Swami Brahmananda,

39. The source of this incident is the *Udbodhan*—Jaistha, 1329 B.S.

and came to see him one day at the Balaram Mandir. When they came, they saluted him, touching his feet. Obviously, the Swami knew about their unclean pasts by his spiritual power, but he didn't object to their touching his feet, nor did he show any sign of hesitation. They had brought some fruits as a gift, which he later distributed to the servants.

A few days later they came to see him a second time. He was then sitting on his cot. Harimati saluted him and sat quietly at a distance. But Kusum put her hand on his feet, and sitting on the floor, told him the sad story of her life. It looked like the daughter had come to her father and was telling him the story of her troubles and tribulations. It seemed at long last she had found one who was her own. Her eyes were swimming in tears. Swami Brahmananda said, "Kusum, you are a singer. Won't you sing a devotional song for me?"

Kusum started singing. She sang, "O Lord, why should you deprive me of the opportunity to touch thy holy feet? I've been waiting for such a long time with the hope that I'll be allowed to do that at least after my death, if not in this life." Singing these two lines of the song, she put her head on Swami Brahmananda's feet and burst into tears and he tried to comfort her by softly stroking her head with his hand. Harimati also began shedding tears. Then they both saluted him and left.

Swami Brahmananda said, "Harimati is a very good girl. It's hard to understand why they had to lead that kind of life."

During this second visit also they brought a basketful of fruits and sweets for Swami Brahmananda. The nephew of Sri Ramakrishna, Ramlal, was present and Swami Brahmananda said to him, "If you permit the devotees and monks to eat these fruits and sweets and also distribute them with your own hands, the impurity of the food will be eliminated."

To the devotees of Sri Ramakrishna, Ramlal was known as Ramlal Dada (Big Brother Ramlal). Ramlal Dada said to Swami Brahmananda, "While you are present here, why should I do it?"

Then picking up two mangoes from the basket, Swami Brahmananda gave them to Ramlal Dada and said, "No, you do it please!" Then Ramlal Dada distributed the fruits and sweets to the monks and devotees who were present there.

[Note: Once a lady and a gentleman came to see Swami Brahmananda at the Balaram Mandir. On inquiry Khudumani came to know why they had come to see the Swami. He told Swami Brahmananda that the couple owned two or three houses in Calcutta. They wanted to donate them to Belur Math to defray the expenses of Sri Ramakrishna's daily worship at Belur Math Temple. As soon as Swami Brahmananda heard that he said, "No, as long as we are alive we won't accept such donations. After we are gone, I know that you will do whatever you want to do!"

Then Khudumani said, "Why don't they donate these houses to our Sevashrama in Varanasi?" Hearing this suggestion, Swami Brahmananda said, "All right. Go and bring them to me."

The lady saluted Swami Brahmananda and said that she had bought those houses with the money that she had earned from singing kirtans. He said, "We can't accept your donation for meeting the expenses of Sri Ramakrishna's daily puja at the temple. But if you insist on our accepting your donation, then the income from that property may be used for the virat bhoga during Sri Ramakrishna's birthday celebration." The lady agreed to that proposal.

Swami Brahmananda used to say, "Sri Ramakrishna accepts all kinds of offerings only once a year, during the virat bhoga." It is obvious that even before the lady told him how she had earned money, Swami Brahmananda by his spiritual power knew everything about her. He could not approve of anyone earning money using religion, such as singing the holy name of God. That's why he hesitated to accept her money.]

◊ ◊ ◊ ◊ ◊

On invitation Swami Brahmananda, accompanied by Nirad Maharaj and Ishwar, went to see the play *Ramanuja*. They were all charmed. At the end of the performance, while they were still seated in the box, one person came to Swami Brahmananda and said, "Kindly come downstairs; the actresses want to salute you." Accompanied by Nirad Maharaj Swami Brahmananda then proceeded toward the green room downstairs. Ishwar decided not to accompany them, because being a young monk, he thought that it wouldn't be proper for him to go to see the actresses in the green room.

After walking a short distance Swami Brahmananda looked back and noticed that Ishwar was not following them. He called him and said, "Ishwar, you must also come with us."

Ishwar responded, "I needn't go there. Please go without me."

Surprised, Swami Brahmananda said, "Why not? They want to have blessings from all of us."

◊ ◊ ◊ ◊ ◊

This incident is about Nabadwip Chandra Basak, a resident of the city of Dacca. He was mischievous from his very childhood. He told us that had he not been the only son of his father, his father would surely have disowned him as his son! Having become tired of the burden of his misdeeds, Nabadwip was lucky to see Swami Brahmananda at an auspicious moment in his life. He then surrendered his body and soul to him.

Swami Brahmananda had dispelled his fears saying, "Nabadwip, there is nothing that I can't give you!"

One day Nabadwip asked him, "On some nights, when I am sitting alone in my room, suddenly the entire room becomes filled with a beautiful fragrance. Why does that happen?"

The Swami replied, "Sometimes the saints come. They come to those whom they love. They come to ensure the well being of those whom they love. The room becomes filled with the sweet fragrance that comes from their bodies."

◊ ◊ ◊ ◊ ◊

Another story. Tabu (Matishwar) came almost every day to give a massage to Swami Brahmananda. The Swami was very affectionate to him. Tabu felt so much attraction for him and his sevaks that he sometimes spent the night at the Balaram Mandir, ignoring the discomfort of not having an adequate place to sleep. In spite of having so much holy company, something very unexpected happened in his life. After that unfortunate incident, he was embarrassed and naturally hesitated to come close to Swami Brahmananda. He would still come some evenings and sleep at the Balaram Mandir, lying near the feet of the sevaks. But he would never go to see the Swami.

In this manner some days passed. Then one day Tabu came to the Balaram Mandir just before dusk. He thought that he would spend some time there with his friends and then go home. While there, he was very careful about avoiding Swami Brahmananda. So he stealthily went and peeked in his room to see if he was there or not! The Swami was just coming to his room from the inner quarters of the house. Seeing Tabu he said, "Hello Tabu! What brings you here?" As he approached, Tabu, speechless with embarrassment, tried to move away from him. Swami Brahmananda sat on the bench in the corridor and asked, "Tabu, have you ever seen a big-horned buffalo?"

Tabu replied, "Yes, Maharaj."

The Swami asked, "How large were those horns that you saw?" Tabu spread out his arms to show how big they were.

The Swami then said to Tabu, "There are buffaloes with even bigger horns." Stretching his arms wide he said, "They are this long and this thick." Then he said, "Well, if a lot of mosquitoes sit on the buffalo's horns will the buffalo even know it or feel any discomfort? Know us to be like that."

[Note: The readers should understand that Swami Brahmananda and other God-realized saints never crave creature comforts. Their minds as well as their bodies are full of God consciousness. The body of such a saint is called in our scriptures a *Chinmaya Tanu*. One who touches such a body derives great spiritual benefit. These great souls, who are personified compassion, sometimes allow those who are dear to them to touch their bodies under the pretext of getting personal service from them. Giving them the opportunity to massage their bodies is one of them.]

◊ ◊ ◊ ◊ ◊

One morning in Dacca Swamis Brahmananda and Premananda were seated side by side on two chairs. Swami Premananda said, "Swamiji was the liberator of the fallen and the lowly."

Swami Brahmananda immediately commented, "I am also the liberator of the fallen and the lowly."

CHAPTER VII

SWAMI BRAHMANANDA—AN ADMIRER OF LOVING SERVICE

In those days many people used to go to Bhubaneswar for a change. While there, some of them also visited the Bhubaneswar Ramakrishna Math. Once a gentleman named Kshitish Babu, accompanied by his brother-in-law Yogesh, came for a visit from Khulna.

They often used to come to our Bhubaneswar Math. Swami Brahmananda liked them. He was particularly fond of Yogesh. Once during a conversation Yogesh remarked, "We grow very high quality rice in the rice field at our country home."

Swami Brahmananda then told him, "That's very nice. Why don't you arrange to bring some of that rice to be offered to Thakur in our shrine?"

So a few days later Yogesh came to the Math carrying a small postal parcel containing rice and said to Swami Brahmananda, "Maharaj, this rice has come from our country home."

Seeing the small size of the packet, the sevaks were not too happy. It most probably contained only one or one and a half seers (three pounds) of rice. Every now and then the Math used to receive several maunds of rice (One maund is equal to 82 lbs.) as a gift from Ram Babu's estate in Jhankar. But when Swami Brahmananda saw the rice brought by Yogesh he was very pleased and said, "Excellent! This is very good quality rice! The payesh for Thakur will be made with this rice."

Throughout the week he went on praising the quality of the rice brought by Yogesh. On some days he went to the storeroom to check if the rice was all right. He would also warn the monk in charge of the storeroom and kitchen, "Make sure that not a single grain of this rice is wasted or eaten by mice. If that happens you will face the consequences. I shall break your head with my cane!" (This was just a humorous way of asking them to be very careful. Surely the Swami wouldn't hit anyone with his cane!) While praising the rice, he would also praise Yogesh. Eventually, the rice was used to prepare payesh for Thakur. Swami Brahmananda praised that rice so highly because it had been given with great love and devotion by Yogesh.

◊◊◊◊◊

Another incident. One evening Ram Babu's middle daughter, Madhavilata, came from her in-laws' home. She brought a dish that she had cooked for Swami Brahmananda. While eating that dish at night, Swami Brahmananda asked her, "Have you yourself cooked this?" Then he praised it highly. Later, the other ladies present there tasted the dish and discovered that the dish lacked the right amount of salt, and that it had not been uniformly cooked—a portion of it still remained uncooked. Madhavi felt very embarrassed thinking that she had served that inferior dish to Swami Brahmananda.[40] But he was pleased to eat it, because she had prepared it with great love and devotion.

◊◊◊◊◊

Another anecdote. Ram Babu took his mother from Cal-

40. In Bengal as well as in other parts of India, there is a tradition that any dish offered to a holy person or a deity must not be tasted before it has been offered to them. That must have been the reason why Madhavilata could not know that she had not put the right amount of salt in it. The same reason may apply to why the dish had not been properly cooked by her.

cutta to Varanasi for a visit. The day after they left, Swami Brahmananda said to his cousin Nityananda Basu, "Nitai (Nityananda's nickname), I am going back to Belur Math."

Nitai asked, "Why, Maharaj? Are you going back because you haven't been feeling well?"

He replied, "No, I'm quite all right."

Nitai asked, "Then why are you going?"

He replied, "I'm going back because Ram isn't here."

Nitai saluted the Swami, prostrating before him with great devotion and said, "Under the influence of liquor I'm often not in control of myself. But if you forgive me and give me a little chance, I assure you that I'll serve you wholeheartedly." Nitai saluted him again, touching his feet and said, "Maharaj, please tell me that you won't hate me!"

He reassured him saying, "Not at all. Why should I hate you?" Thereafter Nitai enjoyed the blessed privilege of devotedly serving Swami Brahmananda for a number of days.

◊ ◊ ◊ ◊ ◊

Another episode. Yogin Ma[41] was extremely fond of feeding Swami Brahmananda. Whenever he was staying at the Balaram Mandir, Yogin Ma used to come to see him almost every afternoon. Seeing her he would become very happy and would cheerfully ask, "Yogin Ma, what food have you brought for me today?"

She would reply, "My child, I have brought only a little something for you. Do please eat it." She would usually bring luchis, curried potatoes, and chum chums in a large container.[42]

---

41. Yogin Ma was one of the spiritually exalted women disciples of Sri Ramakrishna.
42. Luchis are flattened wheat dough deep-fried in ghee. Chum chums are sweets that are made by boiling small balls of fresh cheese in syrup.

◊ ◊ ◊ ◊ ◊

On the eve of Swami Brahmananda's departure to Madras, a farewell feast was arranged for him at the Balaram Mandir. After the feast, he went to the Udbodhan Ashrama at the invitation of Brahmachari Ganendranath. As wished by the Swami, ginger beer (a kind of non-alcoholic drink), soda water and tender coconuts had been kept there for his use. Just then Yogin Ma came with a large container with eight or ten Bengali sweets in it. As soon as he saw her, like a young boy he said to her eagerly, "Please give me quickly what you've brought for me."

Yogin Ma's face radiated intense motherly love. Swami Brahmananda took the container of sweets and one by one ate all the sweets she had brought.

◊ ◊ ◊ ◊ ◊

This incident happened in the year 1905. Lakshminarayan Datta of Baghbazar had a dream in which he saw Lord Narayana appearing before him as Gopala and eating khir, chhana, and sugar from his own hand. After having that dream, the idea came to his mind that if he could feed the disciples of Paramahansa Dev it would be as good as feeding Gopala. So his youngest son, Kiranchandra, went to Belur Math and informed Swami Brahmananda of his father's wish.

The Swami accepted their invitation, and on the chosen day went to Mr. Datta's home along with other monks from Belur Math. After eating khir (thickened doughy milk), chhana (fresh cheese, also called panir), sugar, butter, payesh, and sweets made of kshir, he commented, "I've been invited to many places, but nowhere else have I found such sattvika food."[43]

---

43. Source: Brahmagopal Datta.

CHAPTER VIII

SWAMI BRAHMANANDA AND WOMEN DEVOTEES WITH DIVINE ATTRIBUTES

Swami Brahmananda was then staying in the Bangalore Math. One day the accountant general, Mr. Krishnalal Datta, came to Swami Brahmananda and informed that his daughter was critically ill. She was twenty-seven or twenty-eight years old and was unable to even sit up in bed. As she had no hope of recovery she wanted to see the Swami once. Most probably she had come to know from the newspaper that he was staying at the Bangalore Math.

Swami Brahmananda wouldn't easily agree to go and visit private homes. But this time he said, "All right, I'll go." Then he went immediately with Mr. Datta to his home. Returning in the evening, he said to Swami Hariharananda, "You and Ishwar go right now to Mr. Datta's home and sing some devotional songs for that girl. I've told her that our boys sing devotional songs very well. When you go there sing: 'O Lord, when I see thy incomparably beautiful face...' and 'O Lord, please fill my day and night with the joy of thy love....' She is a very good girl. She belongs to Thakur. It's hard to understand where and how He has hidden all his devotees!"

The monks (Swami Hariharananda and Ishwar) went to Mr. Datta's home and saw the girl. Her entire body except for her face was covered with sheets. Her beautiful lotus-like face radiated goodness and purity. Hearing the songs she said, "I am Maharaj's daughter. You are not strangers to me. I have come to like you very much. I would like to hear more of your singing. Please come again."

As ordered by the Swami, they went again to the girl's home and sang for her. At the end when they sang the song: 'Look, there is the Abode of Peace...,' tears of joy rolled down her cheeks.

When Swami Brahmananda heard the news of her death, he said, "She was expelled from heaven by a curse, so she came down to earth. But such a soul cannot live long in this dirty and polluted world."

◊ ◊ ◊ ◊ ◊

Another story. Nityananda Basu's wife, Kamala, was on her deathbed. Swami Brahmananda was very affectionate to her. He went to see her two or three times because Kamala wanted to see him.

One afternoon when he went to see her, she was about to die. He sat by her bedside and said sympathetically, "Why should she die at such a young age?" Then he told his sevak, "Please bring my rosary." The sevak brought the rosary and handed it to him, but he did not do any japa. Instead, he suddenly stood up and said, "Nitai won't be able to keep her here any more. She is leaving this world due to mistreatment. She is a devi. Perhaps she came down to earth because of a curse. Don't you all feel that the entire house now is filled with a divine spiritual mood?" The sevak then became aware that the whole house was full of the fresh fragrance of Arabian jasmine. Yet, nobody had brought any flowers into the house.

Kamala was an initiated disciple of the Holy Mother Sri Sarada Devi.

◊ ◊ ◊ ◊ ◊

I have already told the story of Mr. Atal Maitra, the deputy magistrate of Puri. Swami Brahmananda had great regard for his eldest wife, whom Mr. Maitra would address as "Bada-Ma." The Swami once said about her, "Once I saw a devi come and enter her room. Immediately before that I smelled the fragrance of Arabian jasmine all around."

At the Swami's suggestion, Atal Babu once arranged for the worship of the Divine Mother Kali in his home. Shashi Maharaj was visiting Puri at the time. He performed the worship in Atal Babu's home.

◊ ◊ ◊ ◊ ◊

A certain lady lived in Varanasi. Swami Brahmananda used to call her "Bangal-Mayee." Due to the untimely death of her two daughters, she became overwhelmed with grief. Then somehow she came to know that a saint (Swami Brahmananda) had come for a visit to Varanasi. When she heard that news she came to see Swami Brahmananda to find peace. Through his blessings she gradually got over her unbearable grief. She also started making fast spiritual progress under his guidance. Referring to her, he once commented to our monks there, "There is a lady here who has made a lot of spiritual progress. Even you monks haven't been able to make that much progress!"[44]

◊ ◊ ◊ ◊ ◊

The newly-married Amiyabala came for a visit to Varanasi from her parents' home in Muzaffarpur. The Holy Mother Sri

---

44. Most probably Bangal-Mayee practiced vatsalya bhava. She used to look upon the sadhus of our Order as Gopala. Shukul Maharaj (Swami Atmananda), who was a disciple of Swami Vivekananda, didn't usually talk with ladies. But he would talk with Bangal-Mayee, sometimes even for two hours. As instructed in her dream, she presented a silver flute for Thakur to the Sri Ramakrishna Advaita Ashram in Varanasi.

Sarada Devi was then in Varanasi. On the day after her arrival in Varanasi, Amiyabala, accompanied by Golap-Ma, went to see and salute Swami Brahmananda at the Advaita Ashrama in the morning. In the afternoon Golap-Ma asked him, "What did you think of Bibhuti's wife, Amiyabala?"

He replied, "She is a fine girl. I wonder how a girl raised in Muzaffarpur on a diet of kalai pulse could turn out to be this good!"

Golap-Ma asked, "When you blessed her, what gift did you give?"

He humourously replied, "I gave her only the dust of my feet."

"Only that?" asked Golap Ma.

He replied, "Golap-Ma, don't you know how valuable the dust of one's feet is? Aside from that, I blessed her, saying many nice things such as, 'May you have this, may you become that, etc.'"

The next day the Holy Mother arranged for a bhandara[45] at the Advaita Ashrama. Swami Brahmananda, Hari Maharaj and Mahapurush Maharaj sat down together to have their meal. Immediately after sitting down to eat, Swami Brahmananda said, "I would like to see Bibhuti's wife again. Yesterday I couldn't see her well."

The Holy Mother sent her niece Maku to bring Amiyabala. After she arrived, Swami Brahmananda asked her, "What's your name?" Out of bashfulness she kept quiet and didn't reply. He said to her, "Why are you so shy? I'm like your father."

---

45. A 'Bhandara' is a feast for sadhus usually arranged by devotees.

Immediately Hari Maharaj said, "And I'm your uncle."

Mahapurush Maharaj joined in saying, "I'm your big uncle."

Swami Brahmananda said to Amiya, "Don't you see that Brahma, Vishnu and Maheshwara are sitting together in front of you?"[46]

Then Amiyabala said, "My name is Amiya."

He teasingly asked her, "Did you say 'homoeopathy'?" She laughed when she heard him say that. Then he said to her, "You may go now, my child!" Unfortunately, this good-natured girl didn't live long. Just a few days after her spiritual initiation from the Holy Mother she passed away.

◊ ◊ ◊ ◊ ◊

Rani (Sarvamangala) was the granddaughter of Navagopal Ghosh, a close devotee of Sri Ramakrishna. When she was just twelve or thirteen years old, her grandmother Nistarini Devi finalized the date of her marriage and then took Rani to Belur Math to seek Swami Brahmananda's blessings.

Nistarini Devi was one of the closest women devotees of Sri Ramakrishna. She liked Swami Brahmananda very much. When they came to see him, he approved of the young girl's marriage and blessed her by patting her on her back. And as soon as they left, he said to Mahapurush Maharaj, "This girl will be only nominally married. She won't really have a family life."

---

46. Swami Brahmananda said this humourously because his own name started with the word "Brahma," and Hari is another name of Vishnu. The name Shivananda also started with the word "Shiva," who is also called "Maheshwara."

After her marriage she returned to her parents from her in-laws' home, and didn't want to go back anymore. She was overwhelmed by an unknown fear and entering her family's shrine, prayed to God saying, "O God, please save me!"

Nistarini Devi again came to see Swami Brahmananda and said to him, "Maharaj, Rani is married, but the problem is that she doesn't at all want to go back to her in-laws' home!"

He said, "You have not been feeling well lately. Who will take care of your shrine work at home? Don't worry; from now on she will do it."

Nistarini Devi said, "If you already knew that she wouldn't have a family life, why didn't you tell me about it? Then we wouldn't have had to spend so much money for her marriage."

He replied, "What was predestined has happened. She was destined to go through this experience of marriage."

The Swami gave Rani spiritual shelter by giving her diksha. When the Holy Mother heard her story she said to her, "My child, this world is a frying pan. Out of his infinite grace, Thakur has taken you out of this terrible world, otherwise you would have been fried in it." Indifferent to all worldly enjoyments, and always remaining engaged in the service of God, Rani's life flowed quietly like a river toward the ultimate goal—the lotus feet of God.

CHAPTER IX

SWAMI BRAHMANANDA'S ABILITY TO UNDERSTAND PEOPLE

The inner nature of a person can be determined through physiognomy and other external physical signs and symptoms. Physiognomy and palmistry were considered the best means of judging human nature in ancient India. Before accepting anyone as his disciple, Sri Ramakrishna would come to know about their past, present and future by his yogic power. He would also know their inner inherent tendencies (samskaras) by examining the physical signs of their entire bodies from their hair down to their toenails. That's why whatever he predicted about anyone would always come true. Swami Brahmananda inherited this power from Sri Ramakrishna.

It is not possible for ordinary spiritual teachers to know the inner tendencies of a person by seeing only the outer signs. For this reason the ancient teachers of India took the help of astrology as the best means of determining the inherent tendencies of a person. This way they also were able to infallibly determine who was the Ishta or chosen deity of a person. Neglect of these two sciences gave rise to cracks in the basic foundation of renunciation in the monastic orders. Thus people with higher secular education and worldly ambition got the opportunity to enter the monastic orders and eventually brought about their degradation.

Since the Buddhist period all the monastic organizations in India have had these unfortunate experiences. Yet they do not seem to have learnt to protect themselves from this danger.

97

The fascination for numbers or for other selfish gains encourage these monastic orders to indiscriminately allow anybody and everybody to join. Swami Brahmananda was free from this kind of fascination.

It was often seen that Swami Brahmananda treated very cordially some people who were not considered good by others. At the same time he was seen to ignore some people of whom others had a high opinion. He used to say, "Some shallow pools of water may look very clean and clear, but if a goat walks in them, they turn muddy. Then again, some pools of water may have a dirty scum on their surface, but they are deep and clean at the bottom. The dirt on the surface cannot affect the purity of the water underneath." Once he commented about one of his sevaks, "He has a multi-layered mind."

There was a young man who was physically disabled and had a speech impediment. He also walked with a limp. Most of the residents of the Math called him by the nickname "Uncle" and thought rather poorly of him, in spite of the fact that he was a disciple of the Holy Mother. But Swami Brahmananda said that he had the ability to understand the deeper significance of spiritual matters. The Swami invested him successively with brahmacharya and then sannyasa, and accepted him as a member of the Order.

A friend of Swami Videhananda, Pra—, was just as humble as he was learned. He used to visit Belur Math every Sunday. Baburam Maharaj treated him with great fondness, and Pra— also respected Baburam Maharaj highly. As Swami Brahmananda was then staying in Varanasi, Baburam Maharaj talked about him a lot with Pra—. He used to say to the monks of the Math, "We need young men like him. It will be nice if some educated and trustworthy young men like Pra— join our Order to preach the message of Thakur.

One day after Swami Brahmananda's return to the Math, Baburam Maharaj told him about Pra—. Then Swami Brahmananda said, "Well, let me see him first. Then I'll see what can be done."

Sometime later, when Pra— came to the Math, Baburam Maharaj became very happy. He almost dragged him upstairs to Swami Brahmananda and said, "This is Pra—. After getting his M. A. degree he has become a deputy magistrate. He is not married. He is a fine young man." Pra— was by nature a little shy. He became quite embarrassed hearing those words of praise. He saluted Swami Brahmananda, and it appeared that he would feel relieved if he could escape from that embarrassing situation. However, he talked a little with him. Then the Swami asked him to go and salute Sri Ramakrishna in the shrine.

After Pra— had left, Baburam Maharaj said to Swami Brahmananda, "Maharaj, you've got to shower your grace on this young man. Did I not tell you before that he was a very good young man?"

Swami Brahmananda replied, "Yes, he is a fine young man. But what's the need to rush? Let him pass through some imminent obstacles that he is going to face, then we'll see what can be done." Hearing that Baburam Maharaj became grave.

Did Swami Brahmananda see into Pra—'s mind that day and come to know his hidden desires? Because, after some days the news came that he had married. After his marriage, he did not come to visit Belur Math for quite sometime.

◊ ◊ ◊ ◊ ◊

This incident happened in June 1917 when Swami Brahmananda was visiting Puri and staying at the Shashiniketan. One day a dark-complexioned young man came to the Shashiniketan carrying a small suitcase and saluted Swami Brahmananda.

The Swami exclaimed, "Hello Kanti, how come you are here? What happened?"

The young man replied with much emotion, "Maharaj, I have now clearly understood that worldly life is useless. The path of renunciation is the best. I've come here giving up everything. Please invest me with sannyasa."

The Swami said, "We'll see to that later. Now go and take a shower. As you were in the train the whole night, you couldn't sleep. It's very likely that you didn't eat anything either."

Kanti said, "What you say is true! For the past seven or eight days I've been in such a mental state that I can't sleep, nor do I find joy in eating, resting or walking. I don't enjoy anything! This time I have made up my mind to live with you and have sannyasa." Swami Brahmananda gestured to his sevak who took Kanti to the inner quarters of the house and gave him some snacks to eat. On inquiry the sevak came to know from him that his full name was Kantichandra Ghosh and that he was the younger brother of Purnachandra Ghosh, one of the intimate disciples of Sri Ramakrishna.

The next morning, after ablutions, Kanti came to see Swami

Brahmananda, who said, "Hello Kanti, did you have good sleep last night?"

Kanti replied, "I had excellent sleep. I haven't slept this well for several days."

The Swami said, "Very good! Are you going back home today?"

Kanti scratched the back of his neck and ran his fingers through his long hair nervously two or three times. Then he answered, "Maharaj, may I go back by the evening train today?" He never came and met the Swami again. A few years after this incident, he married a Western lady, and later acquired some fame by translating the *Omar Khayyam* into Bengali poetry.

◇ ◇ ◇ ◇ ◇

Another incident. Pavitranath Das, a middle-class zamindar of Sylhet, was looking for a guru. He came to Calcutta and started visiting Swami Brahmananda for a while, but could not understand him. He always saw him indulging in small talk, such as in which place good yogurt was available or how to cook a sweet and sour dish, etc.[47] As a consequence, Pavitra Babu felt sad and disappointed. The Swami saw into his mind and said to him, "Your time for spiritual initiation hasn't yet come. Please go home and start doing philanthropic activities for the good of our country." Pavitra Babu followed the advice of Swami Brahmananda.

◇ ◇ ◇ ◇ ◇

A rich merchant in East Bengal was extremely aggrieved

---

47. He used such behaviour as a disguise to hide his spirituality.

at the death of his only son. He decided to lead a retired life of prayer and contemplation, after donating all his property to the Ramakrishna Mission. Many monks were in favour of accepting the gift, because it was often hard to collect enough funds for the relief activities of the Mission.

Swami Brahmananda knew this gentleman and hearing of his intention said, "His present spirit of renunciation is temporary; it won't last long." Then he talked to him and said, "Please go on helping our Ramakrishna Mission off and on as you have been doing. Without making an outright donation of the property, keep it with you, and whenever you wish, spend some money for a good cause. You will get much more satisfaction that way." He decided to follow the advice of Swami Brahmananda, and after adopting a son, continued leading his worldly life as usual.

◊◊◊◊◊

During the Freedom Movement in India some of its leaders wanted to join the Ramakrishna Order as monks. But they couldn't do so because Swami Brahmananda would not approve. It was later seen that they all married and became householders.[48]

◊◊◊◊◊

---

48. Mr. Upendranath Banerjee, a past editor of the *Dainik Vasumati*, was one of them. For a while he lived in the Advaita Ashrama in Mayavati as well.

It is also well known that Netaji Subhas Chandra Bose, whose hero from boyhood was Swami Vivekananda, came to Belur Math and expressed his desire to become a monk. Swami Brahmananda discouraged him saying, "You can't be a monk. You have to serve our country."

CHAPTER IX

Once Dr. Kanjilal brought a distant relative of his to the Balaram Mandir. The boy was only fourteen years old, but he looked like he was twenty, and was very handsome. Swami Brahmananda made kind inquiries of him. It was evening then. An electric bulb covered with a green shade was giving off a dim light in the room. The Swami told the doctor, "I would like to see the boy more carefully, please bring him here tomorrow morning."

When the boy came, Swami Brahmananda took him to his own room and examined his physical signs thoroughly. Then the boy left. The Swami said to Dr. Kanjilal, "What I thought about him at first sight has been confirmed. He has some very bad physical signs. People with such signs turn out to be criminals and murderers." Within a few years, several events associated with the boy confirmed Swami Brahmananda's prediction.

◇ ◇ ◇ ◇ ◇

Another incident. One gentleman, Ma—, came to Bhubaneswar from Calcutta and was staying close to the Ramakrishna Math. He would come to see Swami Brahmananda with his wife every morning and evening. One evening his wife came alone, started talking nonsense, and asking many questions. Suddenly the Swami told his sevak, "Bring a lantern and take her home." Then he said to the lady, "My child, you may go home now. This is a heavily forested area. Sometimes tigers attack people here. Listen, a tiger is growling outside." We could hear hyenas' laughter at a distance. Hearing the laughter, the lady became scared and quickly left for home.

The sevak escorted her home and returning, sat close to Swami Brahmananda. It was a quiet night except for the

103

sound of crickets and the occasional laughter of the hyenas. While smoking, the Swami said, "Mr. Ma— is a fine man, but his wife is very restless. She is not steadfast in holding onto a single idea. She goes to all the ashramas and monasteries in Bhubaneswar in search of sadhus. And when she finds them, she tires them out with her incessant babbling. She cannot follow even one spiritual instruction properly, but wants to try more. Digesting even one idea is too hard for her, yet she asks for more. People of her nature can't grow spiritually. Nothing is achieved by those who go on tasting sermons here and there. You meet all kinds of people in the world, so you have to be cautious."

◊ ◊ ◊ ◊ ◊

Swami Brahmananda used to say, "There are some people who are neither here nor there! They won't marry, but remain in the world and take all kinds of worldly advantages. Occasionally, they go to ashramas to have holy company and ask the sadhus all kinds of big questions about religious life. They try to take advantage of both ashrama and worldly life. The lives of such people are terrible."

◊ ◊ ◊ ◊ ◊

Swami Bhumananda was busy conducting relief operations in Noakhali, Silchar and Brahmanbaria, when Ganendranath, Chhakku and a few others complained about him to Swami Saradananda. He dismissed their complaints saying, "Forget it! In big activities of this kind such lapses happen."

After finishing the relief operations Swami Bhumananda returned. Then Mr. Kiran Datta came to Swami Brahmananda with the proposal that the Ramakrishna Mission start a home for destitute widows. As soon as the Swami heard the proposal he said with heavy irony, "Well, Kiran Babu, shouldn't we open an orphanage as well, along with the home for widows?" Then pausing a little he became extremely grave and said, "Who will do that work? You yourselves won't come forward to do it! And we don't have women workers. No matter whom we send to conduct the work, you will surely blame him." Pointing to Swami Bhumananda, he then told Kiran Babu, "Just see, this monk worked as hard as he could to conduct a relief operation, and people are saying so many things against him."

◊ ◊ ◊ ◊ ◊

Another incident. One morning some monks were in the Belur Math kitchen busy peeling potatoes, Swami Brahmananda told them, "Each of you peel a potato and bring all of them to me. By checking them I'll be able to tell who among you can really meditate." Accordingly, they peeled the potatoes, put them on a platter, and brought them to him. Glancing at the potatoes, he picked one up and said, "The one who has peeled this potato alone can truly meditate." That potato had been peeled by Sudhir Maharaj (Swami Shuddhananda).

◊ ◊ ◊ ◊ ◊

One of the sevaks of Swami Brahmananda used to address a woman disciple of Swami Brahmananda named Ranu as "Mother." Swami Brahmananda once said to her, "Your son (referring to the sevak who called her 'Mother') is a nice boy. Everything about him is nice except that he is a little lustful and short-tempered. Had this son of yours married, his big nose would have become completely flat."

Ranu asked with surprise, "Why, Maharaj, how would that happen?"

He replied, "From kissing the dust of his wife's feet all the time!"

CHAPTER X

SWAMI BRAHMANANDA'S WAY OF DISCIPLINING AND TRANSFORMING MONKS

Swami Mukteswarananda said, "At that time Sanat used to come occasionally from Khardah to Belur Math and stay. Baburam Maharaj was fond of him, but Swami Brahmananda didn't like him at all. Later he became pleased with Sanat when he saw him nursing Swami Turiyananda during his illness in Puri, and he told us, 'Have you seen how well Sanat has been serving Hari Maharaj? He gets so many scoldings from him. He has even asked Sanat to leave a few times, still he continues to quietly serve him! This is what I call the true spirit of service!'

"The birthday celebration of Sri Ramakrishna was just over. Sanat came to some of us and said, 'Let's go to Khardah by boat. There we will make food offerings to Lord Shyamasundar and have His prasad.' So we got permission from Swami Brahmananda to visit Khardah. It was decided that a party of seven, made up of Sanat, Sachin, Satish, Chapta ("flattened", so-called to differentiate him from another Nagen who was fat and roly-poly) Nagen, Tarini, myself, and the Kala (meaning "deaf") doctor who was a little hard of hearing, would go to Khardah and would return to the Math in the evening, after visiting Lord Shyamsundar's temple.

"We arrived in Khardah in the Math's rowboat and went to Sanat's home. There we ate the prasad of Lord Shyamsundar that had been brought from His temple. After our meal, we decided to go to Halisahar and see Ramprasad's residence. Sanat and Sachin were the most enthusiastic to go.

"After we arrived in Halisahar and visited the residence of Ramprasad, we all wanted to go to Bansberia and visit the temple of Hamseswari. Sanat manned the rudder and the six of us rowed the boat. The boat moved at great speed. By the time we reached Bansberia and had offered our worship at the temple of Hamseswari, it was already evening. It would have been good if we had controlled our urge to go and see other places and had returned to Belur Math. But the thought of returning didn't even come to our minds. We decided to go to Tribeni instead, but a severe storm and incessant rain prevented our reaching Tribeni that night.

"We moored our boat midway at an ancient landing ghat. The steps of the ghat were all broken. A banyan tree had grown on the steps and there was an old, dilapidated temple on the ghat. We took shelter in the temple and somehow spent the night there.

"Our clothes were soaking wet from the rain. As we had no change of clothes, they dried on our bodies. At daybreak we rushed toward Tribeni. Arriving there, we managed to bathe in the river, but we couldn't find any food. We had brought some prasad of Lord Shyamsundar from Khardah for the monks in Belur Math, but we had eaten most of it during the night we spent at the ghat. In the morning we ate what little remained of that prasad to assuage our hunger. Around that time we suddenly realized that we had to return to Belur Math. (Perhaps the bath at Tribeni had cooled off our heads!)

"We quickly arranged for the return of "flattened" Naren and the "deaf" doctor by train. On our way back, we rowed the boat until our arrival in Rishra around evening time. By then we were totally exhausted from lack of food and sleep. The boat was hardly moving at all. We were scared of facing severe consequences after our return to Belur Math. Tarini and I were let off in Rishra. But we couldn't catch a train that night; the last train had already left. We approached different homes seeking shelter for the night. But they thought that we might be anarchists, so they told us to go away! At last we found a dilapidated mud hut in a jungle. We spent the night in it, and in the early hours of the morning, while it was still dark, we started for Belur Math on foot.

"As we crossed the brick factory and entered the Math by the western backdoor, we saw Mahapurush Maharaj rinsing his hands after using the toilet. He said, 'Swami Brahmananda is very angry with you two!'

"Very scared now, we entered the Math courtyard, and saw Swami Brahmananda coming downstairs to have a walk. As soon as he saw us, he burst out in anger. After giving us a good scolding he said, 'Get out of the Math! Do you want us all to be arrested by the police? Do you want us to go to jail in our old age?'[49] Then he called Chhakku and said, 'Bring all their belongings here. They won't be allowed to enter their rooms. They have to leave right from here!'

"Chhakku immediately obeyed his orders. We owned only a few little things. He bundled them together and handed them to us. As we were about to leave, we saluted Swami Brahmananda, touching his feet. He didn't object to our touching his feet nor did he move away from us. So we sensed that

49. Both Satish and Sachin were freedom fighters. Although both had joined the Ramakrishna Order as monks, because of their past seditious activities, the police watched them carefully. Satish was released from prison on parole and had to go to the police station once every day. The police used to come frequently to the Math to see if he was still there.

inwardly he was not too displeased with us. So still holding my small, bundled-up belongings under my arm, I folded my hands together and said, 'Maharaj, please forgive us this time. We won't do it again!'

"He remained grave and silent for a little while. Then he said, 'All right, I forgive you this time. If you do that ever again I'll drive you out of the monastery.' We saluted him again and entering our rooms, put down the bundles of our belongings.

"But from our rooms we could hear Swami Brahmananda's voice. He was saying, 'They (our other companions) don't realize that a sword is hanging over their heads! Let them come back. Then I'll ask the gatekeeper to give that kele (dark-complexioned) rascal (Sanat?) a good beating with shoes and drive him out of the compound! Baburam Maharaj has given shelter to these worthless fellows in the monastery! He tells me, "Let only those whom you think to be good stay at the Math. You may ask the others to leave." Look at the fun! It's he who lets them stay at the Math, and it has to be me who has to ask them to leave!'

"Meanwhile, Baburam Maharaj repeatedly went to the bank of the Ganga to see if they had arrived or not. Around ten o'clock in the morning, he saw from upstairs the boat coming. Then he went down to the riverbank and said to Sanat, 'After mooring the boat, go home immediately.' He also warned Satish not to go and see Swami Brahmananda. But Sachin straightaway went inside the Math compound. He was not the least bit afraid or hesitant. Swami Brahmananda was in the courtyard. One minute he would sit and smoke, the next minute he would rise and pace back and forth. His face looked extremely grave.

"Sachin saluted him and said, 'Maharaj, it was all my fault. It was I who encouraged them to go up to Tribeni. Give me whatever punishment I deserve, but please forgive them!'

"He gazed at Sachin, standing tall and erect in front of him, from head to foot. It was this Sachin who had in the past gone to sacrifice his life to liberate his motherland from foreign occupation! And now he was asking to be punished on behalf of his friends! He immediately said, 'No, no, it's not your fault! I know that it's that kele rascal (Sanat) who was at the root of all this. Where is he?

"Sachin replied, 'No, Maharaj, it's all my fault; they didn't do anything!'

"Swami Brahmananda regained his usual composure and said, 'All right, you may go.' The episode ended there.

"Another incident. Ta— hadn't then become a monk, yet he had been living at the Math for several months. He was an adept in music and could sing well. Swami Brahmananda used to call him Ostad (Maestro).

"One morning Ta— saluted Swami Brahmananda and said that he was going to see the Holy Mother in Calcutta that day. The Swami said, 'That's all right. But take some flowers in a basket for her. You yourself must carry them there. Tell the Holy Mother that I've sent the flowers for her.' Then he asked someone to pluck the flowers.

"Ta— signaled to a boatman to come and pick him and his companion up in his boat. Then suddenly he remembered that he had forgotten to bring something along with him. He tried to hand the flower basket over to his companion, but in his hurry the basket dropped to the ground and the flowers scattered all over.

"Swami Brahmananda saw this from the upstairs veranda and immediately called Ta—. After he came the Swami gave him a severe scolding, and wouldn't permit him to go to the Holy Mother's house in Calcutta. Instead he asked another person to pluck more flowers and take them to the Holy Mother.

"He was so displeased with Ta— that for nearly two weeks after that incident he didn't want him to come close or to salute him. This made Ta— so sad and depressed that one day he decided to jump into the river at midnight and end his life. The fact that Swami Brahmananda was so displeased with him made Ta— feel that Sri Ramakrishna must also have become displeased with him. That's why he thought that his life would serve no worthwhile purpose. But at the same time, he also thought that he should go and salute the Swami before giving up his life. But as the Swami would be greatly displeased at the sight of him, Ta— thought that he would go and salute him from a distance, unnoticed in the darkness of the night.

"As he came near the open door of Swami Brahmananda's room, he saw a dim light burning there. Nothing in the room could be seen clearly. The Swami was sitting on his small cot. Ta— entered the adjacent room slowly, and from the threshold of the room saluted him. There was a desk in front of the door, so it was not possible for the Swami to see Ta—. But as soon as Ta— saluted him, he said to Ta— in a most pleasant voice, "Hello, Ostad, don't you sing devotional songs anymore? I haven't heard you sing any songs lately!"

"Then Ta— entered Swami Brahmananda's room and with tears rolling down his cheeks, he saluted him, touching his feet. The Swami said, 'A sadhu's anger is as short-lived as a line drawn in water. Does his anger last long? Go downstairs and sing some devotional songs. I'll listen to them from here.' Shortly thereafter, the nocturnal silence was broken by Ta—'s melodious singing and the atmosphere at Belur Math was filled with its sweet reverberation.

"Another anecdote. Swami Brahmananda was shaping his disciple Ba—'s life by giving him various kinds of spiritual instruction. As a result Ba— developed a false ego. Thinking that he was a great spiritual aspirant, he joined the Order without even taking his guru's permission. He also began wearing the robes of a brahmachari. The Swami was very displeased with his behaviour and started ignoring him so much that Ba— was compelled to leave the Math. Returning home he married.

"Shortly thereafter he started thinking that he had ruined his life by getting married. He wrote a long letter to Swami Brahmananda about it. Then Swami Brahmananda invited Ba— to come and see Durga Puja at the Madras Math. After he arrived, the Swami said, 'What's the harm if you've married? You needn't be afraid even if you marry one hundred times.'

"In spite of getting such blessings from Swami Brahmananda, Ba— could not shake off his depression. In a weak moment he made up his mind to jump into the Ganga and kill himself. On the day he chose to commit suicide, the Swami, for no apparent reason, became very worried and started enquiring about him. Everybody whom he met that day was asked to go and bring him the news of Ba—.

"But no trace could be found of him, even after thoroughly searching everywhere. The Swami then told them that he would go to Sankharitolla that day. Ba— was expected to sing in a small musical session there. Toward evening one of those people looking for Ba— was driving toward the Chandpal ghat. He saw Ba— sitting very depressed under a tree close to the river. He forced Ba— to get into his car and brought him to Swami Brahmananda in Sankharitolla.

"The Swami said to Ba—, 'I have been looking for you since the morning. Nobody could find you. Come, they are all waiting to hear you sing.'

"Ba—, with tearful eyes and folded hands, tried to say something. But Swami Brahmananda stopped him, saying, 'That's all right. Tell me later. You look so thin. Haven't you eaten anything today?' Then he had a lot of 'prasadi' (consecrated) fruits and sweets brought for Ba—to eat.

"Ba— recovered from his depression sometime later.

"Another incident. Swami Brahmananda's disciple Ka— had just returned to Belur Math after doing tapasya in Hrishikesh. Seeing him, Swami Brahmananda said, 'I can't even look at your face! What have you gained through your austerities in Hrishikesh? You've learnt to imitate the Hrishikesh-brand sadhus, but lost your character!'

"The remnants of this scolding continued for two more days. The Swami repeatedly said to the other monks, 'I can clearly see that those who stay at the Math and do their spiritual practices along with their allotted duties, and work in the shrine serving the Lord, are far better! It is very difficult to become a true sadhu. The outgoing tendencies will manifest more and more unless one's mind is kept immersed in spiritual thoughts. Some of those who don't do this turn insane; some even commit suicide. Some lose their character to get money.

114

Others go on rattling out the teachings of bhakti or jnana, but internally turn into atheists.'"

◊ ◊ ◊ ◊ ◊

Swami Prashantananda said: "Swami Brahmananda was at that time staying in the Sevashrama in Varanasi. In the mornings he would come to the Varanasi Advaita Ashrama and scatter rice bran on the ground under the berry tree. Many birds would come and eat that bird feed. One day he asked me to bring some rice bran to him. As asked, I brought it on a glass platter and held it out before him.

"Meanwhile, hearing something funny that he had said, the assembled sadhus burst out into laughter. I also joined in the laughter and momentarily became distracted. As a result, the platter dropped from my hands to the ground and broke into pieces. At this he became very silent and grave.

"Thereafter, if anyone would ask me to do some work, Swami Brahmananda would at once say, 'Don't ask him to do that work. He will break everything to pieces!'

"His behaviour made me extremely uneasy and fearful. I stopped going near him. This way some fifteen or twenty days passed. One morning I was reading a book in the small room at the south end of the Ashrama hall. Someone came outside my room and started noisily rattling the door's handles. Swami Brahmananda's servant, Bulbul, often came and disturbed me by rattling the door handles that way. Thinking that it was he who was shaking the handles, I gave him a severe scolding from inside my room.

"After a short pause the rattling started again! Then I gave an even more severe scolding. But the intermittent shaking of the door handles continued without stopping. This made me extremely irritated. Losing my temper and using all the unkind words in my vocabulary, I gave him a terrible scolding. Still the door rattling went on! I finally went to open the door to teach Bulbul a good lesson. But I couldn't open it, because he was holding both the handles of the double door shut together with great strength.

"Then putting pressure on one door with my leg to keep it shut, with all my strength I tried to pull open the other door. The person on the other side of the door suddenly released the handles. The door that I was pulling on flung open and I fell backwards onto the floor with a big thud. The fall hurt my head and back. In spite of that I somehow managed to stand up and saw Swami Brahmananda walking away from the door of my room toward the flower garden in the courtyard. I was almost thunderstruck! I realized that I had given *him* all those terrible scoldings, thinking that he was Bulbul! Extremely embarrassed and scared, I shut the door and waited inside until he left for the Sevashrama. After a short while I came out, thinking that he must have left, but I saw him standing right in front of me!

"He said, 'So…how did you like that! Will you scold me again?'

"Embarrassed, I ran away from him. I had stopped going near him before because I was scared of his grave exterior. But from that day on, that fear disappeared."

CHAPTER XI

TEACHING AND TRANSFORMING DISCIPLES THROUGH LETTERS

Swami Brahmananda had a disciple named Swami Amritananda. His nickname was Nalin. He was placed in charge of the Bhubaneswar Math. Nalin was extremely devoted to his guru and laboured very hard for the development of the Bhubaneswar Math. Two days before his passing away, Swami Brahmananda blessed his sevaks and disciples in an ecstatic mood. At that time he said, "Nalin is my devotee."

While Swami Brahmananda was in Madras and Nalin in Bhubaneswar, he heard some unpleasant news about Nalin. To rectify his behaviour, the Swami wrote several letters full of innuendo and irony, and sent them, assuming fictitious names such as Paramatmananda and Niranjanachaitanya. He himself did not write them; he dictated them to others and they wrote.

Some of the letters were in the form of poems. It is impossible to translate the unique language in which the letters were written without ruining their subtle humour, innuendo and double meaning. A sample letter written by Swami Brahmananda from Madras is given below.

Respected Kedarbaba,

I have arrived. I'm being shown around. Nice place! Good. Everything is very good! Yet, I remain, as before, the same darvesh (all-renouncing sadhu). Now, I'd like to tell you that I want to perform some tapasya (spiritual austerities). What will I gain by wandering here and there? About this I have written to my dearest friend Nalin also, and am waiting for his reply.

117

As soon as I get his reply, I shall go there (to Bhubaneswar) and begin doing the most intense tapasya. But I have to do tapasya only for mundane reasons. There will be four goals for my tapasya: dharma, artha, moksha, and kama. I have realized now that without artha (money), everything becomes anartha (disastrous or meaningless). I know that the word "artha" has many meanings. You may interpret its meaning as you like. However, please request my dearest friend Nalin to permit me through a letter to come and stay there for a while. I am eagerly looking forward to getting his letter. Please also tell him that it will be extremely difficult for him to find another good soul like me anywhere.

…Please forgive me for my impertinence, because (to practice my austerity) I need to live under a tree with a mosquito net over me. But it will be nice if a good person can be engaged to set up my mosquito net every evening. Please give special attention to this need of mine. Kindly accept my humble salutations. Are you all right?

Your servant,

Paramatmananda

It is obvious that Kedarbaba (Swami Achalananda) was staying at the Bhubaneswar Math at the time. Swami Brahmananda knew that this funny but meaningful letter would be shown to Nalin (Swami Amritananda) by Kedarbaba.

Although the translator is unable to translate the other letters, he is happy to inform the readers that the funny letters written by Swami Brahmananda produced the desired effect on Nalin.

CHAPTER XII

THE VARIOUS TEACHINGS OF SWAMI BRAHMANANDA

Swami Shyamananda said: "At the time of this incident a Ramait sadhu came to Belur Math. He would make a dhuni fire in front of Swami Vivekananda Temple, and sitting there would chant 'Sita Ram' day and night. Whether it was in the morning or in the afternoon—whenever Swami Brahmananda would walk past him, the sadhu would always say, 'I need a smoke.'

"One day, when I was going to the market to shop, Swami Brahmananda said to me, 'Buy eight annas'[50] worth of hemp for the sadhu.' Returning from the market, I couldn't find the Swami. So I asked Dr. Bipin, 'As Swami Brahmananda asked, I have bought some hemp, but what shall I do with it now?'

"The doctor said, 'Go and give it to the Ramait sadhu.' I did what he told me to do. Hearing later what I had done with the hemp, Swami Brahmananda gave me a scolding and said, 'You are so stupid! As punishment you won't be allowed to eat tomorrow at the Math. You have to beg for your food elsewhere, and also have to procure eight annas' worth of hemp by begging.'[51]

---

50. An 'anna' used to be one sixteenth of a rupee in Indian currency

51. According to monastic tradition, monks can go and beg for cooked food from peoples' homes. But they are not permitted to approach more than eight homes. However, monks living in a monastery may get their food in the monastery itself, as is the case of monks living in Belur Math. Swami Brahmananda wanted to remind Swami Shyamananda of that monastic tradition through the punishment that he gave him.

119

"I carried out his orders exactly. Then he said, 'Make as many little packets of hemp as you can and put them on the desk in my room. Remember this: whenever anyone orders you to do some work, you will ask only him about that work, not others.' Those little packets of hemp were to be given to the Ramait sadhu one packet at a time.

"Another incident. Bhim and his three brothers worked at Belur Math as day-labourers. Once the young son of one of them was getting wet in the rain while playing on the bank of the Ganga. While pacing back and forth on the veranda of the Math, Swami Brahmananda saw the boy and told me, 'Bring the boy out of the rain.' I brought the boy to the Math building and began drying his body with a towel. Seeing me doing that, the Swami said, 'You don't have to go through all that trouble. They are children of hardy day-labourers; they grow up exposed to the sun and rain.'

"Once I picked some litchi-fruits from the orchard in Belur Math. From a distance Swami Brahmananda saw me carrying the basket of fruits and asked, 'Khudu (my nickname), what are you carrying in your basket?' When I showed him the fruits in my basket, he asked me, 'What will you do with them?'

"I replied, 'They are for us to eat.'

"He said, 'All right. But before eating them, first soak them in water for an hour or two.'

"Another day, in the evening, Nirad Mazumdar was singing and I was accompanying him on the tabla. Swami Brahmananda sent someone downstairs to find out who was playing on the tabla. He came to us and said, 'So it's you who is playing on the tabla! Swami Brahmananda liked it.' As soon as he said that, the Swami himself came down to us. Seeing him, Nirad began to sing a classical song using an intricate tala (rhythm). As it was too hard for me to play that tala, I stopped playing.

"Swami Brahmananda sat down on the floor and said to me, 'Don't worry, I'll teach you how to play it.' Then he began playing on the tabla and articulating the bol (oral imitation of the sound of the drums). In this manner he showed me how to play the tabla in jhamptala and choutala. Not only that, he also made me play those two difficult talas on the tabla.[52]

"Another incident. According to the lunar calendar it was Swami Premananda's birthday. Krishnalal Maharaj, accompanied by a brahmachari, brought back to Belur Math lots of sweets, such as rasagollas, sandesh, sweet curd and rabri from Calcutta. Then he told us, 'Put all these things in the shrine storeroom. Do you have papadam, beson flour, etc.? Can you also make begunis?'

"We said, 'We'll have them all. Please give us money.' As he

---

52. Tabla and pakhoaj are similar percussion instruments. That Swami Brahmananda was trained in playing both will be obvious from the following incident. A pakhoaj made for use in the Bhubaneswar Math was delivered to the Balaram Mandir in Calcutta. Bhavani put the layer of flour dough on the pakhoaj and took it to Swami Brahmananda to see if the instrument was all right. The Swami said, "I am out of practice. Will I be able to play it?" Then he hit the drum once and said to Bhavani, "Sing a song." He began singing the song starting with the words, "*Sab dukha dur kariley...*" in surphakta tala, as Swami Brahmananda accompanied him on the pakhoaj. After singing for a little while, Bhavani became worried that playing on the pakhoaj might make the Swami's arms ache. So he stopped singing and took away the pakhoaj. The muscles of the Swami's body had lately become as soft as butter!

was taking money out of his pocket, some coins dropped to the floor.

"Swami Brahmananda was walking nearby. Hearing the jingling sound of the coins he said humourously, 'What's the matter? It seems your money has been making a loud noise!' Krishnalal Maharaj saluted Swami Brahmananda and told him what their plans were. Swami Premananda's mother sent some money every year to celebrate her son's birthday. But without letting anyone know, Swami Premananda used to deposit all the money in the shrine account for Thakur's worship. Coming somehow to know this, Swami Premananda's mother made sure that the money wouldn't fall into her son's hands. That's why she sent the money to Krishnalal Maharaj. Listening to all this while pacing back and forth in the courtyard, Swami Brahmananda joyfully said, 'Very good! Let's celebrate! It is Baburam Maharaj's birthday today! Cook some nice polau.'

"As we were taking out beson flour, papadam, etc. from the storeroom, Swami Brahmananda said, 'When you ask the cook to prepare the batter for the beguni ask him to prepare a paste of kalai pulse and rice flour and mix that with beson. The begunis will be very crisp if a small amount of poppy seeds and a little kalo jira are also added to the batter. And since it is big brother Baburam Maharaj's birthday, let special polau mixed with chhana be prepared today.'

"During Swami Brahmananda's stay in Belur Math, every day would be a day of festivity. So many devotees would bring so many things at that time!

"Baburam Maharaj was not at the Math at that time. He had gone to East Bengal. I asked Swami Brahmananda, 'We

122

have to make the food offering to Thakur, but we don't have enough food. What shall we cook?'

"He replied, 'Ours is a family of monks. Why should we worry about which dish to cook? Show me what food you have.' In those days we used to buy a lot of potatoes. There were a few left in our stock. And we had some pumpkins on the rope-shelf. We were also able to get some greens from our vegetable garden. With all that Swami Brahmananda concocted a mixed vegetable dish.

"I used to go by boat to shop at the fair in Vaidyabati. Sanat manned the rudder. Chhakku, two or three others, and I did the rowing. One day Swami Brahmananda asked, 'Where are you going?'

"I replied, 'To the fair in Vaidyabati.'

"He asked again, 'Do you know the song of the fair?'

" I said, 'No.'

"Then he said, 'Listen, I'm going to sing it.' He sang the song, which had a deeper spiritual connotation:

> You can't buy from this fair any suta (thread) other than the suta (child) of Nandarani. Pashupati is the principal weaver here, others are all uninvited traders...[53]

(In this song there is a play upon the different meanings of the word 'suta.' The deeper meaning of the song is that in this mart of the world, for the salvation of one's soul, only the son of Nandarani (Sri Krishna) can be bought by one's devotion.

53. The original song in Bengali is: "E hāte vikāy nā anya suto, vikāy Nanda Ranir suta. E hāter pradhān tānti Pashupati, vād vāki shab ravāhuta...."

123

Lord Pashupati (Shiva) is the principal weaver (Ishwara/God) in this mart of the world, etc.)

"Then he asked, 'At what time will you return?'

"I replied, 'After doing the shopping.'

"He said, 'Start at the beginning of the high tide. Finish your shopping as fast as possible, and then head back to the Math at the beginning of the low tide.'"

◊ ◊ ◊ ◊ ◊

The source of the following is Swami Prashantananda. He said, "In 1913, after giving up my studies and in broken health, I came to join the Order at Belur Math. Swami Brahmananda was then in Varanasi. Swami Saradananda sent me there with an introduction letter to him. In that letter he requested that arrangements for my education and recovery of health be made.

"Accordingly, I had medical treatment at the Sevashrama for eight or ten days and then came to stay at the Advaita Ashrama. Baburam Maharaj had come for a visit to Varanasi. Following his advice, I was admitted to the Sanskrit school run by Annadacharan Tarkachudamani and began studying the scriptures. Every morning before going out on his walk, Swami Brahmananda would teach me some physical exercises. With the help of Muller's book he would show me how to do the exercises. He also taught me a few exercises that he himself had developed.

"Nirad Maharaj (Swami Ambikananda) was an expert singer. But he was a good artist as well. Swami Brahmananda asked him to draw the diagrams for certain exercises. They were hung on the walls of my room. It is due to his training that I am able to do such hard labour in my old age."

CHAPTER XII

[Note: Swami Brahmananda owned a pair of dumb-bells and a pair of small clubs. Every morning after his meditation, he would exercise with them. Until his last illness he followed this routine. He used to tell the monks, "Every day, after doing your japa and meditation, you should have a little physical exercise. Then start doing Thakur's work." In Belur Math, he would take his daily exercise inside his room.

In his younger days the Swami took up wrestling as a sport. One day while in Belur Math he saw Chhakku standing on the veranda and said, "Hello Chhakku, do you want to wrestle with me?" Chhakku was a trained wrestler. Nodding his assent he went to grab Swami Brahmananda's arms, but the Swami lifted him and spinning him above his head, put him down on the floor.]

◊ ◊ ◊ ◊ ◊

Swami Mukteswarananda said: "I was working in the shrine storeroom in the morning. Suddenly Swami Brahmananda entered and asked, 'What are you doing?' I was busy arranging flowers, red and white sandalwood pastes, basil leaves, durva grass and vilwa leaves on the platter for worship. Seeing my work he was pleased and said, 'Very good! While doing your work, mentally chant Thakur's holy name. Also while making garlands for Thakur always remember him and chant his holy name.'[54]

---

54. Swami Jagadananda mentioned how carefully one should serve Thakur. He said that someone had been rinsing utensils used for Thakur's worship under an open faucet, and water had splashed out of the utensils and fallen onto the feet of that person. Swami Brahmananda saw it and said, "You seem to have a lot of courage! We sat on Thakur's lap and sometimes even climbed on his shoulders, still we are afraid of letting water from his utensils splash on our feet." (According to Hindu tradition, touching anything with the feet shows disrespect toward it.)

◊◊◊◊◊

"Swami Brahmananda was walking at a small distance from the wooded portion of our property where I was busy peeling off the bark of a tree. Suddenly he came over and asked, 'What are you doing?'

"I replied, 'I am collecting the bark of the babla tree.'

"'Why?' he asked.

"I replied, 'Mahim Babu has been taking an ayurvedic medicine. Along with it he has to drink the juice from the bark of this tree.'

"Then he asked, 'Why didn't you take my permission first before debarking the tree?' Hearing his words I wondered why I needed his permission to do such an insignificant thing. He said, 'Everything in the monastery belongs to Thakur. You are not to do anything here according to your own sweet will. You mustn't do anything without the permission of the head of the monastery.'

"Once I asked someone to give me a shaving razor. Swami Brahmananda came to know of it and said, 'Why did you go and ask somebody else to give you a razor? You should ask me for whatever you need. If someone else wants to give you anything, don't accept it.' He asked me to give him the razor. He took it and touching it once to his face, returned it to me.[55]

---

55. Our scriptures forbid spiritual aspirants from accepting gifts from all kinds of people. This is called *aparigraha* in Sanskrit. Swami Brahmananda wanted his sevak Mukteswarananda to practice aparigraha. Also, when a spiritual aspirant accepts a gift from someone who has given that gift with the expectation of earning merits, a portion of the spirituality of the receiver goes to the giver. To save his sevak from that hazard Swami Brahmananda accepted the gift instead.

"Mr. Mudaliar, an elderly devotee from Madras, and we, the three sevaks of Swami Brahmananda, stayed in the room opposite to his room in the new building of the Madras Math. One of the sevaks heard that good satoranchas (carpets made of cotton) were available in Madras. He requested Mr. Mudaliar to buy three of them for us. With much happiness he bought them and gave them to us. He gave an extra one to me as well. As soon as I closed the door of our room and laid my satarancha out on the floor, Swami Brahmananda unexpectedly entered and asked me, 'Ishwar, where did you get this satarancha? It seems to be of excellent quality!'

"We were stunned. It was his rest hour and we hadn't expected him. Mr. Mudaliar said, 'I gave the carpets to them.'

"Swami Brahmananda asked, 'Why did you all of a sudden give these to them? Did they ask you to give them?' Then he turned toward me and pointing at my satarancha asked, 'Ishwar, did you ask him to give that to you?'

"I replied, 'No, Maharaj, he gave it to me on his own.'

"Then he asked the sevak who had requested Mr. Mudaliar to give the carpets, 'Why did you ask him to give them? Did I not tell you not to ask anyone else to give you anything?' The residue of this incident lingered on for a number of days. The sataranchas, of course, had to be returned.

"When the monks were sitting in front of Swami Brahmananda in the evening after saluting him, he said, 'What we've enjoyed is nothing! You have no idea what tremendous enjoyment awaits you in the future! There will be so many Maths, so much property, so many mattresses and cushions! Just keep yourselves under check for a while, practice a little restraint!' At that time Abani (Prabhavananda), Nirod (Akhilananda),

127

Yogesh (Ashokananda), Jiten (Vishwananda), etc., were present in Madras Math.

"Occasionally Nitai Babu would give me very expensive gifts for Swami Brahmananda and say, 'There is no need to tell him that I have given them.' Usually he gave Pears brand toilet soap to use for his shower. This soap wasn't that expensive.

"One day, seeing an expensive soap given by Nitai Babu he asked, 'Where did you get that soap?'

"I replied, 'Nitai gave it.'

"He asked, 'Do you know how much it costs?'

"I said, 'I've heard that it costs between two and a half and three rupees.'

"Then he said, 'Look at this! Should one waste so much money on such things!'

"I said that I had asked Nitai not to give such expensive soaps, but Nitai said, 'I myself use much more expensive soaps than this. Can't I give Maharaj a little better quality soap?'

"Swami Brahmananda said, 'See how large-hearted Nitai is! Can't you pray for him a little? All right, give him a gift.'

"I said, 'Maharaj, while you are here, who am I to give him anything?'

"Then he said, 'He is fond of you. If you pray to God for those who love you, God gives them His blessings. Aside from that, Nitai doesn't get the chance to come close to me.'"

◇◇◇◇◇

Rheumatism had made Chandra Maharaj (Swami Nirbharananda), the head of the Varanasi Advaita Ashrama, almost

128

an invalid. In spite of his incapacitation, he took good care of the Ashrama until his death. Building the sandstone temple and the installation in it of a marble statue of Sri Ramakrishna are proofs of his extraordinary organizing ability. It was Swami Brahmananda who had asked him to construct the temple. As head of the Ashrama, Chandra Maharaj had to economize in everything, because the Ashrama had no fixed income. Aside from that, he was frugal by nature.

One day Swami Brahmananda said to him, "You know, Chandra, being the head of an Ashrama is a very difficult job. One is supposed to do 'sadhu-seva' (serve holy men) with the money people donate. Money should be used for the purpose for which it has been donated. If one fails to do this, one will have to be born as a dog in the next incarnation. (It seems to have been mentioned in the *Ramayana*.) Shouldering the responsibility of the head of an Ashrama is indeed very difficult."

◊ ◊ ◊ ◊ ◊

The source of the following anecdote is Shrish Chandra Ghatak. He said, "It was the year 1912. The Holy Mother Sri Sarada Devi was then visiting Varanasi. I was happy to spend a few days with her and some direct disciples of Sri Ramakrishna. On the eve of my departure from Varanasi to Ranchi, the city where I worked, I went and saluted Swami Brahmananda. With a smile on his face he said to me in Sanskrit, 'Punarmushiko Bhava!' (Be a mouse again!) When I asked him to explain why he had said that, he replied, 'You are the child of the Divine Mother. You are a lion's cub. You spent a few days here with your mother—the lioness (the Holy Mother). Now you are going back to do only paper work in your office. Isn't it like turning back into a mouse again?'

"I asked, 'What else will I do?'

"He replied, 'Keep holy company.'

"I asked, 'Where will I find holy people?'

"He said, 'Then read holy books. You've got a lot of friends. Ask each one to contribute two annas a month. With that money buy good books and read them.'

"After my return to Ranchi I began collecting books. In this way the Brahmananda Public Library was founded in Duranda."

◊ ◊ ◊ ◊ ◊

Gokuldas Dey said, "The proprietor of the Minerva Theatre gave me a free pass to his theatre, because I had given them the idea for the play *Kinnari*. When I told Swami Brahmananda about it, he gave me a severe scolding. He said, 'Why did you want a pass from them? Even if they have given it on their own, you shouldn't have accepted it. Don't you know that the proprietors of theatres look down on people who use free passes?'

"I felt extremely humiliated by his scolding. With tearful eyes I went to the bank of the Ganga, but even there I couldn't find any peace of mind. After that I went to the Udbodhan Ashrama.

"Seeing me Sharat Maharaj asked, 'Why do you look so sad today?'

"So I told him why I was so upset. He said, 'That shouldn't have made you upset. Swami Brahmananda looks on you like his own son, that's why he scolded you that way. He never scolds others like that. Go back right now and salute him.'

130

"When I returned to Swami Brahmananda he was in a completely different mood. With a beaming face he greeted me saying, 'You must come with us to visit Bipin-Jamai's home in Baruipur tomorrow!'"

◊ ◊ ◊ ◊ ◊

Another incident. But before narrating the following anecdote, it should be mentioned here that the word rāgi in Bengali means short-tempered. When the prefix anu is added, it becomes anurāgi, meaning "devoted."

At the invitation of the maternal uncle of his disciple Ranu, Swami Brahmananda went to their home. Ranu's mother complained to him saying, "Maharaj, your daughter Ranu is very rāgi. Any little thing makes her angry."

Swami Brahmananda said, "Rāgi? It is good to have rāg."[56] Then he turned to Ranu and said, "You should add anu to your rāg." (anurāg means "devotion.")

This remark made Ranu's mother and grandmother very happy.

---

56. The word *rāg* has another meaning: love and devotion. That's why Swami Brahmananda said that it was good to have rāg.

CHARLES MATHIAS

SWAMI BRAHMANANDA

CHAPTER XIII
SWAMI BRAHMANANDA'S VERSATILE WISDOM

Swami Mukteswarananda said: "One afternoon Swami Brahmananda came downstairs to take a walk. He stood near the tea table and asked me, 'Where are you going?'

"I replied, 'I'm going to bring Ganga water.'

"Then he said, 'It's not hard to give up lust and gold. If you do a lot of japa and dhyana they will go away. But do you know what's most difficult? It's most difficult to give up the false ego, pride, fame, honour, etc. Toward the end of one's spiritual journey, people may get trapped by these things.'"

◇◇◇◇◇

"At the time of this incident I was in Puri. But due to the pressure of my work, I couldn't find time to go to the temple of Lord Jagannath. So I asked Swami Brahmananda, 'May I go to the temple?'

"He said. 'You may go at 3 o'clock in the afternoon.'

"As soon as I arrived at the temple, an unknown family came and surrounded me. An elderly lady from that family pointed to me and said, 'This is our Haripada.'

"No matter how many times I told them that I was not Haripada, the old woman couldn't be convinced. She repeatedly said, 'His mother will surely recognize him when she sees him.'

"They grabbed me and took me to their rented house in Narendra Sarovar. Seeing me, the mother of the missing Haripada said, 'No, he is not my Haripada.'

"They gave me Lord Jagannath's prasad, jive-gaja, (a sweet-

133

meat) to eat. When I returned after dusk, Swami Brahmananda gave me a scolding and asked, 'Where were you all this time?'

"Hearing the entire story he said, 'Why did you eat at their home? You shouldn't have eaten anything, even if they said it was prasad. Do you know that some women cast an evil spell on food and then give it to people? Never eat food given by strangers.'"

◊ ◊ ◊ ◊ ◊

The source of the following anecdote is Swami Shyamananda. He said, "Once Swami Brahmananda packed some seedlings into a large wooden box for our Kankhal Sevashrama. Then he told me to take it to Howrah railway station to be sent as a parcel. I took the box in a bullock cart to Howrah. I spent three hours in the parcel office—from 9 o'clock in the morning till 12 noon—but couldn't send it. Then I came back to Belur Math to have lunch. Swami Brahmananda asked, 'What happened?'

"I replied, 'I couldn't send the parcel. The parcel clerk made me wait too long. I'll go there again after lunch.'

"Then he asked, 'Do you know the mantras for the marriage ceremony?'

"I replied, 'No, Maharaj.'

"He said, 'Chant *Notey shāk tulsir pāt, dhar dhemnā dhemnir hāth*. (Notey greens and tulsi leaf! Hey fella! Grab the hand of your bride!)[57] Now go to our office and get two rupees. Give

---

57. This is of course not a real mantra for the marriage ceremony. It is not unlikely that Swami Brahmananda himself humorously made it up or he might have learnt it from other children during his younger days when he lived in his ancestral village, Shikra Kulingram.

the money to the parcel clerk and say that it is for his expenses in making sure the seedlings get enough water and reach their destination soon.'

"I did as instructed. After getting the money, the parcel clerk promptly got up from his chair and asked a few coolies to water the seedlings. Then he sent the parcel by the next train."

◊◊◊◊◊

Swami Prashantananda said: "With Swami Brahmananda's permission, I once had to go to my village home to arrange the distribution of my property. When I came back he asked, 'You went to your native village. Have you done anything for it? The scriptures say that you become fit to strive for liberation only when you have repaid your debts—such as the debt to your native village. Can you have liberation by doing nothing?'

"When I went next time to my native village I followed his advice and founded a girls' school and a night school for adults. Gradually I got involved in many activities, such as establishing the village post office and the Society for Prevention of Malaria, etc.

"But my conscience started telling me that it was not proper for me as a monk to get entangled in all those activities. So I decided to ask Swami Brahmananda's advice. But whenever I approached him a kind of diffidence came over me and I couldn't say anything. But he could read my inmost thoughts. One day he said, 'Is it possible to get out of entanglements in a single day? One should learn to withdraw gradually. In this manner gradually one can become free from attachment.'

"I followed his advice and in six months, after delegating the responsibilities to other people in my village, I was able to

135

become free. This incident took place a short time before his passing away."

◊◊◊◊◊

Swami Brahmananda once expressed what he himself had experienced. He said, "External music is nothing. Spiritually advanced people can hear a kind of sweet music internally which soothes the entire body and mind."

We hadn't heard that he had ever learned music from tutors as Swami Vivekananda did. We never heard him singing. Yet, one may wonder what gave him the ability to understand and judge music so well? Was it because of his inborn sense of music?

Swami Saradananda, an expert singer, used to request Swami Brahmananda to judge if he was singing the songs sung by Swami Vivekananda according to the right melodies or not. He relied on Swami Brahmananda's judgment that highly.

Once a singer was singing a song for Swami Brahmananda. After listening to it for a while, he told the singer, "Please mix a little bit of Gaur (the name of an Indian classical melody) with the melody."

The singer was very much impressed by Swami Brahmananda's knowledge of melodies. In his singing he had been using the melody Sarang.

◊◊◊◊◊

Swami Brahmananda went to a theatre. Hearing a song there, he asked Bhavani, "Do you know what classical melody it is?"

Bhavani replied, "Maharaj, it appears to be Sohini."

136

Swami Brahmananda said, "Yes, you are right."

One evening, before going to supper, he asked someone, "Who is playing on the harmonium and singing?"

The person replied, "It's Sujji."

The Swami said, "Go and bring him here!" When the singer came he said to him, "You sang yesterday also. You see, hearing your out-of-tune singing I couldn't sleep last night. Bring the harmonium here and put it under my cot."

◊ ◊ ◊ ◊ ◊

One day Swami Brahmananda said to Gokuldas Dey: "All sorts of people are writing plays nowadays. You are all university men, why don't you write?"

Gokul Babu expressed his inability. Then Swami Brahmananda said, "Through spiritual practice this little mind of ours has to be merged in the cosmic mind. Then with the help of that mind, we will be able to know the thoughts of every human being and animal. If one can write with that kind of mind, the plays will turn out right. When Girish Babu[58] wrote his plays his mind was connected to the cosmic mind. In that state he could clearly know how and what everyone was thinking or saying."

◊ ◊ ◊ ◊ ◊

Gokul Babu borrowed the plot of a play from the book *Avadāna-Kalpalatā* and gave it to Pundit Kshirodprasad Vidya-vinod. Based on that plot he wrote the play *Kinnari*. It was staged at the Minerva Theatre and was a great success. The Star Theatre of Calcutta later staged the play. The proprietor of

---

58. Girish Babu (Girish Chandra Ghosh) was the most famous playwright of Bengal.

the Minerva Theatre appealed to the High Court of Calcutta, claiming the copyright to the play. In that appeal he claimed that he was the author of the play's plot. Gokul Babu had to go to the High Court to give evidence against that claim. In that connection Swami Brahmananda advised him, "Don't say a single extra word. Only give the right answers to the questions that you are asked."

◊◊◊◊◊

We have heard that a single suggestion given by Swami Brahmananda shed new light on a court case concerning Ram Babu's estate. His lawyers won the case, acting upon that suggestion.

◊◊◊◊◊

Once there was an urgent need for 80,000 rupees for Ram Babu's estate. Learning of it from Swami Brahmananda, Kiranchandra Datta consulted with his elder brother and loaned the money to Ram Babu. Swami Brahmananda gave his opinion that monetary transactions should be formally arranged. So papers were signed and the loan was given at 6 % interest. When the loan was repaid, Kiran Babu only accepted the capital. He didn't want to take the interest. He said that as Ram Babu was his boyhood friend, he could not even think of taking any interest on the money loaned to his friend. Moreover, he argued that he was not in the business of giving loans to people to earn a living.

Swami Brahmananda, however, commented that unless Kiran Babu accepted the interest, Ram Babu would feel insulted, because he would appear to be cheap. Arguments and counter-arguments over this issue between the Swami and Kiran Babu continued for a while, but no solution could be found. Ram

Babu silently sat there as though not involved. The Swami seemed slightly excited and Kiran Babu was feeling helpless.

Just then Krishnalal Maharaj arrived at the scene and with folded hands said, "Maharaj, we have been experiencing some difficulty in bringing the food offerings from the kitchen to Thakur's shrine, because they sometimes get contaminated on the way by the touch of people. My humble proposal is that the interest on the loan be used to construct a back staircase for Thakur's shrine."

Kiran Babu agreed to that proposal. Swami Brahmananda also agreed and said, "Let the amount be entered in our books as a donation from Kiran Babu."

◊ ◊ ◊ ◊ ◊

When Amulya Maharaj went to supervise the construction of the buildings for the Bhubaneswar Math, Swami Brahmananda verbally instructed him about the architectural plans, etc. He said to Gokul Babu, "There will be the statue of a lion on the top of the gate of the Bhubaneswar Math. Please make a model of that lion for us." The lion on the gate of the Bhubaneswar Math is a replica of the model made by Gokul Babu.

◊ ◊ ◊ ◊ ◊

Swami Brahmananda was then busy finishing the construction of the Bhubaneswar Math. He was in need of some money for the work. But nevertheless, if someone offered to give money, he would sometimes refuse it. Or if someone gave a certain amount, he might take only a portion of it; the rest would be returned to the donor.

He used to say that sometimes money is made through swindling people in various ways or causing suffering to others. The curses of those people are on such money. Swami Brahmananda also used to say, "The householders are turning into renunciates by giving away their hard-earned money. And the monks are becoming attached to enjoyment by taking their money!"

◊ ◊ ◊ ◊ ◊

In a farming area at some distance from the Bhubaneswar Math, a piece of land suitable for growing rice was available for sale at a very low price. The sale proceeds from the rice obtained from that property would be enough to meet the annual expenses of the Math. Even after those expenses were met, some rice would be left as surplus. At first Swami Brahmananda was quite enthusiastic about the property, but he later lost interest in buying it. If anybody would raise the topic of buying the land, he would say, "All right, let us think about it." Finally he told everyone, "It is better for the Math not to acquire such properties. If we acquire estates, we may end up oppressing the labourers."

The reason he changed his mind about buying the property was that some complaints had reached his ears about those who were engaged in managing the work at the Math or who were conducting relief work in that area.

CHAPTER XIV

WHAT SWAMI BRAHMANANDA SAID ABOUT THE GREATNESS AND GLORY OF SOME HOLY PLACES

Swami Brahmananda often talked about Kusumsarovar in Vrindaban, and Barshana (the birthplace of Sri Radharani), because they were the two places where he had performed tapasya. He would say that tapasya performed in Vrindaban for two years produced the same results as tapasya done in any other place for ten years. He also used to say that one could experience a heavy downpour of spirituality in Barshana.

While talking about Vrindaban—the place of Sri Krishna's divine play—his face would display great spiritual emotion. He said, "Hari Maharaj and I were together in Vrindaban. He used to regularly do a lot of japa and meditation. Unless absolutely necessary, we hardly spoke to each other.

"After 8 o'clock in the evening we would eat one or two chapatis that we had got by begging and then go to bed. At 12 midnight we would get up, rinse our faces and hands with water, and sit down to do japa. I don't know why one night I slept a little longer than usual. Suddenly a hard push woke me up. I heard someone say to me, 'It's past midnight, aren't you going to sit for japa?' I heard it when I was not completely awake. So I thought that Hari Maharaj must have awakened me. After asking him I learned that he hadn't tried to wake me up. I hurriedly washed my hands and face and as I was sitting down to do japa, I saw a Vaishnava holy man standing in front of me intently doing japa. Seeing him I became a little scared, because the door to our room was bolted from inside.

"While doing japa I kept looking at him every now and then. As long as I did my japa that holy man also did the same, standing in front of me. After that, every night I used to see him doing japa in our room."

◊ ◊ ◊ ◊ ◊

Swami Brahmananda narrated the following two incidents that reveal the greatness and glory of Lord Jagannath. He said, "One day I was gazing intently at the image of Lord Jagannath in His temple. A young man who was standing next to me occasionally nudged me and asked, 'Sir, what are you looking at?'

At first I felt irritated by his behavior. Finally I said, 'Why? I am looking at Lord Jagannath.'

"He said, 'I can't see the image of Lord Jagannath!'

"'Can't you see anything on the altar?' I asked.

"He said, 'I'm seeing a woman standing there.'

"I asked him again, 'Is there some woman whom you love?'

"He replied, 'My aunt brought me up. I used to love her very much. But she isn't alive anymore.'

"Then I said to him, 'Lord Jagannath appeared before you in the form of your aunt. What you have seen is not a hallucination.'

◊ ◊ ◊ ◊ ◊

"A married couple was going by train to Puri with their young son. The little boy was extremely restless. The entire night he kept his parents busy watching over him. In the early hours of the morning the parents felt a little drowsy. Yet the boy's mother caught hold of her son's leg with one hand. Suddenly the boy freed himself from his mother's grip and fell out of the window of the train. Immediately the mother woke up and pulled the alarm chain. The train stopped. It went backwards a little way to help find the boy. But he could not be found anywhere. The train then went on to Puri. The parents informed the authorities at the Puri railway station about the incident. They also reported it to the police. A little later a search party was sent out in a trolley car.

"At last, after a lot of searching, the little boy was found sitting under a date tree near Sakshigopal. The boy was happily playing with some toys. Such toys are made in that part of Orissa. The people in the search party said to the boy, 'Come with us.'

"But the boy said, 'No. My uncle has asked me not to go anywhere.'

"They asked, 'Where is your uncle?'

"The boy replied, 'He has gone to bring my food. Before going, he asked me not to go toward the railway tracks, because I might be hit by a train.'

"The police station in Puri was informed that the boy had been found. The boy's uncle loved the boy very much, but he was then in Calcutta—several hundred miles away. All these are no other than the divine play of Lord Jagannath."

◊ ◊ ◊ ◊ ◊

Swamis Nirmalananda, Shankarananada, Bhumananda, Gopalananda, Durgananda, Yatiswarananda, and Narayan Iengar accompanied Swami Brahmananda on his trip to Kanyakumari in December 1915. He stayed there for nine days.

Swami Bhumananda said, "The image of the goddess Kanyakumari is carved out of touchstone. In the afternoon the priests cover the face of the image with a thick layer of sandalwood paste. They put red color on her lips. This makes the deity appear to smile. Her face looks exquisitely beautiful in the evening with the bright lights shining on it.

"Swami Brahmananda would go to see Her around that time. He would stand and stare intently at the deity. I would stand by his side holding his rosary in my hand. The rosary had 54 beads. Whenever he would stretch out his hand to take the rosary from me, I would give it to him. After telling his beads for a little while, he would return the rosary to me and continue looking at the deity. At that time his lips would quiver, and it appeared from his facial expression that he was afraid. But I would feel a sudden urge to burst out in laughter. Somehow I would control it externally, while inside I was laughing.

"I mentioned this to the other monks who were present with him at the time. They said that they also had had similar experiences. After Swami Brahmananda came to Madras from Kanyakumari, he said, 'I was able to visit Kamakhya and Kanyakumari by the Divine Mother's infinite grace. While visiting the shrine of Kanyakumari I felt like I was bursting with laughter. I saw Mother Kanyakumari as an eight or ten year old young girl who was laughing out loud. Her image was exquisitely beautiful and I felt that it was living.'

"When we heard Swami Brahmananda that day, we realized that it was the laughter inside him that had been transmitted to our minds."

◊ ◊ ◊ ◊ ◊

Swamis Sharvananda and Shantananda, as well as Brahmachari Ishwar, accompanied Swami Brahmananda when he visited Tirupati in March 1917. Inside the Tirupati temple, whenever he would stand with folded hands for a long time and look at the image of the deity, Balaji Venkateshwara, his body would shake with spiritual emotion. He was supposed to spend only three days in Tirupati, but decided to stay there for a week. During that time he was always in spiritual ecstasy and would talk in an ecstatic mood. He later said that Tirupati was a holy place charged with divine consciousness.

The very first time that he saw the deity he said to Swami Sharvananda, "Sharvananda, I see a female deity here!" (Tirupati or Shripati is one of the names of Lord Vishnu.) After returning to their lodging in Tirupati he said, "I very clearly saw that it was a female deity. Please make inquiries about it."

Through inquiry they came to know that in the beginning it had been a temple for a female deity. The word *vālā* also indicates a female deity. When first entering the temple, one sees a large lion (the mount of the Divine Mother) inside the gopuram (ornate temple gate).

Every Friday morning the deity is given an abhisheka or mahasnanam (ritualistic bath). With the permission of the head of the temple, Swami Brahmananda saw the image without its clothes or external decorations. He saw that the image, carved out of black rock, was seven or eight feet tall. The feet were adorned with ornaments commonly used by women. It was obvious that they had tried to rub off the third eye of the deity, but the eye was still visible. This eye was kept covered by the temple priests with the tilak of the Ramanuja sect.

At considerable distance from the Balaji temple, there are meditation huts for holy men on both sides of a mountain stream. Swami Brahmananda was very pleased to see the site and invited a sadhu to come and visit him the following day.

The sadhu came and sang some devotional songs to the accompaniment of his ektara (a single-stringed musical instrument). The Swami became completely absorbed in the music, and borrowing the ektara from the sadhu, began playing it. As instructed by him, Ishwar sang along with the music. He sang a song in Bengali that starts with the line: *Tomāri deoā prāney tomāri deoā duhkh, tomāri deoā bookey tomāri anubhav.*

Swami Brahmananda bade good-bye to the sadhu after offering him a gift of various fruits.

◊ ◊ ◊ ◊ ◊

On the west bank of the Ganga, in the town of Bally, there is the temple of Kalyaneshwar Shiva. Once Thakur went there with Rakhal, and seeing the deity (Shiva), entered into spiritual ecstasy. A long time after that incident, Swami Brahmananda went there from Belur Math and offered his worship to Kalyaneshwar Shiva. Many others accompanied him that day. Since then, as instructed by Swami Brahmananda, offerings for worship have been sent from Belur Math to the temple of Kalyaneshwar Shiva every Monday.

One year, in the Bengali month of Chaitra, the weather was extremely hot. There was no trace of rain anywhere. Swami Brahmananda called Swami Brajeshwarananda and said, "Deven, if you can bathe the image of Kalyaneshwar Shiva with twelve large pitchers of Ganga water, then it will rain."

Swami Brajeshwarananda immediately ran with a pitcher to collect water from the Ganga. By the time he had finished pouring twelve pitchers of water on the deity, dark clouds had come and covered the sky. It rained so heavily that when Swami Brajeshwarananda returned, he found knee-deep water standing on the Belur Math grounds.

CHAPTER XV

SWAMI BRAHMANANDA'S POWER TO SENSE THE SUPERNATURAL

After the dedication of the new Madras Math building, all the sadhus of the Math moved into it on April 24th, 1917. As the house used by the Madras Math all those years was still being rented by the Math, Swami Brahmananda wanted to stay in it for a few more days. Two or three of his sevaks also stayed with him. On the morning of April 30th, when a sevak brought him a smoke, the Swami said to him, "There was a lot of dancing in this house last night."

The sevak asked, "What kind of dancing, Maharaj?"

He replied, "There are ghosts in this house. As Thakur has gone to the other house, they are very happy now. That's why they danced throughout all of last night." That very day he moved to the new Math building.

◊ ◊ ◊ ◊ ◊

It was dusk. Swami Brahmananda was returning from the Madras seaside by a horse-drawn carriage that belonged to Dr. Sitaram Aiyar. He had been taken there for an outing. Ishwar and Dr. Aiyar's two daughters were also in the carriage. As the carriage went past the rented house that had been previously occupied by the Madras Math, the Swami pointed to the second floor of the house and asked, "Do you see anything there?"

Ishwar replied, "Yes, Maharaj. I see a man and a woman running back and forth between the room that was Thakur's shrine and the room where you stayed."

He said, "Those two are ghosts."

On inquiry we came to know later that a man and a woman had committed suicide in that house sometime in the past.

◊ ◊ ◊ ◊ ◊

When Swami Brahmananda was staying in the house of the zamindar of Kashimpur in Dacca, he wanted to know if any-one had committed suicide in that house. Hearing that the only son of the zamindar had committed suicide there, he said, "I saw a Muslim gentleman coming and standing near me with folded hands."

On inquiry we came to know that three persons, one after the other, had committed suicide in a room of that house. And one of them was a Muslim gentleman.

◊ ◊ ◊ ◊ ◊

The sevak of Swami Brahmananda was massaging oil over his body at the Balaram-Mandir in Calcutta. Soon Tabu came and joined in. Swami Brahmananda asked, "Tabu, have you ever seen a ghost?"

He replied, "No, Maharaj."

Then the Swami continued, "I can't tell you enough about the different kinds there are. Do you know what some kinds do? They sit on the shoulders of people and suck their blood like mosquitoes." When the massaging was over, the sevak went to bring some hot water for the Swami. Just then a servant was passing by. Pointing to him the Swami said to Tabu, "If you want to see a ghost, look at him."

CHAPTER XV

Tabu shuddered at the sight of something that was sitting on the shoulders of the servant and really drinking his blood.

◇◇◇◇◇

Swami Brahmananda used to say, "Some think that they have seen ghosts, but what they saw was something they imagined out of fright. Only one or two can see real ghosts. Ghosts can influence the minds of weak-minded people. Some people commit suicide having been influenced by spirits that committed suicide.

"Lustful, angry, and envious ghosts can also influence those who are usually not prone to lust, anger or envy to do evil things. Ghosts satisfy their evil urges using such people. Sometimes controlling one person, they try to influence other people through him.

"There is a class of 'devatā's[59] who are superior to these ghosts. They lure spiritual aspirants and distract them from their spiritual path. They are called apsarās in the scriptures. But there are some departed illumined souls who try to help genuine spiritual aspirants. They sometimes even materialize to help aspirants."

◇◇◇◇◇

Once there was a proposal to cut down a vilwa tree at the Ramakrishna Mission Sevashrama in Varanasi. Hearing that Swami Brahmananda said, "Why will you cut that tree down? There is someone (a harmless, departed spirit) who lives in it. Why will you make him shelterless?" That's why they decided not to cut it down.

---

59. Such departed souls are also called upa-devatās.

◊ ◊ ◊ ◊ ◊

At the Shashiniketan in Puri the residents were once suddenly awakened at midnight by a very strange, loud noise. Swami Brahmananda came out of his room and wanted to know where the sound had come from. Hari Maharaj had been awake the whole time. He said, "I think the noise came from somewhere above the cornice of the outer corner of my bathroom."

At this Swami Brahmananda became a little sad, and said in the absence of Hari Maharaj, "This has something to do with ghosts; it is a bad omen."

Hari Maharaj used to wake up at 3 o'clock in the morning. Then, accompanied by Amulya Maharaj, he would go and attend the mangalarati in the Jagannath temple. He would return to the Shashiniketan after taking a bath in the sea. After this incident, one day he cut his foot by stepping on a sharp, broken seashell while bathing in the sea. The injury turned septic. As a result, he had to suffer a lot for two months.

◊ ◊ ◊ ◊ ◊

Swami Brahmananda was at the Balaram Mandir when an outbreak of plague occurred in Calcutta. One day while pacing back and forth on the veranda of the second floor, he saw a four-armed deity holding a sword and a human skull in Her hands dancing up the staircase to the female quarters of the house. He immediately left the Balaram Mandir and returned to Belur Math. Later the news came that Shantiram Babu's wife and their maidservant had died of plague.

◊ ◊ ◊ ◊ ◊

150

After his return from Puri to Calcutta, Swami Brahmananda stayed at the Udbodhan Ashrama for a few days. He stayed in a room upstairs, while Swami Prajnananda stayed in an identical room downstairs. One evening around 9 o'clock, he saw a person with a ghostly body standing on the veranda. A few days later in the morning, he saw a similar apparition. After seeing these two ghosts one after another, he went back to Belur Math. A few days later he got the news that Swami Prajnananda had passed away. Then he said, "I knew this would happen. Another one will also die." After a few days, Swami Prajnananda's assistant, Swami Chinmayananda, who had come to Calcutta for medical treatment, passed away at the Udbodhan Ashrama.

◊ ◊ ◊ ◊ ◊

Allopathic doctors and ayurvedic physicians lost all hope for the recovery of a dying patient. But Dr. Kanjilal, a homoeopathic physician, treated and cured him. Later Dr. Kanjilal came to Swami Brahmananda and told him about the case. Then the Swami said to him, "God has cured the patient. Don't think that your medicine cured the patient. Every disease has a presiding deity, no one can be cured unless the deity is propitiated."

[Note: Swami Saradananda (Sharat Maharaj) also talked about presiding deities of diseases.

Long ago, in the early days of Belur Math, Sharat Maharaj was once standing in the courtyard and saw an ugly, dark-complexioned woman with a towel wrapped around her waist walking rapidly toward the kitchen. He spread out his two arms to stop her and said, "I won't allow you to go in there." Then the woman went towards the neighbouring brick factory through the western back door of the Math. After that incident many labourers from the brick factory died of an epidemic of cholera. Sharat Maharaj said that the woman was the presiding deity of cholera.—Source: Swami Asitananda]

CHAPTER XVI

Swami Brahmananda's Love of Trees and Plants

The compound of the Bhubaneswar Math, previously heavily littered with gravel, was decorated in one year with fruit trees and flowering plants by Swami Brahmananda. To anyone who came for a visit the place was like an oasis in a desert. It is here where Swami Brahmananda once said, "Trees have feelings. They know who takes care of them. They become happy when the person who takes care of them comes near them. They become sad when that person goes away. Their feelings are similar to the feelings of human beings. They are never ungrateful. By offering fruits and flowers they serve the person who takes care of them."[60]

◊ ◊ ◊ ◊ ◊

In those days it was difficult to buy any vegetables other than a few edible roots such as "skanda-mool," taro roots, and pumpkins in Bhubaneswar. That's why a disciple of Swami Brahmananda used to send two parcels of vegetables every week from Calcutta. But even those vegetables were not sufficient for the needs of the monastery. One day while rinsing his mouth after his meal, the Swami saw a seedling growing next to a gutter in the inner courtyard. After examining it he determined that it was a brinjal (eggplant) seedling. He said, "Don't disturb it; let it grow." After

---

60. *Srimad Bhagavatam* (10/35/5) says, "The creepers and trees of the forests have become full of flowers and fruits as if to manifest Lord Vishnu in them. Laden with fruits and flowers and thrilled with joy, they are shedding sweetness all around."

getting good care, the seedling grew and branched out into a large healthy plant. Shortly thereafter it started yielding a lot of brinjals as if to repay for the care it had received from the monks.

◊ ◊ ◊ ◊ ◊

Swami Brahmananda found a cutting of some plant in a corner of the backyard of the Sashiniketan. He asked Mr. Chakravarty, the caretaker of the property, about it and learned that it was the cutting of a particular type of lemon tree (Pati-lemon). Unfortunately, it had not grown at all in the past two or three years. Examining the cutting the Swami said, "It looks like it is still alive!" Then he started taking good care of it. Within a few days new buds appeared on the cutting, and in a few months it grew into a large, bushy tree. While he was in the Shashiniketan blossoms appeared on the tree. After his return to Calcutta from Puri, when he was staying at the Balaram Mandir, a large basket full of large lemons arrived—the first fruits from the tree he had so fondly taken care of in Puri.

◊ ◊ ◊ ◊ ◊

The doctors asked Swami Vivekananda to drink pomelo juice. Swami Brahmananda made inquiries about where good quality Pomelo trees were to be found. Then he brought cuttings from those trees and planted five of them in a straight line on the Belur Math grounds. Under his loving care the plants grew into healthy trees and started producing a lot of fruit. The row of fruit-laden trees looked very beautiful. One could easily pick their fruits while standing on the ground. The fruits of one particular tree were very large, and their white-colored segments were very sweet and juicy. But the trees didn't yield any fruit while Swami Vivekananda was alive. He only saw their blossoms. That saddened Swami Brahmananda a lot.

◇◇◇◇◇

There were an Alphanso tree (a kind of mango tree) and a Bhuto-bombai mango tree in Belur Math. Swami Brahmananda had planted them. The Alphanso tree yielded fruit throughout the year. These two mango and five Pomelo trees (also planted by Swami Brahmananda) are no longer in Belur Math. However, for many years they served the devotees and God by giving plenty of fruit. Now the large Sri Ramakrishna Temple stands where these trees used to stand.

Four trees collected by Swami Brahmananda still stand on the grounds of Belur Math near the river Ganga. They are a white sandalwood tree, Punnag tree, Nagalingam tree, and a Thonga banian tree with its cone-shaped leaves. Under the guidance and supervision of the Swami, others planted two of these trees, while he himself planted the rest.

◇◇◇◇◇

We have heard from Gangadhar Maharaj that seeing a very large rose on a bush planted by Swami Brahmananda, Swami Vivekananda exclaimed in appreciation, "Look what Raja has done!" In later days Swami Brahmananda was able to grow similar roses in the Bhubaneswar Math.

In those days the flower garden in Belur Math was vibrant with the colours of various kinds of roses. Swami Brahmananda didn't like anyone to denude the plants by plucking too many flowers. He used to say, "This flower garden is an offering to Virat—the all-pervading Divinity." He instructed that only those flowers that were hidden behind the foliage should be plucked for Thakur's worship. Once he saw Khudumani about to pluck a large rose for worship in the temple. He said to him, "That flower cannot be used for worship. I have already offered this rose plant with all its flowers to Thakur." When Khudu replied that he was plucking that flower for the worship of the Holy Mother, Swami Brahmananda said, "If it is for Mother's worship you may take it."

◊ ◊ ◊ ◊ ◊

Swami Brahmananda planted several Magnolia Grandiflora trees on the grounds of Belur Math. Without his knowledge Haripada (Swami Pranavananda) plucked a few flowers from them. As a punishment he was asked to feed himself by begging from people's homes for three days.[61]

◊ ◊ ◊ ◊ ◊

Almost every afternoon while in Bangalore, Swami Brahmananda would go for a walk in Lalbag, the famous flower garden owned by the Maharaja of Mysore. There was a German gardener there before the First World War. The Swami would enter into an ecstatic mood looking at the full-blown flowers and the beautiful, harmonious setting of the garden. Pointing at the flowers he would say, "Look, it seems these celestial nymphs are smiling." Pointing at the lawns he used to say, "It seems the Divine Mother has spread out Her velvet carpet here." He would tell the names of the various flowering plants and vines to those who would accompany him. He would sometimes be seen absorbed in reading the catalogues

---

61. Traditionally monks are allowed to get their food by begging from people's homes. However, those who live in monasteries like Belur Math get food provided by the monasteries.

CHAPTER XVI

of plants and flowers.

◇◇◇◇◇

There was an apple tree in the inner courtyard of Bangalore Math. Swami Brahmananda wanted to encircle the tree with balsam bushes. Amulya Maharaj brought some high quality balsam seeds from Lalbag. Shortly after sowing the seeds they germinated and grew into beautiful, flowering plants. The snow-white flowers looked all the more beautiful with traces of different coloured stripes on them.

Once, after taking his meal, Swami Brahmananda came out of the dining room to rinse his mouth in the inner courtyard. As his sevak Ishwar was about to pour water over his hands,[62] the Swami, looking at the flowers, asked him, "How do the flowers look?"

Ishwar replied, "They are very beautiful."

He asked again, "Are they really very beautiful?"

Ishwar replied, "Yes, they are very beautiful."

He then told Ishwar, "Do one thing. Stand here and raising your voice shout three times: 'Balsam flowers are very beautiful.' Shout louder and louder each time!" When Ishwar carried out his orders, Swamis Bhumananda, Gopalananda, Videhananda, and others came out of the building to see what was happening. They saw Swami Brahmananda looking at the face of Ishwar in amazement.

When the swamis asked him what had happened, Swami Brahmananda said, "Just look at this! I came out hoping that

---

62. In India people eat using their hands instead of knives and forks. They rinse their hands well before eating. After eating they do the same.

Ishwar would pour water over my hands so that I could rinse my hands and mouth. But keeping me standing here, Ishwar has started shouting at the top of his voice! Looks like he has entered into an ecstatic mood at the sight of the flowers!"[63]

In this manner, whenever he stayed in a place for even a few days, he would decorate it with flowering plants and fruit trees. If anyone would come from any of those places, he would make inquiries about the plants and trees. The sadhus coming from such places knew that Swami Brahmananda wouldn't be satisfied with a superficial reply. So with great care they remembered all the details about those trees and plants. The Swami wanted all, especially the all-renouncing sadhus, to take care of plants. He used to say that taking care of trees and plants is good for the mind.

At the time of Thakur's birthday celebration, the Vilwa trees (wood-apple trees) in Belur Math were almost denuded of their leaves. The flowers on the flowering trees and plants also became scarce. The Vilwa leaves and flowers had to be collected from outside, going from one neighbourhood to another. Swami Brahmananda saw Khudumani leaving the Math one morning and asked, "Where are you going?"

He replied, "We don't have enough flowers and Vilwa leaves in the Math. I am going to look for them outside."

The Swami said, "Dig the soil around the roots of our trees. Put some clay at their roots collected from the gutter of our

---

63. Swami Brahmananda was the emperor of the domain of spiritual bliss. His mind had a natural tendency to remain absorbed in Brahman (God). But by Divine Will he had to remain conscious of this world to serve humanity. Though extremely difficult, he would try to bring his mind down to the awareness of this world by sometimes indulging in playful jokes and humour.

cowshed. Also water the trees a little. Then they will burst into blossoms. And if you go near Kalyaneswar you will find a Vilwa tree with new leaves coming out. Near the Paramanik ghat next to the Cossipore cremation ground, you will find another Vilwa tree which still has many leaves on it."

◊ ◊ ◊ ◊ ◊

Swami Brahmananda wrote the following in a letter from Bhubaneswar on November 25, 1921:

In Bangalore I procured from Lalbag, seedlings and seeds of several kinds of good plants and sent them here. I couldn't bring much along with me. I brought only a few seedlings of different varieties of hibiscus. Such hibiscuses are rarely seen in this part of the country. There is a kind of hibiscus that looks like a large land-lily.

Swami Shivananda
(also known as Mahapurush Maharaj)

CHAPTER XVII

SWAMI BRAHMANANDA—A LOVER OF FUN AND FROLIC

Swami Brahmananda was fond of fun and frolic throughout his life. Perhaps this was because Rakhal was the "mind-born child" of Sri Ramakrishna, a master of wit and humour. The ocean maintains the undisturbed silence of its depths even when its surface is noisy and restless. So also the personality of Swami Brahmananda, which was always immersed in the ocean of Brahman, displayed those two characteristics. A part of his personality remained immersed in the silent depths of samadhi, while another part occasionally interacted with the external world using wit, humour, and fun. Below are various anecdotes illustrating this.

◊◊◊◊◊

At the public celebration of Sri Ramakrishna's birthday in 1912, Swami Brahmananda decided to dress up Swami Shivananda in an unconventional style. When the vast grounds of the Math were almost packed with people, he said to Swami Shivananda, "Big Brother Tarak, let's have some fun. I have a white dhoti, shirt (punjabi) and chuddar for you. Take off your orange robe and put these on, then stroll about on the grounds of the Math. When the devotees see you in these clothes they'll be speechless with wonder!" He agreed to the proposal with a smile and walked around the grounds of Belur Math wearing those non-monastic clothes.

◊◊◊◊◊

One morning as Swami Brahmananda was walking on the grounds of Belur Math, a young man came up to him and said with folded hands, "I want to see Swami Brahmananda. I want to become a monk."

Swami Shivananda was sitting at the breakfast table drinking tea. Swami Brahmananda pointed to him and said, "Go to him. He is Swami Brahmananda."

The young man went to him and after saluting him said, "I have come to see you."

Swami Shivananda asked him, "Do you know the name of the person whom you've come to see?"

The young man replied, "His name is Swami Brahmananda."

Swami Shivananda pointed to Swami Brahmananda and said, "That's Swami Brahmananda walking over there."

The young man said, "But, sir, he told me that you were Swami Brahmananda."

Swami Shivananda said again, "No I am not him. He is walking over there."

Then the young man went to Swami Brahmananda and told him what Swami Shivananda had said. Hearing that, the Swami said, "No, no, I'm not Brahmananda." Pointing to Swami Shivananda he said, "Go to him again. Great saints like him sometimes use pretence to hide their saintliness; they don't want to reveal their true identity to others. Go and grab him. Don't leave him ever!" When the young man went back to Swami Shivananda he gave him a severe scolding. Then he again returned to Swami Brahmananda, who said, "I told you that great saints like him use pretence. Sometimes they even beat those who come to disturb them. No matter what happens, you must not leave him. Grab his feet and stay there."

The young man became completely puzzled. He was about

to shed tears when Swami Brahmananda said to him, "All right, go to the monastery. You will be allowed to join our Order as a monk."

◊ ◊ ◊ ◊ ◊

One funny incident. Baburam Maharaj was then ill and staying at the Balaram Mandir. Accompanied by his sevak Ishwar, Swami Brahmananda came from the Udbodhan Ashrama to see him. Ishwar and Baburam Maharaj had a bittersweet relationship based on the loving scoldings that Ishwar frequently got from Baburam Maharaj. So, as much as possible, Ishwar tried to avoid him. That day, looking much thinner, Baburam Maharaj was lying in bed. After making inquiries about his health Swami Brahmananda said, "Baburam Da, do you know that our Ishwar is a poet? Have you heard any of his poems?" Then turning toward Ishwar he said, "Ishwar, come here. Have you never read out your poems to Baburam Maharaj? Recite one now." With trepidation of heart the poet began reciting the following poem:

> *A strange kind of love from an unknown, strange land*
> *Has come and overpowered me today.*
> *That's why my heart is leaping with joy.*
> *While dreaming*
> *I was immersed in an intense darkness and forgot myself.*
> *I don't know whose soothing touch has awakened me. ...*

As soon as the recitation was over, Swami Brahmananda told Ishwar, "Recite another poem of yours."

Baburam Maharaj immediately sat up in bed and before Ishwar could recite the poem, gave him a scolding and said, "Stop!" Then he said to Swami Brahmananda, "Don't you know that he has almost no education? He certainly can't write po-

SWAMI ABHEDANANDA

ems! Many similar poems are published in monthly journals. Lately I have been reading them while lying in bed. He must have copied them and recited them to you." Then turning to Ishwar he said, "Get out of my room!"

Swami Brahmananda said, "No. No. I know it is he who wrote them. He doesn't read journals or magazines."

Baburam Maharaj said, "Do you really think he can write poems? I'm telling you that he can't. He is an ignorant fool."

[Note: A few days before his passing away, Baburam Maharaj sent for Ishwar. But for fear of being scolded, he was hesitant to go to him. Then Baburam Maharaj gave his word that he wouldn't scold Ishwar. When he came to see him, he made Ishwar sit close by him and said, "You fellow! Do I really scold you? Swami Vivekananda wanted you all to shape your lives according to the teachings of the *Bhagavadgita*. When I don't see that happening, I scold. I scold them more whom I love most."]

◊ ◊ ◊ ◊ ◊

Swami Abhedananda returned to Belur Math from America. Whenever he asked the junior monks at the Math to do anything they would say, "We'll do it if Swami Brahmananda orders us. Please ask him." Hearing this again and again he became displeased. One day he went to Swami Brahmananda's room as he was eating and said, "What have you done? They won't do anything others ask them to do! They will do only what *you* ask them to do! Have you turned them into so many slaves? Their only excuse is 'Please tell Swami Brahmananda!'"

At this Swami Brahmananda said, "Do you know one thing?

165

None of them really obeys me. They really and truly respect and obey Hari Maharaj. They also obey and respect Sharat Maharaj. Now that you have returned to Belur Math, you and others take over and manage the Math. I have become old. I would like to retire peacefully in some place. Let me go and stay in Bhubaneswar.

"By the way, you were saying that they obey me here. Do you want to know why?" Then pointing to the bowls of food that had been given to him, he said, "I eat very little. They will eat most of it. It is only for this food that they obey me!"

The funny way he said these words made everyone burst into laughter. Swami Abhedananda also laughed and said, "You joke about everything!" Then smiling he returned to his room.

◊◊◊◊◊

Sitting upstairs on two chairs on the Math's veranda, Swamis Brahmananda and Vijnanananda would humourously bandy words with each other. One day, for fun, Swami Brahmananda took the position of a believer while Swami Vijnanananda took the position of an atheist, and they started debating with each other. Swami Vijnanananda lost the friendly debate, because Swami Brahmananda refuted all his arguments. The following day Swami Brahmananda took the position of an atheist and Swami Vijnanananda that of a believer. Then the debate started. But that day also Swami Vijnanananda couldn't defeat Swami Brahmananda. The debate continued till dusk.

At dusk Swami Brahmananda would rinse his hands with holy Ganga water to prepare for his evening prayers. That evening as his sevak was pouring water over his hands, Swami Vijnanananda noticed that and said, "What's this? You're be-

SWAMI VIJNANANANDA

having just like a believer!"

Swami Brahmananda replied, "You know, it's just an old habit! Touching holy Ganga water at dusk has become a habit. You can't call it believing in God!"

◊ ◊ ◊ ◊ ◊

Sometimes the pranks that Swami Brahmananda played on Gangadhar Maharaj (Swami Akhandananda) would exceed all limits. Once Gangadhar Maharaj was going to leave Kothar and go to Calcutta. In spite of Swami Brahmananda's request to stay on for a few more days, he insisted on leaving, saying that he wouldn't stay even one more day. The distance between Kothar and the nearest railroad station to go to Calcutta is ten miles. Gangadhar Maharaj had to travel those ten miles by palanquin. Shortly after he started, he fell asleep. Following the instruction of Swami Brahmananda, the palanquin bearers then turned around and returned to the house in Kothar. Without disturbing the sleep of Gangadhar Maharaj, they quietly went to their own rooms to sleep.

◊ ◊ ◊ ◊ ◊

The following story was told by Ramkrishna Basu's daughter Mahamaya: "One day Swami Brahmananda gave me a sealed envelope and said, 'Go and give this letter to Gangadhar Maharaj.'

"Gangadhar Maharaj opened the envelope and found that it contained something that was a very bad omen for starting on a journey. So he had to cancel his trip that day."

◊ ◊ ◊ ◊ ◊

Chinmayi, a close friend of Mahamaya, said, "Swami Brahmananda had got a picture of a crab from somewhere. He

CHAPTER XVII

SWAMI AKHANDANANDA
(ALSO KNOWN AS GANGADHAR MAHARAJ)

gave it to me and said, 'Go and give it to Gangadhar Maharaj.' Some in Bengal consider a crab to be a very bad omen. So Gangadhar Maharaj didn't leave his room that day."

Chinmayi then narrated another incident. "Mahamaya and I went to Gangadhar Maharaj's room and said, 'Good morning, Gangadhar Maharaj.' He turned his face away and would not look at us. We said again, 'Gangadhar Maharaj, good morning.'

"He said, 'I won't look at you. I know Swami Brahmananda wants you to trick me!'

"We said reassuringly, 'No, Maharaj. We've only come to salute you.' Gangadhar Maharaj was a trusting person. He believed our words and turned his face towards us.

"Then we winked at him. Winking is considered a very bad omen. So he couldn't go on his trip."

◊ ◊ ◊ ◊ ◊

On a particular day Gangadhar Maharaj got all packed up and ready to leave Belur Math to go to Sargachhi. Swami Brahmananda requested him to stay on that day, but he was determined to go.

Then as instructed by Swami Brahmananda, the young monks of the Math came and surrounded Gangadhar Maharaj. Some of them started ringing bells, clanging cymbals, and blowing conches. Others chanted, "Crab! Turtle! Washerman!"—all considered terribly bad omens for starting on a trip. Some monks winked at him.

He closed his eyes and began chanting, "Durga! Durga!" to ward off the evil influence of the bad omens. Then Swami

Brahmananda came up to him and innocently asked, "Ganga-dhar, aren't you going to Sargachhi?"

Seeing him, he heaved a sigh of relief and said, "Get these mischievous boys away from me."

Swami Brahmananda replied, "See how much they love you! They want you to stay. Do you think they'll listen to me?"

As a result, Gangadhar Maharaj's trip was postponed.[64]

◊ ◊ ◊ ◊ ◊

Swami Brahmananda was seated in an easy chair on the ve-randa of the Bangalore Math. The spacious betel-leaf shaped garden in front of the veranda had many flowering plants, bushes, and several varieties of leafy vines. Those seated on the veranda were able to see visitors coming to the Math, but people on the street in front of the building couldn't see any-one on the veranda.

When Swami Brahmananda saw Miss McLeod coming to-ward the Math to see him, he immediately entered his room and told Tulsi Maharaj, "Tell her that I'm not feeling well to-day."

On three consecutive days Miss McLeod tried to see Swami Brahmananda, but he wouldn't see her—always giving the same excuse. This made her determined to see him. On the fourth day she covered her entire body with a green cloth with a leafy design, and crawling under the bushes, suddenly jumped up in front of Swami Brahmananda and said, "Naughty boy, where will you escape to now?"

A little embarrassed, Swami Brahmananda said, "I'm feeling

64. Source: Swami Gaurishananda

fine today."

Smiling, Miss McLeod said, "I knew you would say that, because I caught you this time."

◊ ◊ ◊ ◊ ◊

The source of the following anecdotes is Swami Prashantananda. He said, "Swami Brahmananda came to know that there was a misunderstanding going on between the monks of our two ashramas in Varanasi.

"There is a tradition among devotees in India of feeding holy people. Following that tradition, our devotees would sometimes give money to our ashramas requesting that feasts for our monks be arranged there. Such feasts are called 'bhandaras.' During Swami Brahmananda's stay at our Varanasi Advaita Ashrama, devotees would give him money to arrange bhandaras for our monks.

"To remove the misunderstanding between the monks of the two ashramas, Swami Brahmananda would occasionally arrange bhandaras at the Advaita Ashrama and invite the monks of the Sevashrama to come there and eat. At other times, he would arrange for bhandaras to be held at the Sevashrama and would ask the monks of the Advaita Ashrama to go there and eat. He gave a funny name to these bhandaras. He would call them 'harernamah'.

"One day Swami Brahmananda dressed me up in very fancy Hindustani clothes. He had me wear a turban and nagra shoes, and asked me to hold a long thick cane. This outfit made me look like the orderly of a king of some native state of India or that of an aristocratic landlord (zamindar). Then he gave me a sealed envelope addressed to the head of the Varanasi Sevashrama and said, 'Go to the Sevashrama and give this to Charu Babu.[65] Make sure he doesn't recognize you. If he does, I'll break your head!' Swami Brahmananda taught me how to salute him in Mughal fashion before handing him the envelope.

"Very rarely did messengers from the princely states of India come to the Sevashrama. When I went and saluted Charu Babu, he returned my salutation with a nod. Then he took the envelope from me. Thinking that it might contain some urgent message, he carefully cut it open with a pair of scissors. The envelope held a small piece of paper on which was written *harernamah* and nothing more. After reading the note Charu Babu looked at me and laughed. Then I said to him in Hindi, 'The sender expects your reply.'

"He wrote *accepted* in English on a piece of paper and gave it to me.

"Another incident. The head of the Advaita Ashrama was Chandra Maharaj. Something had happened between him and me, and he wouldn't talk to me anymore. But as I was a monastic worker in that ashrama, I just went on doing all my duties as before. The only difference was that we were not talking to each other.

"One afternoon Swami Brahmananda was sitting on the lawn at the Sevashrama and I was gently stroking his feet. Then he asked me. 'Do you know what the myna bird says?'

"I replied, 'No, I don't.'

"He asked me to repeat after him: 'Ri ri ri, kot, kot, kot, pāpich, pāpich, khendi-kirkich, kidār-kich, ishon-mishon, dhyap dhyap, kishto-kishor, kishto-kishor, doog doogādoog, pleeng ply.'

---

65. Charu Babu was the head of the Sevashrama.

For several days after that he trained me how to say those words properly. He also taught me how, at the end, to take a bow and disappear, saying, 'Pleeng ply.' He also had me rehearse this a few times in front of other residents of the Sevashrama.

"It was a celebration day at the Advaita Ashrama. The Ashrama hall was full of people. Suddenly I heard Chandra Maharaj calling me. I went to him and he said, 'Swami Brahmananda wants to see you.'

"Swami Brahmananda was seated in the hall. He said to me, 'Tell all of us here what the myna bird says.' But I hesitated. After he had asked me two more times, I did my little act, and all, including Chandra Maharaj, burst into loud laughter. From then on Chandra Maharaj was pleased with me and started talking to me normally. This is how Swami Brahmananda tactfully solved the problem between Chandra Maharaj and I.

"Swami Brahmananda would write many teasing letters from Varanasi to Dr. Bipin in Belur Math. The letters would be sent using Chandra Maharaj's name as the author. So Dr. Bipin would send angry replies to Chandra Maharaj, thinking that it was he who had written the letters. Swami Brahmananda would write back in Bengali, Sanskrit, as well as in French. A multi-linguist lawyer of Allahabad would come to see him in Varanasi. The Swami used him to write some letters in French. They were then mailed to Dr. Bipin. To know their content, he had to run to Calcutta to find someone who knew French. Once the Swami used me to write a letter in Sanskrit poetry to send to Dr. Bipin. I only remember one couplet of that letter. The English translation is given below:

> Do you want to defeat me in battle? It is a futile hope. You being a wild goat can never hope to win a battle against a lion like me!

(Dr. Bipin's first name was Bipin-bihari. The word *Bipin-bihari* means *wild*.)

"Sometimes Swami Brahmananda would send gift parcels to Dr. Bipin. As soon as he would open one, a big rubber snake might burst out, raising its hood, or maybe a mechanized rubber lizard would leap out at him.

"Another incident. Swami Brahmananda was then in Bhubaneswar. From Calcutta Kaiser (Lalit Chatterjee) wrote to him praying for an easy technique for spiritual salvation. Kaiser wrote the letter in poetry. The Swami came to know that at one time I used to write poems in Bengali. So he said, 'You have to draft a reply to Kaiser's letter in poetry. In that letter include two names: Noree and Poree.' (Noree and Poree were two actresses on the Calcutta stage and Kaiser knew them well.)

"The first line of the letter I drafted was, 'O, you have granted salvation to so many sinners like Noree and Poree.' The underlying idea was: 'You yourself have granted salvation to so many people like Noree and Poree. Why do I have to prescribe any technique for your salvation?'

"Aside from that, Kaiser had promised that he would arrange for a theatrical performance to benefit the Bhubaneswar Ashrama, but had done nothing about it up to then. I therefore suggested to Swami Brahmananda, 'Why don't I write at the end of the letter—'Benefitted by your benefit night. Yours, Kaschit Ānanda—?' (This funny name was concocted just to hide the identity of the letter writer.)

"He said, 'That's just right.'

"Kaiser showed this letter to one or two very important

members of the Bengal Literary Society (Bangiya Sahitya Parishad). They remarked that the quality of writing was first class. Kaiser wrote a letter to Swami Saradananda quoting their remarks. When I went to salute Swami Brahmananda in the morning, he told me, 'A certificate has come for you.'

"I had, in fact, appeared in an examination in Calcutta, the results of which hadn't come out yet. So I eagerly asked, 'Where is it, Maharaj?'

"He replied, 'It is with Sharat Maharaj'. Sharat Maharaj had come for a visit to Bhubaneswar and was staying at the Lakshmi-Nivas. So I went to see him immediately.

"Seeing me he asked, 'What brings you here so early in the morning?' When I told him that I had come for the certificate he was quite surprised. However, knowing that Swami Brahmananda had told me about the so-called certificate, he understood everything. He knew the Swami's humourous side very well. He said to Swami Bhumananda, 'His certificate is in that stack of letters. Please bring it here.' Swami Bhumananda searched thoroughly, but couldn't find it. Then Sharat Maharaj himself found Kaiser's letter and gave it to me."

◊ ◊ ◊ ◊ ◊

Swami Mukteswarananda said, "It was around 2 o'clock in the morning when Bhavani and I returned to the Balaram Mandir after having a late supper at the Sukia Street home of Dr. Kanjilal. The newly-hired gatekeeper was sleeping under a blanket on the other side of the closed front door. We were afraid of making a loud noise, because Swami Brahmananda was upstairs. So we softly called the gatekeeper through the open window a few times. But that didn't wake him up. Then we began throwing small pieces of broken bricks through the iron bars of the open window at him. As that didn't work, we threw bigger pieces of brick at him. Still no response. Then we broke off a branch of the thorny 'madar tree' (coral tree), stuck it through the window bars and hit his head with it once or twice. That worked. He immediately got up and opened the door for us. When we asked him why he hadn't responded earlier, he replied, 'I thought you were ghosts.'

"Bhavani got up in the last part of the night and offered Swami Brahmananda a smoke (hubble-bubble). After smoking, he began walking back and forth in the morning on the veranda next to the inner courtyard. Meanwhile the gatekeeper had come and was standing at the entrance to the staircase. He was waiting there to complain to Swami Brahmananda about us. He held the branch of the madar tree in one hand and big pieces of brick in the other. Some scratches from the thorny branch were noticeable on his face. The Swami didn't seem to notice the gatekeeper. When the Swami moved away a bit, Bhavani grabbed the gatekeeper and dragged him downstairs. Then he told him, 'Don't complain to Maharaj, take this tip.' The gatekeeper was given the one rupee that I had with me. This made him very happy.

"Another incident that I want to narrate happened some time later. It was the day of Sri Ramakrishna's birthday celebration. Swami Brahmananda became tired after walking on the grounds of Belur Math and listening to the kirtan. So he went upstairs and said to his sevak Bhavani, 'I would like to rest now. Let no one come and disturb me.'

"Two volunteers were asked to stand downstairs at the bottom of the staircase to make sure that no one went upstairs to disturb him. Bhavani himself remained upstairs. A little later Bashi appeared before Bhavani. He had somehow bypassed the volunteers and had come to Bhavani to get his permission to see the Swami. Bhavani resisted him initially, but considering his very close relationship with the Swami, he allowed Bashi to go and see him. The Swami was pleased to see Bashi and asked him to massage his body a little. He said to him, 'Did they let you come? I asked them not to allow anybody.'

"Bashi replied, 'They asked me not to come. But they permitted me when I fervently appealed to them!'

"Swami Brahmananda with his thumb and forefinger made the gesture of flipping a coin and asked Bashi with a smile, 'Did you bribe them?'"

◊ ◊ ◊ ◊ ◊

Gokuldas Dey wrote as follows: "Once I couldn't stop laughing when I saw Swami Brahmananda coaching a matchmaker on how to conduct his business. I don't think I ever saw anyone else as humourous as the Swami. He was the supreme emperor of the domain of eternal bliss. Is it any wonder then when we see him sprinkling a drop or two of that bliss upon us on earth?"

CHAPTER XVIII

Swami Brahmananda's Fun and Frolic with Children

Swami Brahmananda's childlike simplicity was natural with him. There was a photograph of him wearing a sleeveless shirt in Pulinbehari Mitra's room. Pointing like a child at that picture, he said to Pulin Babu proudly, "Look at me sitting there like a hero!"

Once Swami Brahmananda was being driven in a car on Cornwallis Street in Calcutta. A young boy named Kartik was then walking on the footpath returning home from school. When the Swami met him the following day, he said to him with childlike pride, "Did you see me in the car yesterday? Wasn't it great that I was in a car?"

◊ ◊ ◊ ◊ ◊

Many young children used to come to the Balaram Mandir. Swami Brahmananda would play with them as though he himself was a child. He used to play "hide and seek" and card games with them. Sometimes he would suddenly appear before them wearing a mask. Getting scared, the children would run helter-skelter, screaming for their mothers.

◊ ◊ ◊ ◊ ◊

One day Nitai Babu's little son brought a wooden elephant to play with. When he saw Swami Brahmananda he appealed to him again and again saying, "Maharaj, ride my elephant!"

The Swami was walking on the veranda upstairs. He took the elephant from the little boy and putting it against his back, pretended to ride it for a little while. Gokul Babu, who was

179

close by, enjoyed the sight. The Swami looked at him and burst into laughter.

◇ ◇ ◇ ◇ ◇

Shyam Babu brought a bearskin from Kashmir and gave it as a gift to Swami Brahmananda. Anyone wearing it would look just like a real bear.

It was a little after dusk. Swami Brahmananda's room was lit with a subdued light. He had asked all the children of the Bose family to come and they came running to his room. There were quite a few children in the extended Bose family. As soon as they entered the Swami's room, they saw a terrible bear standing there baring its teeth and shaking its arms. Even the grown ups found it scary.

The children ran screaming with fear out of the room as fast as they could. But the young son of Tulsiram Babu's daughter, Vishweswari, didn't run away. The Swami was very fond of the boy. With tears in his eyes the little boy, though afraid, stretched his arms out to him and said crying, "I know you are Maharaj."

The Swami immediately took off the bearskin and picking him up, hugged him tightly.

◇ ◇ ◇ ◇ ◇

When Swami Brahmananda visited Varanasi for the last time, Balaram Bose's daughter Krishnamayee and some of her children accompanied him. Krishnamayee would cook some dishes and send them for Swami Brahmananda and Hari Maharaj every day through her daughter Chinmayee. Her nickname was Chini, a Bengali word that means *sugar*. One morning she came to the Advaita Ashrama. As soon as Swami

Brahmananda saw her he said, "I want to drink sharbat (a cold drink) made of chini."

Then the other monks present began saying, "Chini has come. Drop her into a big bucket of water. We will then have plenty of sharbat for everybody!"

Chini became very angry and said to Swami Brahmananda, "I won't bring your food anymore!"

Swami Brahmananda said, "No, no, no! I promise I won't say it again!"

BALARAM MANDIR (HOME OF BALARAM BOSE)

CHAPTER XIX
SWAMI BRAHMANANDA—A LOVER OF PLAYFUL DISGUISES

Ramprasad used to sing: "The divine Mother Kali is present in all the letters of the alphabet. Every letter is nothing but Her holy name."

Addressing the Divine Mother, Sri Ramakrishna said, "O Mother, Thou art all the letters of the holy Vedas and the Vedanta. Aren't you also the letters used in vulgar and obscene language?" The words that rouse animal tendencies in impure minds would lift His mind to the highest level of samadhi. This proves that words have power. Depending upon the kind of mind a person has, it produces either good or bad effects.

For a very small number of powerful saints all words, whether holy or profane, are equally holy. These saints have the power to lift the minds of ordinary people around them to great heights of spirituality, sometimes by using profane or vulgar language. Sri Ramakrishna, a divine incarnation, had that power in abundance. His "mind-born son" Swami Brahmananda inherited that extraordinary power. He used it to spiritually transform many souls by removing the barriers they encountered on their spiritual paths. Once Swami Jagadananda told the author that after the passing away of the Swami, there was no one in the Ramakrishna Order who displayed that kind of power.

While talking about his own spiritual state Sri Ramakrishna said, "The Divine Mother has put me in the state of a devotee. She has also put me in the state of a 'vijnani.' That's why I indulge in light-hearted fun with youngsters like Rakhal. Had She placed me in the state of a 'jnani' it would not be possible." Once he said, "When the Divine Mother puts me in the state of a child I go through three spiritual moods—childhood, adolescence and adulthood. In adolescence one indulges in frivolities."

◊ ◊ ◊ ◊ ◊

A young man named Gopal came to Bhubaneswar with his uncle and was staying at the Sanatorium. This roly-poly, dark-complexioned young man was very guileless. He was going through a period of great sadness due to his wife's death. So he came to see Swami Brahmananda, who naturally felt great compassion for this sad, young man.

Whenever Gopal would come to see him, Swami Brahmananda would narrate the love story between Lord Krishna and the gopis with a lot of humourous embellishments. He would do this while walking back and forth on the veranda of the Math building. Gopal would roll on the floor in laughter.

Then Swami Brahmananda would say, "How can I tell the story if you laugh so much!"

At this Gopal would say, "Please tell me. I won't laugh any more!"

But no matter how much he tried, he could not stop laughing. His grief at the loss of his wife completely disappeared. He didn't want to stay away from the Bhubaneswar Math even for a day. Except for going home to have his meals or to sleep at night, he would spend all his time at the Math. He came to Bhubaneswar to stay only for a month, but he ended up staying there for three months.

CHAPTER XIX

◊◊◊◊◊

Kedarnath Bhattacharya of Baruipur had great respect for Swami Brahmananda. One evening he came to the Balaram Mandir accompanied by a friend. The Swami was sitting together with two or three people of his own age group and indulging in light-hearted fun. Seeing the visitors he said, "Hello Kedar Babu. Welcome! Please take your seats." Then he went on indulging in frivolous conversation as before. Kedar Babu was wondering how his friend would interpret the Swami's behaviour. His friend was becoming more and more restless. Noticing it, he left with his friend.

On the way back the friend said to Kedar Babu, "So this is the President of your Belur Math! He behaves like a zamindar, lives in a rich man's home, smokes from a golden hubble-bubble, (It was actually a brass hubble-bubble.) and kills his time in frivolous talk." Kedar Babu tried to change his friend's opinion in so many ways, but failed. Thereafter, whenever Kedar Babu met his friend, he would criticize the Swami.

However, six months later the friend came to him and said, "All these days I have been trying to forget that gentleman (Swami Brahmananda), but I haven't been able to. I also recall that he was not at all embarrassed at seeing a total stranger like me, nor did he change the topic on seeing us. Therefore, I feel that I must see him again. Would you please take me to him?" The two friends went to see the Swami that afternoon.

As soon as they arrived, the Swami said to Kedar Babu's friend, "So you have come! You came the other day also, isn't it? You see, I am not as spoiled as you think I am." After that he talked to that gentlemen for some time, but did not at all talk about God or anything spiritual. The curiosity of the gentleman kept on increasing. At first he would come with his friend Kedar Babu, and then he started coming alone. Eventually he surrendered to Swami Brahmananda completely and with great yearning of heart prayed for spiritual initiation.

◊ ◊ ◊ ◊ ◊

A gentleman in Varanasi was often overpowered by vulgar thoughts. He decided that he would go to Swami Brahmananda and would think those vulgar thoughts in his presence. His sick mind made him think that in this way he would be able to judge the saintly calibre of the Swami. But when the gentleman came and sat in the presence of the Swami, his mind was lifted to such a high plane that in spite of trying to bring his mind down, he couldn't do so for two hours.[66]

◊ ◊ ◊ ◊ ◊

It has been seen that the people in whose presence Swami Brahmananda used to indulge in light banter and frivolous conversation were greatly benefited spiritually. They discovered a great, loving friend in him and felt that he loved them unconditionally, ignoring all their defects. They felt that he would not mind getting caught in their bonds of love.

◊ ◊ ◊ ◊ ◊

Pa— and La— were long-time devotees. Both were very large-hearted. They had great intimacy with the actors and actresses of the Calcutta stage. Swami Brahmananda loved them and would lightheartedly chitchat with them. One day he said, "Two cargo ships arrived at the port of Calcutta carrying a cargo of lies. But they couldn't find any buyers. At last they found two buyers: Pa— and La—"

---

66. Source: Swami Jagadananda.

◊◊◊◊◊

The source of the following story is Swami Prashantananda. We are narrating it in his own words:

"In the early morning I went to the Balaram Mandir to salute Swami Brahmananda. Gangadhar Maharaj was also staying there then. I saw Swami Brahmananda going through the hall to Gangadhar Maharaj's room. He beckoned to me to follow him. A few minutes later, as soon as I entered the room, Gangadhar Maharaj gave me a scolding and said, 'What do you want here? What business do you have here?'

"I replied very humbly, 'I have come to hear the conversation between two saints.'

"He said, 'Get out of here. We are having a private conversation.'

"Swami Brahmananda interrupted us and told Gangadhar Maharaj, 'Ignore him. Let him stay.'

"They had been chitchatting lightheartedly before I entered the room. But seeing me, Swami Brahmananda increased the intensity of his bantering and joking. Being irritated due to my presence there Gangadhar Maharaj repeatedly told me, 'Get out of this room.'

"However, Swami Brahmananda, without saying anything to me, kept on joking and bantering as before. Realizing his intent, I took out a piece of paper and a pencil from my pocket and pretended to write something. Greatly annoyed, Gangadhar Maharaj asked me, 'What are you writing?'

"I replied, 'I have a mind to write a book on the teachings of saints. So I am taking notes.' This made him really angry.

Raising the cane he was holding, he wanted to chase me out of his room. Swami Brahmananda immediately grabbed his cane and stopped him.

"Then Gangadhar Maharaj said, 'You must not pamper these boys like this. Don't you see how obstinate he is! I am asking him to leave, but he won't listen. Then again he is writing something.'

"With a twinkle in his eye, Swami Brahmananda said, 'Let him write. Using the teachings of Thakur, *Kathamrita* (*The Gospel of Sri Ramakrishna*) has been written. Let him write a book containing the teachings of saints. Why should we care?'"

CHAPTER XX
SWAMI BRAHMANANDA'S PLAYING OF CARDS AND GOING FISHING

[Note: Unless a person himself is a saint it is not possible for him to recognize or understand a saintly soul. There is a saying in India that saints are like elephants. Elephants have tusks that can be seen from outside, but they have teeth inside their mouths that cannot be seen. Similarly, saints have their *inner* and *outer* personalities. Without knowing their inner personalities it is impossible to understand them correctly.

For the above reason, a saintly soul of a very high calibre like Swami Brahmananda may appear to be an enigma to many. He may often be considered strange, whimsical, eccentric, and even crazy!

Usually we judge people by their actions. But no action is either good or bad. With which attitude an action is performed determines whether it is good or bad. A good attitude makes an action good, and a bad attitude makes it bad.

The minds of saints are usually at such high levels of spiritual consciousness that unless we know *why* they are doing certain things, it is very easy to draw the wrong conclusions. One example from the life of Swami Brahmananda is given below to clarify this point.

Swami Brahmananda was then visiting Varanasi. The Swami had a woman disciple in that city. He often praised her great love and devotion to God.

She invited her guru Swami Brahmananda and the other monks to come and have a meal at her home on a certain day.

189

The Swami accepted the invitation. But on the day of the invitation he said to the other monks, "I'm not going there; you all go without me."

Accordingly, the monks went to the lady's home. She had arranged for a sumptuous feast for them. But the monks could not enjoy the food seeing how disappointed and sad she was because her guru hadn't come to her home.

Upon their return to the ashrama, a young monk went to Swami Brahmananda's room and after saluting him said with much feeling, "Maharaj, none of us could heartily enjoy the meal at her home. Although she was most hospitable to us, no matter how much she tried, she couldn't hide her great sadness because you hadn't gone there with us! Maharaj, you accepted her invitation, why then didn't you go?"

Then the Swami said to him, "Let me ask you one thing. Had Thakur (Sri Ramakrishna) come to you and said, 'Don't go there!' what would you do?"

The monk replied, "I wouldn't go, Maharaj."

Swami Brahmananda said, "That's exactly what happened to me this morning. Thakur came to me and asked me not to go."

Hadn't that young monk gone and asked the Swami why he hadn't gone to that lady's home, we would surely have misjudged him. We would have thought that he was a whimsical person, or one who wouldn't honour his commitments.

If this is kept in mind while reading the anecdotes included in this chapter, the readers will get to know a very charming side of the Swami's childlike and playful outer personality.]

In those days there were two ponds, Goalpukur and Padmapukur, in Belur Math. Occasionally Swami Brahmananda would go fishing in them with a pole. Two or three times on invitation he went outside to fish as well.

While staying at the Balaram Mandir in Calcutta, he sometimes played cards with his brother monks such as Hari Maharaj, Gangadhar Maharaj or Baburam Maharaj's elder brother, Tulsiram Babu, etc.

Hari Maharaj was grave by nature. Yet to give joy to Swami Brahmananda, he would join in playing cards. But whenever Swami Brahmananda would sneak a look at Hari Maharaj's cards, he would become quite displeased. Once he said to him, "I won't play with you anymore. I often forget that this is all lila to you—mere play-acting—and I lose my temper when we play."

◊ ◊ ◊ ◊ ◊

Sometimes Sharat Maharaj would come to the Balaram Mandir to discuss official matters with Swami Brahmananda, but he would persuade Sharat Maharaj to play cards with him instead. When playing against Swami Brahmananda, Sharat Maharaj would purposely lose. That would make Swami Brahmananda exceedingly happy, and he would say, "Sharat, it seems you don't know how to play at all!"

Sharat Maharaj would respond, "Brother, what can I do? I can't play as well as you. That's why I make all those mistakes and lose."

◊ ◊ ◊ ◊ ◊

Even Swami Shivananda, a senior brother monk of Swami Brahmananda, sometimes played cards at his request. But he tried to dissuade Swami Brahmananda from playing cards or going fishing. He would tell him, "You are the Order's President. What will people say if you do these things?"

Swami Brahmananda wouldn't reply. He would just go fishing when he was sure Swami Shivananda wouldn't find out about it.

◊ ◊ ◊ ◊ ◊

At the invitation of the Maharaja of the state of Cooch Behar, Swami Brahmananda went to his palace in Alipore a few times. Every time he visited, he stayed for three or four days. The caretaker of the palace, Shourjendranath Mazumdar, respected the Swami very much. Shourjendranath spent a lot of money providing comforts for him and his companions.

In 1920, during Swami Brahmananda's visit there, Christmas Eve was celebrated at the palace. Ramlal Dada had to play the role of a Catholic priest. He didn't know a single word of English. But he memorized one or two English sentences, and requested Pundit Kshirodprasad Vidyavinod in English to read the Bible, saying, "I request…etc." Obviously, it was all planned by the Swami to make the event interesting.

◊ ◊ ◊ ◊ ◊

It was arranged by Dr. Haran Banerjee that Swami Brahmananda would go fishing one day at a lake within the compound of the R. G. Kar Medical College in Calcutta. But on the appointed day one obstacle after another appeared. As Swami Brahmananda was about to start, Mahapurush Maharaj suddenly arrived.

Bhavani and Ishwar, two sevaks of Swami Brahmananda, were supposed to go to the lake in advance and make all the preparations. Bhavani knew that Mahapurush Maharaj had come, but without greeting him, he went straightaway to the lake. But Ishwar went to greet Mahapurush Maharaj. After he saluted him, Mahapurush Maharaj inquired about everything and came to know about the planned fishing expedition as well. So Swami Brahmananda had to explain to him that at Dr. Haran Banerjee's earnest request, he felt obliged to go fishing that day.

Then, after arriving at the lake, Swami Brahmananda changed his mind about fishing when he heard that the Principal of the medical college, Dr. Kedar Das, was coming there. Nevertheless, Bhavani and Ishwar were able to catch several fish from the lake that day.

◊◊◊◊◊

Kiranchandra Datta arranged for a celebration in his country house in honour of Swami Brahmananda's visit. Upon his arrival, the Swami wanted to go fishing in the lake there. After casting the line, he sat patiently on the lakeshore holding his fishing rod. There was silence for quite a while. Finally the silence was broken by his excited calls. He called Kiran Babu and all the others to come and see the fish he had caught. They all ran to him and saw that he had caught only a little minnow with his fishing rod!

◊◊◊◊◊

Whenever Swami Brahmananda caught even a single fish, he would be extremely happy. He would say about anyone who was with him at the time, "He brings me good luck. He is my good luck charm." But, on the other hand, if he couldn't catch any fish (and that would often be the case), he would blame the person who was with him saying, "He brings me bad luck.

He is a jinx."

When playing cards the Swami behaved in the same way. If he won the game, he would point to the person who was with him and say, "He is my lucky charm." Then he would turn to that person and say, "You must stay close to me when I play cards!" But if he lost the game, he would blame his companion and say, "He is a jinx. It's because of him that I couldn't win." That's why nobody wanted to stay near him when he was fishing or playing cards.

Occasionally while fishing or playing cards the sevaks had to bring his hubble-bubble for him to smoke. But immediately after delivering the hubble-bubble, they would leave as fast as possible for fear of being considered a jinx.

Swami Brahmananda was very fond of a young man, the first syllable of whose name was Gha—. Apparently the Swami would be happy to see him. He would eagerly answer his questions, and would sometimes take him to his own room and privately advise him on spiritual matters. Once, at the Udbodhan Ashrama, Swami Brahmananda told Sharat Maharaj, "It seems I've at last found a good young man after waiting all these days." Then he referred to Sri Ramakrishna's parable about a ghost who longed for the company of another ghost. But unfortunately he never succeeded in finding any. Swami Brahmananda said to Sharat Maharaj, "So many young men came and left. None of them wanted to become our companion. But this one seems to be very nice. He also has had quite a few spiritual visions."

Sharat Maharaj just listened quietly, and then commented, "Is he really that good? Nice to hear that."

After graduating from college, Gha— came to stay at Belur

Math to become a sannyasi. Nobody objected to his joining the Math, because he was a favourite of Swami Brahmananda. But the Swami did not know about his joining the Order, because he was then in Calcutta. After returning, he was quite displeased to see him in the robe of a brahmachari. His displeasure seemed to increase day by day. He would say, "Why does he come to me? He is a jinx. If I happen to see him, that day no fish will bite the bait!"

Once Charu Babu, from the village of Belur, invited Swami Brahmananda to come and fish in the lake in his garden. That made the Swami very happy. He said to everybody at the Math, "Make sure that Gha— doesn't come close to me tomorrow morning. I don't want to see his face before I go fishing." So Gha— left the Math as soon as he got up from bed the next morning.

In the morning Swami Brahmananda told his two sevaks, Bhavani and Ishwar, "You go first and make all the arrangements for fishing. I'll join you a little later." Around 10 o'clock in the morning he arrived at the lake and announced, "I won't fish today. You fish."

"Why, Maharaj?" They asked him.

He said, "When I started from the Math I was afraid that Gha— might have returned to the Math without my knowledge. To avoid seeing him, I decided to take the circuitous road through the jungle. As soon as I entered the jungle, I heard a rustling noise as if some animal such as a fox was walking on dry leaves. I was making my way through the jungle removing twigs and vines with my cane. Suddenly I noticed something like a white chuddar behind a tree. When I approached I saw Gha— standing there. He was shaking with fear. I asked him,

'Why are you here? I took this jungle road just to avoid seeing you lest my fishing trip ends up in a disaster. And now you are standing here in front of me!'

"He said, 'Maharaj, I was returning to the Math through this jungle to avoid meeting you. I didn't know that this would happen.' Well, this is the story. Now I am sure no fish will take my bait. So you do the fishing."

◊ ◊ ◊ ◊ ◊

Tulsi Babu was an expert card player. It was very difficult to defeat him. Swami Brahmananda would choose him to be his partner and would win most of the games. Having lost several games one after the other, Gangadhar Maharaj said one day, "You win because Tulsi Babu is your partner. Today I'll make him my partner. Let me see if you can win today!"

The Swami agreed to the proposal and said, "All right. I accept the challenge."

Even though another good player like Gour Babu was present, Swami Brahmananda chose Ishwar as his partner. Gangadhar Maharaj smiled and said, "Very good. Let me see if you can defeat me now!"

The game went on in full swing. Swami Brahmananda won the first two tricks. During the final trick Ishwar had two cards in his hand. One was the trump card. It was his turn, but he couldn't decide which card to play. Swami Brahmananda looked at him with a grim face. Seeing that, Gangadhar Maharaj said to him, "Take care! Don't give any hint to Ishwar!

Mustering a little courage, Ishwar played the trump card and the game was over. Winning the game, Swami Brahmananda very excitedly said to him, "Had you not played the trump card I would have broken your head with the handle of my hubble-bubble!" Then he turned to Gangadhar Maharaj and said cheerfully, "Didn't I tell you that I would defeat you with Ishwar as my partner?"

Gangadhar Maharaj was speechless!

◊ ◊ ◊ ◊ ◊

The singer Pulin Behari was closely associated with Swami Brahmananda. He used to say that the Swami didn't know how to play cards well. Nor was he good at fishing. He would do all those things just for fun. His mind had a natural tendency to enter into samadhi or to commune with God. He indulged in all those frivolous activities just to bring his mind down to the awareness of this world. He had come as a companion of the divine incarnation, Sri Ramakrishna, to assist him in his work. Once some gentlemen came to see him in Kankhal while he was playing cards. He folded his hands together to greet them and said, "Although we are playing cards we are indeed sadhus."

◊ ◊ ◊ ◊ ◊

Once a highly-placed official, most probably a judge, came to see Swami Brahmananda. He was then joking and chit-chatting with some people. The arrival of the stranger didn't affect him in the least, nor did he stop his light bantering and joking. As the gentleman was leaving, the Swami said to him with a smile, "There is more to us than what you've seen today. We have other sides also! When you come again, you will see the other sides."

◊ ◊ ◊ ◊ ◊

One afternoon Kedar Babu came to the Balaram Mandir

and asked Swami Brahmananda, "Maharaj, shall we play any games today?"

The Swami replied, "Kedar Babu, should one spend one's entire life in playing games? Is the purpose of human life only playing games?"[67]

◊ ◊ ◊ ◊ ◊

Once Baburam Maharaj said to Jiten Datta, "Thakur used to say that Rakhal was beyond the three gunas—sattwa, rajas, and tamas. That's why he is not at all affected by his fishing, joking or bantering with people."

A devotee from East Bengal (being unable to understand the behaviour of Swami Brahmananda) wrote in a postcard to M. (Mahendranath Gupta), "Sri Ramakrishna used to say that we should be always absorbed in the thought of God. But I saw his 'mind-born son,' Rakhal Maharaj, having fun in the company of youngsters, playing cards, and catching fish!" Mahendranath Gupta showed that postcard to some monks at Belur Math. Some of them reported its content to Swami Brahmananda.

Then the Swami called Baburam Maharaj and said, "Baburam Da, don't you remember how much fun Thakur used to have with us? But we cannot have even a small fraction of that with these boys who have come to us, renouncing their parents, homes and everything else. How many other than us came and stayed with Thakur at that time? During the rainy season the ground of Dakshineswar was damp and soaking wet. The chilly wind of the winter months blew from the direction of the Ganga and shook our very bones. And the ter-

---

67. Source: Swami Gaurishananda.

rible heat of the scorching summer sun was chest-splitting.

"Once in a great while, perhaps during their holidays, one or two people came to see Thakur for an hour or two, either in the morning or in the evening. Very rarely would they spend a night with him.

"Thakur had no body-consciousness. With us he would sometimes remain completely naked, but if a householder devotee would come, he would wrap a cloth around his waist."

Hearing Swami Brahmananda's words Baburam Maharaj responded, "Do you have to remind me? How can I forget those days? Can words ever describe how Thakur was? My entire heart and soul become full of joy when I remember those wonderful days!" Mahendranath Gupta was present and heard this conversation.[68]

---

68. Source: Swami Shyamananda.

SWAMI SARADANANDA AND SWAMI SHIVANANDA

CHAPTER XXI

THE LARGE-HEARTEDNESS AND INGENUITY OF SWAMI BRAHMANANDA

Besides being very broad-minded, Swami Brahmananda did everything on a grand scale. Pettiness was foreign to his character. And in addition, he had great ingenuity. Whatever he did, he did in his own inimitable style. The following anecdotes will throw some light on these sides of his personality.

◊◊◊◊◊

Arrangements were made in Belur Math for the worship of the Divine Mother Jagaddhatri. Swami Brahmananda expressed the wish that food be offered to the Mother on a very large plate. Narayan Datta of Baranagore went out in search of such a plate. He later returned with a plate of massive size. Food for the Mother was put on it and it took four persons to carry it to the shrine upstairs. After the food offering, the Swami came to salute the deity in the shrine.

◊◊◊◊◊

According to the wish of Swami Brahmananda, the worship of the Divine Mother Durga was performed in a rather modest way in the Bangalore Math, without using even the traditional clay image. But the overall grandeur of the worship far exceeded that of Mother Durga's worship in Belur Math.

◊◊◊◊◊

One year during the birthday celebration of Swami Vivekananda, Swami Brahmananda said, "This time we have to arrange for a lavish feast for the poor. We shall serve them 'fish kalia' (a rich fish dish). His sevaks rushed to the Sealdah railway station to shop for fish. They were able to buy a large number of rui (carp) fish. Several fishwives were engaged to cut them up. They came with their large fish knives. The menu consisted of the usual vegetarian dishes that are prepared for the celebration in other years, but this time the fish dish was special and its quantity was sumptuous. [The poor people of Bengal love to eat fish, but they don't get to eat such delicacies as 'fish-kalia.' That's why Swami Brahmananda arranged for that dish.]

Another year Swami Brahmananda ordered that the poor should be fed large-size pantuyas (a delicious Bengali sweet made of fresh cheese). Accordingly, some sevaks went to Howrah to buy fresh cheese, while Khudumani rushed to Ghughudanga. After buying a large quantity of cheese, many pantuyas of extra large size were prepared by the cooks. In the same way Swami Brahmananda in some years ordered huge quantities of beguni to be cooked. In other years he ordered many basketfuls of fried papadam (a kind of thin cake made of chickpea flour) to be prepared to feed the poor.

◊ ◊ ◊ ◊ ◊

There are many sadhus living in the cities of Kankhal and Varanasi. These two cities are full of monasteries and ashramas of the Naga and Paramahamsa sannyasis. During the occasional bhandaras the invited sadhus are served puris, kachauris, laddus, jilebis, balushais, and sour buttermilk—food the sadhus consider delicious.

Once Swami Brahmananda invited all the sadhus of Varanasi to a bhandara in our Ashrama there, and he ordered Bengali style radhaballabhi, several delicious Bengali vegetable dishes, sweet curd, pantuyas, rasagollas, etc. to be prepared, in addition to puris, kachauris and laddus. The sadhus ate to their hearts' content, saying that they hadn't eaten such delicacies ever before. There was a lot of surplus food. It was distributed to the sadhus the following day.

Another time Swami Brahmananda arranged for a similar sumptuous bhandara for the sadhus in Kankhal. He had gone there for the Durga Puja that he had organized at our Sevashrama. The Divine Mother Durga was worshipped there using the traditional clay image.

◊◊◊◊◊

Swami Mukteswarananda related, "Once Swami Brahmananda said to us at the Bhubaneswar Math, 'The kitchen storeroom is empty because you don't do your spiritual practice properly. If you perform spiritual austerities food will be provided by God.'

"He would be as happy as a little boy when he would see the different cooked dishes served to him. But he would only nibble at the food. Most of it would be left uneaten.[69] He used to say, 'When I was younger and able to eat, I wouldn't get food like this. When I performed austerities in Kusumsarovar, my only food was rotis made of millet flour and a little salt. The quantity of food was very small, so I would drink a lot of water to fill my stomach. Now that I can't eat much, all this food is coming!'

"At the end of his meal he would take a little surplus food

---

69. Swami Brahmananda used to eat rice and rotis in the daytime. The dough for the rotis would be prepared with wheat flour mixed with a little curd. Then by sprinkling water on it, it would be kept moist for about two hours before it would be used to make the bread. His two meals during the day consisted of a little milk and fruit along with rice and/or rotis. At night he would take a little fruit, milk and sweets. In addition, sometimes he would take half a roti.

from each serving bowl and mix them in one bowl. He named the concoction 'gal goppa.' We all used to share that dish. Sometimes he himself would serve it to us. Occasionally he would mix the surplus fruit, milk and sweets in one bowl. That mixture he would call by the funny name 'William Bhat.'

"On winter mornings he would sometimes ask the cook to prepare a dish that he had named 'gopal goppa.' It was a delicious rice and lentil dish. The ingredients were mung dal, rice, peas, potatoes, beets, carrots, green coriander leaves, khir and browned butter. Sometimes a sweet and sour dish would also be served with gopal goppa. It would be prepared by smoothly blending together raisins, dates, tamarind, sugar, green coriander leaves, green chili pepper and a little salt. It looked a little bit like the ayurvedic medicine *chyavanprash*.

"Swami Brahmananda also prepared a special kind of tea, which he called 'Moglai tea.' A few pods of small cardamom, cloves and cinnamon sticks would be put inside a small bag made of cheesecloth. Then the bag would be put in boiling milk or the bag of spices would be boiled in water for a while and that water would be added to the boiling milk. A decoction of tea leaves would be prepared in a separate container and then put into the boiling milk. Saffron and sugar would be added at the end. In the winter, during some celebrations, he would order this tea to be made and served to the guests. It would make him very happy."

◊ ◊ ◊ ◊ ◊

Krishnalal Maharaj wouldn't smoke. So he wished that all monks, especially the brahmacharis, should follow his example and not get addicted to smoking.[70] He wanted Swami Brahmananda to ban smoking in the Order. But the Swami said, "Swami Vivekananda made the rule that monks would only be permitted to smoke tobacco. Alcohol and all other intoxicants are banned. So far as I am concerned, I have been smoking since age fourteen. How can I ask the boys not to smoke?"

◊ ◊ ◊ ◊ ◊

A senior monk complained to Swami Brahmananda about the behavior of one of his sevaks. He said, "He smokes cigarettes every now and then. He doesn't respect his seniors. He smokes even in our presence. He goes to Nitai's[71] room for idle chitchatting. He also uses Nitai's face cream and powder."

In response to the first complaint Swami Brahmananda said, "I wonder why he smokes all those cigarettes. Smoking cigarettes is not good; it is harmful to the lungs. Smoking bidis is even worse. It is so much safer to use the hubble-bubble. All right, I'll tell him not to smoke so many cigarettes. I have many kinds of excellent tobacco for the hubble-bubble. If he wants, he can take some from me."

Before responding to the second complaint, Swami Brahmananda maintained silence for a while. Then he said gravely, "How much more will he enjoy? Gradually all these cravings will drop off on their own. And Nitai is fond of him. That's why he goes to him."

◊ ◊ ◊ ◊ ◊

Swami Brahmananda's servant, Bulbul, found an advertise-

---

70. Smoking is allowed in the Ramakrishna Order, but not encouraged. All other intoxicants and alcohol are banned in the Order. The vast majority of the monks don't smoke.

71. Nitai was not a monk. That particular sevak left the Order after the passing away of Swami Brahmananda.

ment for a movie and gave it to Hrishikesh (Swami Prashan-tananda). He wanted to go with Hrishikesh to see the movie. Hrishikesh talked to Swami Brahmananda about it. The name of the movie was *Les Miserables*. Hrishikesh had read the book by Victor Hugo. Swami Brahmananda told him, "All right, both of you may go and watch the movie." When he heard that the tickets would cost one rupee he said, "Go to A— and get the money from him."

But when A— was approached for the money, he became very displeased. Irritated, he said to Hrishikesh, "You have come to become a monk, and now you want to watch movies!" Without entering into a controversy Hrishikesh quietly came away.

Later that afternoon Swami Brahmananda was seated in the courtyard of the Sevashrama. Seeing Hrishikesh he asked, "What happened? Didn't you go to the movie?" After hearing that he hadn't got the money from A—, Swami Brahmananda said to Charu Babu, "Charu Babu, please lend me one rupee." He immediately brought the money and gave it to him. With that money Hrishikesh and Bulbul went to watch the movie.

◊ ◊ ◊ ◊ ◊

Bulbul liked to wear nice clothes and live comfortably; he didn't want to do much work. Swami Brahmananda wouldn't interfere. Rather, he would give Bulbul whatever he wanted. He used to love the paid servant, Bulbul, and the renunciate monks equally. He would look to the needs of both.

◊ ◊ ◊ ◊ ◊

Hrishikesh was preparing for the final graduation examination on Vedanta conducted by the traditional Sanskrit school system. But he was finding it hard to prepare properly for want of the necessary textbooks. He came to know that a two-volume set of *The Brahmasutras* with commentaries on *Shankara-Bhashya* had just been published in Bombay. One volume contained five different commentaries, including the *Ratnaprabha,* and the second volume contained the commentaries *Bhamati, Bhamati-Kalpataru,* and *Kalpataru-Parimal.* He informed Swami Brahmananda about the publication of these two volumes. Swami Brahmananda immediately wrote to Varen Ghosh in Bombay to buy and send them to him.

◊ ◊ ◊ ◊ ◊

It was the year 1916. The Annual General Meeting of the Ramakrishna Mission was in session. Swami Brahmananda said to the members present, "You are all aware that your President[72] is not an educated man. Therefore, in my place Swami Sharvananda will speak on the teachings of Sri Ramakrishna." Swami Sharvananda was one of Swami Brahmananda's disciples.

◊ ◊ ◊ ◊ ◊

Swami Brahmananda founded the Bhubaneswar Math so that monks of the Ramakrishna Order could go there for both rest and the performance of spiritual austerities. He would ask the monks very cordially, "When are you going there for a visit?"

◊ ◊ ◊ ◊ ◊

Someone asked him once, "Why have you made the gate of the Bhubaneswar Math so massive and tall?" Smilingly he replied, "Now I am the President of an Order that has very little financial resources. But in the future the Presidents of our Order will enter this Math in great grandeur, sitting on the backs of elephants. That's why I wanted the gate to be built like that."

---

72. Swami Brahmananda was then the President of the Ramakrishna Mission.

THE HOLY MOTHER SRI SARADA DEVI
(1853 – 1920)

CHAPTER XXII

THE HOLY MOTHER SRI SARADA DEVI AND SWAMI BRAHMANANDA

Birendranath Basu, a disciple of Swami Brahmananda, came to Belur Math to take the Swami to Dacca, a city in eastern Bengal. But in spite of encouragement from Baburam Maharaj, he didn't want to go. Baburam Maharaj said to Birendranath, "Do one thing, go to the Holy Mother. If she approves of his going, he won't say, 'No.'"

Baburam Maharaj asked Krishnalal Maharaj to take Birendranath to the Holy Mother in Calcutta. Krishnalal Maharaj took him to her and said, "Mother, this is a son (disciple) of Maharaj. He has come to take him to Dacca. But Maharaj doesn't want to go." To get Mother's permission, Birendranath caught hold of her feet and lay in front her.

The Holy Mother said, "My child, let go of my feet. The son (disciple) has come to take his father (guru) to Dacca. Of course he will go. But my child, take him there very carefully." Baburam Maharaj's plan worked and Swami Brahmananda agreed to go to Dacca.

◊ ◊ ◊ ◊ ◊

Chandramohan Datta, an employee of Udbodhan Ashrama's publication department, came to see Swami Brahmananda every morning at the Balaram Mandir. Once in a while Swami Brahmananda would ask him to bring one pice's[73] worth of unripe bananas or two pices' worth of greens.

One day Chandra said, "Maharaj, I asked the Holy Mother why you rarely go to see her."

The Swami asked, "What did she say?"

---

73. A pice was the lowest denomination of Indian currency at that time.

209

Chandra replied, "She said, 'Rakhal is no other than Lord Narayana. He is always with me.'" Swami Brahmananda was then seated on the cot in his room at the Balaram Mandir. As soon as he heard that he became so quiet and grave that it seemed he was no longer conscious of his body. Seeing that, Chandra became scared and left the room immediately.

◊ ◊ ◊ ◊ ◊

Swami Brahmananda had a wooden box wrapped in woolen material in his room. The box contained some homoeopathic medicines. According to his own needs he would use them. Sometimes he would dispense them to others also. After the Holy Mother's return from Jayrambati to the Udbodhan Ashrama in Calcutta, he walked there from the Balaram Mandir. In the mood of a little boy, he came upstairs and saluted her, touching her feet. Then he asked, "Mother, how are you?"

The Holy Mother didn't have a veil on her face at the time. She said, "My child, I have pain in my leg. I'm suffering a lot. I also have a slight temperature."

The Swami was listening to her words and at the same time, just like a restless, young boy, kept looking from side to side. It appeared as though he was looking at the pictures on the walls. Then he said, "Mother, I'll give you a homoeopathic medicine to use. I've read a lot of books on homoeopathy. I also have medicines with me. I'll give you a medicine; you'll be cured." Then still in the mood of a child, he saluted the Holy Mother and hurriedly went downstairs.[74]

---

74. The source of this story is Swami Vasudevananda. Swami Brahmananda would be overwhelmed with spiritual emotion whenever he would come into the Holy Mother's presence. He would try hard to suppress his spiritual feelings. That's why he behaved that way in this incident. That's also why he wouldn't go to see her that

◊ ◊ ◊ ◊ ◊

It was July 20, 1920. This was the day when the Holy Mother Sri Sarada Devi left her mortal coil. Swami Brahmananda was then at the Bhubaneswar Math. He got up from bed and asked, "What's the time now? I don't know why I'm suddenly feeling sad. I wonder how the Holy Mother is doing in Calcutta!" On Thursday morning just as he was getting ready to go out for a walk, a telegram came from Swami Saradananda carrying the sad news of the Holy Mother's passing away. Hearing the news, Swami Brahmananda became so overwhelmed with grief that he could no longer stand up. He immediately went and lay down in bed.

He rose a little later saying, "I shall observe mourning." Then he told the other monks, "Those of you who are disciples of the Holy Mother must not wear shoes during the three days of your mourning. You will all eat only havishya." He also ate only havishya during the three-day mourning period, and didn't wear shoes for several days in honour of the memory of the Holy Mother. He kept all his grief inside. Only once he said, "As long as the Holy Mother was with us, I felt like I was in the protective shelter of a mountain."[75]

---

frequently. For the same reason, he would only occasionally enter Thakur's shrine. Before entering Thakur's shrine on his birthday, he would touch holy Ganga water. While inside the shrine, his folded hands would tremble with intense spiritual emotion. Even after saluting Thakur, his hands would shake uncontrollably. In 1915 Swami Premananda requested him to perform Thakur's aratrika. While he was doing the aratrika, his entire body shook with spiritual emotion.

75. Panchanan Babu of Salkia collected some relics of the Holy Mother and kept them in his home. He informed Swami Brahmananda of this in a letter. Swami Brahmananda immediately wrote back saying, "Please go and deposit the relics at Belur Math as soon as possible. Otherwise, immerse them in the Ganga. Such holy relics must never be kept by householders in their homes."

SWAMI VIVEKANANDA
(1863 – 1902)

212

CHAPTER XXIII
SWAMI BRAHMANANDA AND HIS
BROTHER DISCIPLES

Swami Vivekananda, before his passing away, requested Swami Brahmananda to look after his mother, Bhubaneswari Devi. Whenever she called him, he went to her promptly and did what she asked him to do for her. Once she wanted to go on a pilgrimage to Puri. Swami Brahmananda made all the arrangements for her trip and accommodation there.[76]

◇◇◇◇◇

Swami Brahmananda was then in Puri. While talking to Brahmachari Praneshkumar about Swami Vivekananda he said, "Everything about him was wonderful. He was so full of spiritual consciousness that it was not always possible to come near him. Then again, he would sometimes be quite easily approachable. It wasn't possible for us to fathom his deep love for others.

"One morning a drunkard came to Belur Math. He entertained everybody by singing, dancing and joking for an hour. Then he left. While replying to his correspondence from England in his room upstairs, Swami Vivekananda heard the man singing. He knew about every little thing that was happening in the Math. He came near the staircase and asked, 'Where has he gone? He gave us so much joy. What did you give him to eat?'

"When he heard that he had been given only a little prasad

---

76. After returning from the trip to Puri, she contracted pneumonia and passed away on July 25, 1911.

213

(sugar-puffs that had been offered to God), he became very displeased. He said, 'He provided us with a million dollars' worth of entertainment and you've given him only a few sugar-puffs! Take these two rupees and give them to him. Ask him to buy some good drinks.' We were all amazed to see him give money to a drunkard to buy liquor. His actions were always prompted by genuine love. Ours is but an imitation!

"Once a check for Rupees 750/- came to him from the United States of America. Giving that check to me he said, 'Keep this money with you. After I am gone (from this world), Christina will want to go back to her country (the U.S.A.). Then where will you get money to pay for her passage?' Before he passed away he made all kinds of arrangements like this for us."

◊ ◊ ◊ ◊ ◊

Through vatsalya bhava Sri Ramakrishna behaved with his mind-born son, Rakhal, just as a mother behaves with her young child. That's why Swami Vivekananda didn't want to burden Swami Brahmananda with activities that might cause him any physical strain. He wrote to Swami Ramakrishnananda and other brother monks, "Never forget that Rakhal was the object of Thakur's special love and affection." This motherly love of Sri Ramakrishna enabled Rakhal to be free from the feeling of awe that a disciple has towards his guru. The following incident, as narrated by Swami Brahmananda, proves that point.

He said, "During that period I lived on Varanasi Ghosh Street in Calcutta and would often go to see Thakur at the Dakshineswar Kali temple. I went there one afternoon while he was resting on his bed after his meal. As I entered his room, he made me sit on his bed and started talking about various things. Then he told me, 'Please stroke my feet a little.'

"I said, 'Please forgive me, I can't do that! I'd rather ask someone to come and stroke *my* own feet! Why don't we just keep on talking instead?'

"Still he gently repeated two or three times, 'Stroke my feet. I am telling you, serving a holy man has its reward.'

"As soon as I touched his feet with my hand, something strange happened. With my eyes wide open I saw the Divine Mother Kali run into the room as a seven or eight year old girl and circle around his bed a few times. I could hear Her ankle bells ringing. Then She suddenly merged into Sri Ramakrishna's body. He chuckled and said, 'Will you believe now that serving a holy man has its immediate reward?'"[77]

◊ ◊ ◊ ◊ ◊

One day after having his meal in Belur Math, Swami Brahmananda went to rinse his hands and mouth with water. His sevak, Khudumani, had brought a pot of water for that purpose, but he had to go elsewhere for a little while to do some other work. And unexpectedly, the Swami finished eating early. As Khudumani was not there, Baburam Maharaj picked up the water pot and was about to pour water over Swami Brahmananda's hands. At this the Swami said, "Baburam Da, why you? You aren't supposed to do this!"

Meanwhile Khudumani came running and snatched the water pot away from the hand of Baburam Maharaj. Then Baburam Maharaj said to Swami Brahmananda, "We were supposed to serve you, but your sevaks are depriving us of that

---

77. Source: Swami Nirlepananda.

**LEFT TO RIGHT: SWAMI SHIVANANDA, SWAMI VIVEKANANDA,
SWAMI TURIYANANDA AND SWAMI BRAHMANANDA**

opportunity by not letting us do it."

[Note: According to Sri Ramakrishna, Swami Premananda
was a born-free soul or *Nitya-Siddha*. According to Indian
tradition, he was not supposed to give such service to Swami
Brahmananda who was younger than him. But he was endowed with humility—a common characteristic of all genuine
saints. That is why he wanted to serve his younger brother
monk. He was also completely indifferent to worldly possessions. At the same time, his compassionate heart bled at the
distress of others and he wouldn't hesitate giving away whatever little possessions he had.

He had a blue, quilted shirt for use in the winter. Once,

in the winter, Khudumani put it outside in the sun to make it fluffy and warmer. But sometime later, when he went to bring it back to Swami Premananda, he couldn't find it. Swami Premananda saw him looking for something. He asked, "What are you looking for?"

Khudumani replied, "I am looking for your blue shirt."

Swami Premananda said, "I have given it to Gagan. He can't stand the cold."

Khudumani asked, "What will you wear? That's the only warm clothing you had!"

Swami Premananda replied, "I am a sadhu—an all-renouncing monk. Should coldness or warmth matter to me?"—Source: Swami Shyamananda]

One day Swami Brahmananda was sitting at the tea table. Baburam Maharaj came up to him with a garland of flowers in his hand and told him, "Look how beautiful this garland is!" So saying, he put the garland around Swami Brahmananda's neck. Then these two saints looked at each other steadily for several minutes without moving. Who can tell what they were seeing in each other? Were they seeing in each other their own chosen deities?[78]

◊ ◊ ◊ ◊ ◊

In Indian poetics it is mentioned that the nature of love is like the movement of a snake; it follows a winding path. As if to prove that true, Baburam Maharaj and Swami Brahmananda sometimes had friendly quarrels between them. Once Baburam Maharaj gave a gourd from the Belur Math garden

78. Source: Swami Vrajeswarananda.

to a poor brahmin neighbour nicknamed "Jai Ma Kali." That neighbour got this nickname because he used to dance every now and then chanting, "Jai Ma Kali." Swami Brahmananda saw him carrying the gourd home. Aiming for Baburam Maharaj's ears, Swami Brahmananda said, "If everyone starts giving away the monastery vegetables to anybody and everybody, how shall we have enough vegetables for our daily food offering to Thakur?"

As soon as Baburam Maharaj heard those words, he felt very hurt. With his towel still over his shoulder, he headed toward the gate of the Math. He intended to leave for good. But after reaching the gate he had to turn back. He said, "I saw Thakur blocking my path. He told me, 'Where are you going, my darling boy?' Saying that, he wrapped my towel around my neck and pulled me back to the Math."

◊ ◊ ◊ ◊ ◊

Praising the devotees of East Bengal, Swami Premananda requested Swami Brahmananda to visit Dacca and Mymensingh. Then Swami Brahmananda said, "You have an all-encompassing love. But I have selective love. I pick and choose whom to love."

◊ ◊ ◊ ◊ ◊

While travelling in East Bengal, in the village of Gharinda in Mymensingh District, Swami Premananda stayed in the home of Shourjendranath Mazumdar. There a Muslim Maulavi (a Muslim teacher or scholar) challenged Swami Premananda to prove Hinduism's impartiality by eating with him from the same plate. Accordingly, he ate some fruits and sweets (Thakur's prasad) with the Maulavi from the same plate.

Immediately after returning from his trip, Swami Premananda became very ill with kala-azar. Swami Brahmananda became very worried and upset. When he met Shourjendranath he scolded him saying, "Why did you invite him there if you couldn't protect him from all these dangers?"

◊ ◊ ◊ ◊ ◊

On July 30, 1918, Swami Premananda passed away in the large main room at the Balaram Mandir. From morning onwards and throughout the day, he had felt very uncomfortable. Swami Brahmananda had asked one of his sevaks to sit by Swami Premananda's bed and chant hymns from the scriptures. Meanwhile Swami Brahmananda began pacing back and forth in the corridor solemn faced. Repeatedly he would go up to the door of his own room and then would turn back and return to the door of Swami Premananda's room. He kept this up for several hours.

Then suddenly he entered Swami Premananda's room holding a photo of Sri Ramakrishna. He came to him and said, "Baburam Da, please look at Thakur!" As Swami Premananda passed away, he muttered in Hindi, "O traveller, pack your things. You have to go a long way!" [79] Then overwhelmed with grief he left the room. Returning to his own room he began sobbing like a little child. Swami Saradananda, the personification of gentleness and self-composure, came in. He put his arms around the Swami and kept wiping his tears away with his own chuddar.

◊ ◊ ◊ ◊ ◊

79. The original Hindi is as follows: "Chalo musāfir, bāndho gānthuriā. Bahut door jāne hogā."

Swami Brahmananda had a disciple named Swami Umananda (Yogin). When he was in Belur Math he served his guru. Then he was transferred elsewhere. When Swami Brahmananda visited South India for the first time, Umananda was one of the monastic workers at the Madras Math. Unfortunately, he contracted small pox there. He had to be hospitalized and his condition turned critical. Shashi Maharaj, the head of the Madras Math, used to visit him every day in the hospital. Two or three days before his passing away Umananda expressed the wish to see Swami Brahmananda. He said to Shashi Maharaj, "I know that Maharaj may become nervous about coming inside the hospital.[80] Please ask him to come by car; he needn't enter the hospital. Looking out the window, I'll be able to see him in the car."

When Shashi Maharaj told this to Swami Brahmananda he

---

80. When Swami Brahmananda visited South India the second time
he stayed for a while at the Bangalore Math. Plague broke out in
Bangalore at that time. The Swami was childlike. Lest he became
nervous like a child and wanted to return to Belur Math, the news
of the plague outbreak was not given to him. However, the news was
in the newspaper and the Swami read the newspaper daily.One day a
very bad odor filled the Math buildings. On inquiry it was discovered
that some dead rats were lying on the flat roof of the kitchen building.
The odor came from their rotting bodies. The doors of the residential
building were closed. Then they started removing the dead rats
and disinfecting the roof. Everybody took care not to tell Swami
Brahmananda what was happening. But on his own he asked, "What
have you all been doing after shutting the doors of the building? Have
some rats died? Well, isn't that natural when plague is rampant all
around?" He displayed no signs of nervousness whatsoever. After this
incident dead rats were also discovered quite a few times within the
Math premises. Each time Swami Brahmananda asked the residents of
the Math to do the cleaning with due caution, such as masking their
faces with cloth.

SWAMI RAMAKRISHNANANDA
(ALSO KNOWN AS SHASHI MAHARAJ)

221

said, "There are so many patients suffering from all kinds of diseases in the hospital. If I go there, won't I catch some of their illnesses?" Shashi Maharaj requested Swami Brahmananda once or twice again, but he didn't go to see Umananda. When he died, Shashi Maharaj became quite aggrieved.

The following morning, as usual, he went to see Swami Brahmananda, who inquired of Shashi Maharaj's health. He told him that he was well. Then he became quite emotional and said with tears in his eyes, "Maharaj, how could you be so cruel! Umananda is one of us. He wanted to see you only once before his death, but you didn't go!"

Swami Brahmananda became very grave, then after a few moments' pause, said, "Shashi, is going there physically to see him everything? Do you really think that I didn't go to see him? (That means he certainly went to see him in a subtle body.)" Shashi Maharaj fell flat at Swami Brahmananda's feet and said, "Maharaj, it's so hard for us to understand you!"

◊ ◊ ◊ ◊ ◊

Swami Brahmananda was then at the Madras Math. Shashi Maharaj went to his room in the morning and saluted him, touching Swami Brahmananda's feet with his hands and putting his forehead on the ground. Krishnalal Maharaj also went with him. He saluted Swami Brahmananda just with folded hands. He didn't bow down and touch his forehead to the ground, as he should have done. Shashi Maharaj returned to his room and sent for Krishnalal Maharaj. He asked why he had saluted Swami Brahmananda the way he did.

Krishnalal Maharaj explained, "Swami Brahmananda doesn't like me to salute him by touching his feet and putting my forehead on the ground in front of him, because he was born in a lower caste kayastha family and I was born in a higher caste brahmin family."

Shashi Maharaj immediately grabbed Krishnalal Maharaj's hand and pulled him into Swami Brahmananda's room. Then he prostrated himself in front of Swami Brahmananda and saluted him, putting his head on his feet. He said to Krishnalal Maharaj, "Krishnalal, (pointing to his own body) I was also born in a brahmin family. I wasn't born an outcaste. If you want your own well being, salute him as I've done. Otherwise, you will be ruined!" Krishnalal Maharaj followed Shashi Maharaj's instruction immediately.

◊ ◊ ◊ ◊ ◊

Swami Brahmananda and Hari Maharaj were then staying at the Shashiniketan in Puri. After taking his noon meal Swami Brahmananda said to his sevak, "Come outside with the water pot. I'll rinse my mouth and hands over the roots of the sapling we planted in our garden yesterday." The sun was pretty scorching outside.

As Swami Brahmananda began rinsing his mouth and hands in the garden, Hari Maharaj rushed out and held an umbrella over his head, saying to the sevak, "Didn't you see how hot the sun is?"

Then Swami Brahmananda said to Hari Maharaj, "You are not supposed to hold the umbrella over my head! Please give it to him (the sevak). And you've come running barefooted over all those sharp pieces of broken rock. I hope you don't injure your soles, then there will be a disaster." (Hari Maharaj had developed diabetes. That's why Swami Brahmananda was

223

worried about him.) Swami Brahmananda finished rinsing his mouth and hands as fast as he could, because he didn't want Hari Maharaj to stand in the scorching sun for long.

◊ ◊ ◊ ◊ ◊

Ram Babu's mother passed away in Varanasi. Nitai Babu and several others were going to Varanasi to attend her post mortem shraddha ceremony. As Nitai Babu was fond of Swami Brahmananda's sevak Ishwar, he wanted to take him along to Varanasi. When Ishwar told Swami Brahmananda about this, he said, "All right, go with Nitai and offer your salutations at the Vishwanath temple. On the way back visit Ayodhya, Allahabad and Vindhyachal."

Ishwar was to stay in the building where Hari Maharaj was staying in the Varanasi Sevashrama. Immediately after his arrival, he went to salute Hari Maharaj, who was on his bed, half reclining. As soon as he saw Ishwar he sat up and asked, "So you have come? Where is Maharaj?" When he heard that Ishwar had come alone to visit the Vishwanath temple, he said. "When I saw you I thought that as you had come, Swami Brahmananda must also have come with you. But now I see that you've come here to visit Lord Vishwanath leaving behind the *real* Vishwanath!" He said the last sentence so emphatically and in such an excited tone that Ishwar became quite nervous. He briefly saluted Hari Maharaj and left the room hurriedly.

◊ ◊ ◊ ◊ ◊

During her last illness the Holy Mother expressed the wish to eat crispy puffed rice mixed with toasted chickpeas. Someone brought a bowlful of it and gave it to her. Sharat Maharaj heard about it, and considering the condition of her health, decided that it wouldn't be good for her to take that food. So he entered the Holy Mother's room and begged her to give the bowl of puffed rice to him.

Although he did it out of a sense of duty, he later suffered intensely from remorse, because he hadn't let the Mother eat what she had asked for. After her passing away, Swami Brahmananda came one morning to the Udbodhan Ashrama. Then Sharat Maharaj said with great sadness to him, "Maharaj, the Mother is present inside you. Would you please eat a little crispy puffed rice mixed with toasted chick-peas today?"

He replied, "All right, Sharat, that's what I'll eat today. Please give me!" He started eating the puffed rice and Sharat Maharaj, crossing his arms across his chest, kept looking at him with his eyes filled with tears.

◊ ◊ ◊ ◊ ◊

A gentleman from East Bengal named Gi— used to visit Sharat Maharaj at the Udbodhan Ashrama. He would sit close to Sharat Maharaj in his small room downstairs and listen to the conversation. One day Sharat Maharaj said to Gi—, "You come to see me frequently, but why don't you go to see Swami Brahmananda who lives so close to us? Please go and see him." In spite of his request, Gi— only went to see Swami Brahmananda once or twice. He didn't like him that much. Nor could he understand him. Sharat Maharaj came to know this and became very displeased. He told Gi—, "If you don't want to go to see him, please don't come to see me anymore!"

So Gi— went to see the Swami one evening at the Balaram Mandir. He was smoking his hubble-bubble, sitting quietly in his room. Two gentlemen were seated on a rug in front of him.

It seemed that Swami Brahmananda was not even aware of their presence. Gi— entered the room, saluted the Swami and sat down by those gentlemen. After about an hour the Swami noticed them. He made personal inquiries about Gi—. Then said to him slowly, "Please think of Thakur all the time and pray to him. Then you will get everything. What more will I say! May Thakur shower his grace upon you. May you all have spiritual awakening." Gi— felt very much blessed and had an inner sense of fulfilment. Later he went to Sharat Maharaj and told him everything.

◊ ◊ ◊ ◊ ◊

It was the year 1917. Swami Brahmananda was then staying for a while at the Udbodhan Ashrama. Sharat Maharaj looked upon him as the very embodiment of Sri Ramakrishna and behaved with him accordingly. When Swami Brahmananda returned to the Balaram Mandir from the Udbodhan Ashrama, Kartik (Swami Nirlepananda) went to salute him one day. Swami Brahmananda said to him, "Hello! Don't you have gopal goppa there (at the Udbodhan Ashrama) anymore?"

Kartik said, "It is up to you, Maharaj. Please come there again. Then we'll have gopal goppa."

Swami Brahmananda humourously said, "Can two lions live in the same forest?" (Sharat Maharaj was the head of the Udbodhan Ashrama. That's why he said this.)

CHAPTER XXIV
INCIDENTS REVEALING SWAMI
BRAHMANANDA'S DIVINE NATURE

Swami Mukteswarananda said, "Some Marathi ladies lived in Madras. They worshipped God as Baby Krishna or Valagopala. If they would come to hear of a saint, they would invite him to their home and worship him as Valagopala. No man other than the master of their household and saints had access to their home. One day they came to the Madras Math with the master of their household and sang devotional songs in Thakur's shrine. They wanted to take Swami Brahmananda to their home, but he didn't agree because he was not feeling well. At their insistence he requested Swami Shivananda to go there instead.

"Ramlal Dada, Swami Sharvananda, a few brahmacharis of the Madras Math, and I accompanied Swami Shivananda. After our return, Swami Brahmananda heard from us what had happened in their home. When he heard that one by one the ladies had rinsed the feet of Swami Shivananda with cold water, he exclaimed, 'No sir, I'm not going there!' He wouldn't normally wet his feet except when taking a shower. Nevertheless, eventually he had to agree to visit their home; he couldn't ignore their earnest request. Sharvananda and I accompanied him. I was not that willing to go, because I hadn't liked the earlier visit to their home. But Swami Brahmananda said, 'Come with me. If they start washing my feet repeatedly, ask them not to do it.'

"In their home there was a beautiful picture of Valagopala on an altar. They made Swami Brahmananda sit on a beautiful chair and put in front of him various articles of worship, such as sandalwood paste, flowers, incense, an oil lamp, water in a silver pitcher, fragrant water in a few smaller pitchers, and milk

227

in several small, silver containers with little gold cups fastened to each one of them. They first saluted the Swami and sang the Sanskrit hymn in adoration of the guru. Then they worshipped Valagopala in the picture, and bringing little cups of milk near his mouth, mentally offered them to him. Then they saluted the Swami again and stood around him in a semicircle. The ladies looked like goddesses. They were wearing saris of different colors and all of them had unbraided, flowing hair.

"They put Swami Brahmananda's feet in a large silver bowl and were about to pour water over them. I said, 'Please don't wet his feet.' Completely overwhelmed by their devotion, they seemed not to have been aware of my presence there. Then hearing my words, they became completely bewildered. Swami Brahmananda said to me with compassion, 'Let them do this just for one time today. I'll be all right. Don't say "No" to them.' The ladies then began their worship.

"Using the water from the larger pitcher and then the fragrant water from the smaller pitchers, one of the ladies washed Swami Brahmananda's feet. She dried his feet with her hair. Then placing his feet on a velvet cushion she worshipped them with sandalwood paste and flowers. She also put a small garland on his feet. In this manner about ten or twelve ladies worshipped him in the same way. After the worship, each took a pot of milk along with the little gold cup and started singing and dancing around him. They sang a famous song composed by Namadeva that starts with the following words:

> Please drink this milk, my little Prince Gopala (Baby Krishna)
> Please drink this milk Nandadulala (Krishna—the darling of
> Nanda)...

"While singing, each one came to Swami Brahmananda, and one after another fed him milk from the small silver pitchers with the little golden cups. He became immersed in the depths of his spiritual mood. He appeared to be the living Valagopala. A heavenly mood permeated the atmosphere, and the room filled with a sweet fragrance. The ladies also appeared to have lost their body-consciousness. As I was standing very close to the Swami, their hair was brushing against my body, but for the time being I lost the awareness that I was a man. The thought came to my mind, 'Is it Vrindaban? Is Swami Brahmananda the Gopala of Vraja? Are these ladies the dairymaids of Vrindaban? And are they immersed in vatsalya-bhava?'

"In this way time passed, but none of us was aware of time anymore! Eventually the dancing, singing, and the feeding of milk came to an end. Swami Brahmananda gradually came out of his deep spiritual mood. The ladies saluted him one by one. He suddenly said to me ecstatically, 'Ishwar, sing a song.' Out of a strange emotion I burst forth singing a song on Lord Shiva: 'Lord Shiva has started playing his tabor, etc.' Swami Brahmananda's spiritual mood suddenly changed and he regained his normal composure.[81]

81. The ladies distributed the prasad of Valagopala to the companions of Swami Brahmananda. They would come and visit him at the Madras Math with gifts of fruits, such as bananas, coconuts, etc. Every time they came they sang devotional songs for him. They came the day before his departure from Madras. In a letter written from Madras on October 22, 1921, Swami Brahmananda wrote, "Some Maharashtrian devotees invited us yesterday evening. Almost everyone except me went to their home. The devotees later came to the Math twice and sang devotional songs. Most of the devotees are ladies from respectable families. They sing in a chorus. There is only one man in that singing group. They sing very well, and the women devotees are very devoted to God. I heard that they came to the Math yesterday and sang devotional songs. Later our monks sang the short version of *Ramanama Sankirtananm*, which they liked."

"When Sharat Maharaj heard all the details of this incident, he remarked about Swami Brahmananda, 'That incident triggered his memory of who he really was. He came to remember that he was one of the spiritually exalted companions of Lord Krishna in Vridadaban.'"

◊◊◊◊◊

Swami Brahmananda returned from Madras to the Balaram Mandir in Calcutta via Bhubaneswar. One day, in the main room of the building upstairs, a singing session was being held. Ramlal Dada dressed himself as a dhopwali (a woman singer) and began singing *Mathur* (a singing narrative on Sri Krishna's life in Mathura). He sang:

> *O Krishna, please come back to Vrindaban at least for a day or two. If you wish, please stay here, or else you may return to Mathura. The water in the river Jamuna is overflowing now from the tears shed in it by the milkmaids of Vrindaban, who are pining for you,…*

Ramlal Dada was dancing and singing in front of Swami Brahmananda, who was slowly swaying his body to the rhythm of the singing. Both were in a lighthearted mood. Gradually the singer became emotional while singing, and tears appeared in his eyes. The Swami also suddenly became very grave. His eyes were half closed, while his body slowly swayed with intense spiritual emotion. The room became filled with an indescribable, solemn mood. The singing revived the Swami's memory of his past incarnation, when he had played with Sri Krishna as his companion. It triggered his yearning to go back to Vrindaban. Then the singing stopped and gradually his spiritual feelings also subsided.

CHAPTER XXV

SWAMI BRAHMANANDA'S POWER
OF ATTRACTION

The derivative meaning of the word *Krishna* is "the Lord who attracts His creatures to Himself." Sri Krishna's divine power of attraction in Vrindaban attracted not only human beings, but animals and plants as well. Rakhal, the companion of Sri Krishna in his past incarnation, also displayed this power of attraction. No matter where he was, he created around him an atmosphere of joy. Anyone who came within its perimetre felt that joy. That's why when it became known that he would be coming to Belur Math, to another ashrama, or to a devotee's home, everybody there would be extremely happy.

When the Swami stayed in Belur Math, both in the mornings and in the afternoons he would walk over the entire grounds of the Math from the gate in the south up to the northeastern rear gate of the property. Sometimes he would go to the flower garden or to the vegetable garden and inspect the condition of the plants and trees there. He would also give necessary advice to those who cared for the gardens.

When he would visit the pasture inside the Math compound, the cows would stop grazing and come to him. They would encircle him and raising their heads, wait for his caresses. He would touch each one of them fondly with his cane. But that kind of caressing wouldn't satisfy Nagri, a cow of the Hariyana breed. So Swami Brahmananda had to stroke her neck with his hand. Whenever he would call Nagri from a distance, she would raise her tail and come running toward him like a young calf.[82]

◊ ◊ ◊ ◊ ◊

Kedarnath Basu, an initiated disciple of Swami Brahmananda, returned home one evening at 9 o'clock from his work. Shortly after his arrival he started for Belur Math. His wife pressed him hard not to go, but he didn't listen to her. When he came to the Lahiritola ghat on the bank of the river Ganga, he met his friend Suren Sen. He was also going to the Math. Hiring a boat, they reached the Math at midnight. As they arrived, they saw two other boats coming. Dr. Kanjilal was coming by one boat, while Kalipada Banerjee was arriving by the other. Both were initiated disciples of the Holy Mother Sri Sarada Devi.

---

82. To the south of the Balaram Mandir there was a cattle shed owned by a milkman. One day Ram Babu saw that the milkman was about to sell a young calf of the Hariana breed to a butcher. The calf was apparently not allowed by the milkman to drink enough milk from its mother, so it was very emaciated. Ram Babu bought the calf for five rupees and arranged to send it to Belur Math as his gift to Swami Brahmananda. The Swami ordered the calf to be given one seer (four cups) of milk every day. When the calf became a little stronger, it was given half a seer of milk and two large rotis daily. He used to feed the young calf with his own hands. He named it Nagri.

When the cows would see Swami Brahmananda, they would simply stand still. But when they would see Baburam Maharaj, they would come running and compete with one another for his caresses. Some of them would lick his hands, feet or face. But Nagri would gently push him with her horns. He would caress all of them by stroking their bodies. One day, during a celebration, the monks and devotees were sitting in the courtyard, eating their food from leaf plates. Suddenly Nagri came running from somewhere, and went straight to where Baburam Maharaj was sitting and eating. She ate all the food on his plate and walked away. She didn't even care to look at anyone else's plate.

232

They were all surprised to see one another coming to Belur Math so late at night. To explain, each of them said, "What to do? I didn't feel like staying at home." Thinking that Swami Brahmananda was sleeping, they wondered how to inform him of their arrival. But when they came to the second floor of the monastery building, they saw him standing on the veranda. As soon as they saluted him, he said, "Now go and eat prasad." He had already arranged enough prasad to be kept for four or five people.

◊ ◊ ◊ ◊ ◊

In February 1922 Swami Brahmananda came to stay for three days in the home of Sachin Roy, the maternal uncle of his disciple Ranu. Ranu, although married, lived like a brahmacharini. She studied Vedanta philosophy under the tutorship of her sister's husband, Professor Kanailal Pal. Swami Brahmananda used to say that Ranu was not only a very good spiritual aspirant, but also a brahmavadini. He was very fond of her, because she had great faith and was completely dedicated to him as her guru.

No other member of Sachin Babu's extended family was a disciple of Swami Brahmananda, but all of them respected him highly and were eager to serve him wholeheartedly. His visit to their home made them exceedingly happy, and that happiness was evident from the expressions on their faces. At one time Durga Puja used to be celebrated in their large residence with great pomp and grandeur. Swami Brahmananda's visit created a similar heart-warming, festive atmosphere for them.

The first two days of Swami Brahmananda's visit passed in an atmosphere of great joy. On the third day, in spite of their happiness, the undercurrent of thought that he would leave the following day made everybody sad. In the evening this sadness became manifest on their faces. With tears in her eyes, a little girl came to Swami Brahmananda's sevak and asked, "If tomorrow doesn't come, will Maharaj always stay with us?"

All the others began pressuring him hard to stay two or three more days. Swami Brahmananda said, "Do I want to leave you? I must go because there is a business meeting at the Math. Sharvananda is coming to pick me up." In the afternoon of the next day, Swami Sharvananda came in a car to take him to Belur Math. Everyone in the Roy household began shedding tears. Swami Brahmananda asked Swami Sharvananda to go and wait outside. Then he began telling such a funny story that everyone burst into laughter. It created a strange sight; they were laughing with tears still rolling down their cheeks! While laughing, one old lady rolled on the floor.

Meanwhile Swami Brahmananda signalled to his sevak to carry his things to the car. Still continuing to tell the funny story, he came down from the third floor of the house, where he had been staying, to the carport. He finished telling the story just before entering the car. As he entered the car, everybody suddenly realized that he was really leaving. Then unable to control their emotions, they burst out crying.

◊ ◊ ◊ ◊ ◊

In the early part of the book, we talked about Nistarini Devi, the wife of Nabagopal Ghosh. She used to have the spiritual attitude of a Vrajagopi. She fed Sri Ramakrishna with her own hands, looking upon him as Lord Krishna. When Swami Vivekananda visited their home in Ramakrishnapur in connection with the installation of the marble image of Sri Ramakrishna there, with a mother's feelings she fed him a few spoonfuls of polau. The Swami used to address her as "Baudidi" (an endearing and respectful term meaning the elder brother's wife).

Several members of Nistarini Devi's family were disciples of Swami Brahmananda. He visited her home in Ramakrishnapur many times. Whenever he went there, they wouldn't let him leave unless he had stayed with them for a few days. Once during his stay with them, Sharat Maharaj arrived from Belur Math carrying some official papers and said, "Please come back to the Math. We can't take action on some important, official papers without you."

Swami Brahmananda said, "Sharat, can't you bring those papers here? The devotion of Nirad's mother (Nistarini Devi) has tied me to this place!" By the way, she would often shed tears out of spiritual emotion just looking at him.

Swami Bhumananda said, "Anyone who would come to see Swami Brahmananda usually didn't want to leave him. Everyone felt an undercurrent of spiritual joy in his presence. This joy was like the intoxication caused by opium. Anyone who came to see him even once, wouldn't be able to resist the wish to come back and visit him again and again. Words cannot describe the mysterious atmosphere created by his presence. It can only be said that it was not possible to ignore his spiritual influence and wonderful power of attraction."

SWAMI BRAHMANNANDA

CHAPTER XXVI

EVENTS ON THE EVE OF
SWAMI BRAHMANANDA'S PASSING AWAY

Swami Brahmananda took Swami Bhumananda along with him as one of his sevaks when he visited South India for the second time. After his return to Calcutta, Sharat Maharaj asked Swami Bhumananda, "This is the first time you acted as Swami Brahmananda's sevak. How did you find him?"

Swami Bhumananda replied, "He doesn't follow any specific routine as you do. To serve him one cannot act according to one's own ideas; one must act according to his wish. You lead a very orderly life, but he doesn't care for that kind of orderliness. He has infinite spiritual moods. Even his eating habits are not monotonous. He is a person of great originality."

Sharat Maharaj was very pleased to hear his words. He said, "I see that you've observed him correctly."

◊◊◊◊◊

In 1920 Dr. Bidhubhushan Roy visited Bhubaneswar for a month and enjoyed the holy company of Swami Brahmananda. He stayed at the Sanatorium and visited the Math every morning and evening. Coming to the Math, he would sit quietly for a long time near the Swami. He said, "We are scientists. We judge things through external observation. Having seen Swami Brahmananda closely all these days, I've realized that he is quite unlike any other person in this world."

But due to this extraordinariness and originality, many of his contemporaries found it hard to understand him correctly. This also happened in the cases of Sri Krishna, Sri Nityananda and many other great saints and divine incarnations. Uddhava, the playmate and companion of Sri Krishna, lamented, "Alas! How unfortunate are the people of this world, particularly those who belong to the Yadava family. They lived with Sri Krishna but couldn't understand his glory at all!"

Sri Ramakrishna said that his manasa putra, Swami Brahmananda, was the companion of Sri Krishna in Vrindaban in his previous incarnation. The more I reflected on his personality, the more obvious it became to me that it closely resembled the multifaceted personality of Sri Krishna. His love for everybody irrespective of gender, his compassion for the distressed and the lowly, his childlike fondness for fun and frolic, his wonderful originality in his day-to-day behaviour, and above all, the depth and profundity of his spiritual personality, make it impossible for us to understand his spiritual greatness using the criteria for judging average saints. What to speak of others, even some senior monks of Belur Math found it hard to understand him.

◊ ◊ ◊ ◊ ◊

Once in the Udbodhan Ashrama, Kiran (Swami Aseshananda) was massaging the body of Sharat Maharaj. Then Sharat Maharaj said to him, "Do you think Swami Brahmananda is like anybody and everybody? He can mould our minds like dough and give them whatever shapes he wants!" Towards the end of his life Swami Brahmananda also said more than once, "In the Order no one understands me except Sharat."

◊ ◊ ◊ ◊ ◊

About one year before his passing away, he said one day to his sevaks in Belur Math, "You have been with me for all these years, but you haven't been able to understand my spiritual

238

attitudes. You haven't been able to adopt any of them. Many people don't hesitate to blame me for putting up with your deficiencies. Because of you I've been put in this uncomfortable position."

◊◊◊◊◊

Swami Brahmananda told his sevaks never to ask others to give them anything. Once he rebuked one of them in Madras because he had not followed that instruction. After his return from Madras to Bhubaneswar, a similar incident perturbed him very much. Mahapurush Maharaj was visiting Bhubaneswar at the time. With great pain and sorrow Swami Brahmananda told him, "Tarak Da, I've told them so many times not to ask others to give them anything, but they never listen to me. I can't describe how pained I am because of their behaviour."

Then he recounted the pains and troubles he had had to endure for the sake of the Order, such as trying to bring about reconciliation between monks with conflicting views, efforts to rectify through forgiveness the behaviour of those who defy discipline, etc. At the end he said, "I can't do this anymore! You all take over now and run the Order. I just want to live quietly in some place. I can no longer endure the headaches of being the President!" He said this to Mahapurush Maharaj in Bangalore, Madras, and other places as well.

◊◊◊◊◊

This incident happened two months before his passing away. He and Hariprasanna Maharaj were seated on chairs on the upstairs veranda of the Math. They were surrounded by other monks, some of whom were sitting on the floor, while others were standing.

Swami Brahmananda said, "Many think that if Swami Vive-kananda were present he would have guided us properly, and the Ramakrishna Mission would have had much more expansion. But who is there who has really understood Swamiji, or who even could hope to understand him? Getting to know him by reading his books is one thing, but trying to know him being close to him was another thing. They don't know how difficult it was to live with him, nor do they know how difficult it was to put up with him! Unable to stand his severe scolding, at times even I thought of leaving the Math. One day after getting a scolding from him, I felt extremely sad and was weeping in my room.

"A little later, Swamiji knocked at my door. When I opened the door, he saw tears in my eyes and immediately hugged me. He said, 'Raja, Thakur was so fond of you and loved you so much. Yet, I scold and talk to you harshly. I am not fit to live with you anymore!' As he was saying this, tears rolled down his cheeks.

"To comfort him, I gently stroked his head and back and said, 'I know that you scold because you love me. But I can't remember that always, that's why I sometimes shed tears.'

"Then Swamiji said, 'What can I do! It's as though my body is always burning. That's why I can't keep my head cool. If I live any longer I'll most probably hurt you even more. Raja, can you do one thing? Do you know what they do in the West? They shoot a racing horse when it becomes worthless. Can you shoot me if I get a gun and give it to you? There won't be any harm if you kill me, I've finished all my work.'"

◊ ◊ ◊ ◊ ◊

Another incident. Swami Brahmananda was having his

meal in Mahapurush Maharaj's room, who was watching him eat, while Ishwar was waiting on him. While eating, half-absorbed in himself, he suddenly said to Mahapurush Maharaj, "Tarak Da, I won't ever be able to give up my fondness for Belur Math. Even after my death, I'll be watching it from above."

◊ ◊ ◊ ◊ ◊

Swami Brahmananda's indrawn mood became more and more intense as the end of his life was drawing near. While pacing back and forth on the grounds of the Bhubaneswar Math, he would be seen talking to himself. Sometimes he would talk quite loudly. It would appear that he was talking to someone else. His mind had a natural tendency to enter into samadhi and remain immersed in it. By talking to himself, he tried to bring his mind down to the awareness of this world. While talking about Sri Ramakrishna he once said, "After coming down from samadhi he used to talk to himself unintelligibly. It would seem then that he was talking to someone else."

After the construction of the Math buildings in Bhubaneswar, he wanted to stay there quietly. He wanted to be away from the problems of administrative work and remain absorbed in his own spiritual moods. But his administrative responsibilities wouldn't allow him to do this. He always responded to the call of duty whenever any urgency needing his presence would arise. In 1921 he visited our ashramas in Varanasi and South India in connection with such duties.

◊ ◊ ◊ ◊ ◊

During Swami Vivekananda's birthday celebration, Swami Brahmananda said to Sharat Maharaj, "One day you should offer South Indian cooked food to Thakur at the Udbodhan Ashrama."

Sharat Maharaj said, "It will be offered any day you choose. But you have to be present with us that day." On January 29, 1922, Swami Brahmananda visited the Udbodhan Ashrama (also known as Holy Mother's House). His presence created a mart of joy. His sevaks began cooking several South Indian dishes. After the food had been offered to Thakur in the shrine, the two brother disciples, Swami Brahmananda and Swami Saradananda, sat down together and enjoyed the prasad.

The following day was the birthday of Swami Brahmananda. To celebrate his birthday the monks and devotees decorated his small room with flowers and garlands. He was made to wear new clothes by the devotees. Garlands of flowers were put around his neck and his head was decorated with a beautiful crown. And he was smiling like a little child. Sharat Maharaj came and saluted him, touching his forehead to the ground.

On this joyous, festive occasion arrangements for serving various kinds of delicacies were made. Swami Brahmananda had ordered large quantities of radhaballabhi and ladykenny to be prepared. Once, for a little while, he went to see the devotees and monks happily eating together. After having their midday rest, the women devotees came to him and said, "We never had this much joy in our entire life. Everything, including your holy presence and the sumptuous food, has created a kind of atmosphere we have never experienced before."

◊ ◊ ◊ ◊ ◊

Toward the last days of his life Swami Brahmananda seemed to display an all-encompassing love and compassion. While living in Belur Math, he would go out every morning for a walk. He would ask his sevak to carry with him some fruits and sweets. Coming out through the southern gate of the Math, he would enter the neighborhood where some Muslim families lived. He would distribute the fruits and sweets to the children of that neighborhood. Then he would proceed toward Belur Village and would make kind inquiries of the villagers before returning to Belur Math.

◊ ◊ ◊ ◊ ◊

Gokuldas Dey wrote in his memoirs, "In the early days Swami Brahmananda would converse only with those whom he knew or who were of similar spiritual attitude. He could never associate with those who had negative religious views.[83] But before his passing away, he mixed with all kinds of people without any reservation."

---

83. Swami Brahmananda didn't like to meet people with negative religious views. Aside from that, we must not forget that he had the ability to see through the innermost depths of a person's mind. In 1918, around 8 o'clock in the morning, Kartik was reading a book in his room on the third floor of the Udbodhan Ashrama. Suddenly Swami Brahmananda burst into the room and said to Kartik, "Leave this room. Don't tell anybody that I am here." As soon as Kartik left, he bolted the door from inside. Some wealthy person was to come and see him around that time.

SWAMI SARADANANDA
(ALSO KNOWN AS SHARAT MAHARAJ)

CHAPTER XXVII
Swami Brahmananda's Final Departure From This World

Swami Brahmananda used to say, "Brahman alone is real. This world is illusory." Yet, he was seen to be interested in the minor details of mundane activities, and often took part in discussions on apparently insignificant, worldly topics. He would sometimes quote the Upanishadic statements, "All is Brahman; there is no multiplicity in this world." "The world is unreal; everything that exists is Brahman." Many cannot properly comprehend these two utterances from the scriptures. That's why they become confused and speak against the authors of the scriptures. When they finally receive the grace of God and their guru, they will realize that the world is not real in its tangible form, but it is real as the eternal Brahman.

Sri Shankaracharya said in one place in his commentary on the *Bhagavadgita*, "This world is real as the eternally existing Atman (Brahman)." Those who experience the external form of this world, and also Brahman as its essence, are alone able to enjoy the lila of Brahman in the world. They experience this universe as full of divine consciousness. It is not indulging in poetic fantasy. It is their direct experience. Sri Ramakrishna had this experience when he worshipped Mother Kali at the Dakshineswar temple. His manasa-putra, Swami Brahmananda, also had that experience. Sri Ramakrishna left him behind to help unworthy devotees like us to ascend to Brahmaloka (the abode of Brahman).

Swami Brahmananda said, "Some experience both the noumenon (nitya) and the phenomenon (lila).... During His rash-lila, when Sri Krishna was dancing with his gopi companions, one of them said to the other, 'My friend, the one who is dancing with us is the Ultimate Reality or Parabrahman as talked about in Vedanta philosophy.' That means Sri Krishna, who was dancing, was no other than the Parabrahman. Here the noumenon and the phenomenon are the same."

◊ ◊ ◊ ◊ ◊

Swami Brahmananda once wrote to a woman disciple, "Train your mind in such a way that nothing will remain unknown to it. Merge your mind in that Great One who is your inner controller. Then your mind will be filled with tremendous power and nothing will remain unknown to you. The world has been manifested by that Glorious Being using His two modes: nitya (the noumenon) and lila (the phenomenon). Sometimes He exists as nitya; sometimes He enjoys His divine play, lila, in this tangible universe. Read about Him, hear about Him, and meditate on Him."

◊ ◊ ◊ ◊ ◊

While Swami Brahmananda was staying in Calcutta at the Balaram Mandir, Swami Saradananda would go there and see him almost every day. Every morning Swami Brahmananda went out for a walk. During those walks he sometimes went to the Udbodhan Ashrama to see Swami Saradananda. On March 22, 1922, he came to the Balaram Mandir from Belur Math. The following day he went for a visit to the Udbodhan Ashrama. Then Swami Saradananda took him upstairs to his own room.

◊ ◊ ◊ ◊ ◊

On Friday, the 24th of March, Swami Brahmananda had an attack of cholera. While out for a walk that morning, he felt exhausted after walking only a short distance. So he returned to the Balaram Mandir. He said to his sevak, "No matter what the doctor says, you can never trust this illness. Chant the name of Lord Shiva repeatedly!"

246

From this it appears that at the very beginning of his illness he knew what would happen to him. Yet, sometimes in conversations he seemed to have expressed the wish to live a little longer. With childlike simplicity he said to Dr. Nilratan Sarkar, "Please cure me. I want to be well." Sometimes he would say, "Take me to Bhubaneswar, I'll be all right if I drink the well water there." Four days before his passing away he said, "I don't like the stagnant atmosphere of Calcutta, let me go to Bhubaneswar. The air is free and clean there."

When the sevak said, "You are still very weak," he said, "I'll be able to go after three or four days."

Two days before he passed away he said to Swami Saradananda, who was seated at his bedside, "Sharat, do I have to go in spite of you being here with me?" Swami Saradananda just kept on looking at his face silently. He couldn't understand what he had meant by those words, not then and not at any time later.

Even during his illness the characteristics of Swami Brahmananda's keen sense of humour were quite evident. After his condition improved, he was given normal, solid food to eat on the first of April. The following day, as wished by him, he was being carried by his sevaks to the main, big room of the house. Even though he had become emaciated from his illness, the sevaks found it a little hard to carry him. Quoting from a popular Bengali proverb he humourously said, "The elephant, though dead, still costs one hundred thousand rupees."

He was all right for two days. Then suddenly the symptoms of diabetes appeared. He had had this problem for a while, but this time it manifested itself with virulence. The doctors gave up all hopes of his recovery. Then Swami Saradananda suggested that ayurvedic treatment should be tried. Hearing that, Swami Brahmananda humourously commented, "Why not try the hekimi (Islamic system of treatment) also?"

Nevertheless, a very famous ayurvedic physician named Shyamadas Vachaspati came and started treating Swami Brahmananda. On Sunday, the day before his passing away, Shyamadas Vachaspati came at 11 o'clock in the morning and examined the Swami's pulse. After the examination, he lost all hope of his recovery. Until that morning he was able to talk, now he lay limp and silent in his bed with his eyes wide open. Everybody thought that he had lost his speech. But seeing the sad expression on the ayurvedic physician's face, in his inimitable way he asked with a smile, "Hello, Doctor, how is your patient?" Then he himself replied to the question, saying, "You won't be able to do anything more! Now my medicine, as the scriptures say, is the holy water of the Ganga, and my physician is Lord Narayana!"

That morning he had said to Dr. Bipinbihari Ghosh, "Brahman alone is real; the world is illusory." On an earlier day he said to the ayurvedic physician, "Lord Shiva alone is the Truth; medicines are a big lie!"

On Saturday, April 8, 1922, his thirst and the burning sensation in his body increased very much. The whole day, until 11 o'clock at night, he took only little quantities of ice and lemonade. He suffered from extreme restlessness. That day around noon, the women of Balaram Bose's family came and began crying. He said to them, "I am giving you my blessings. You needn't have any fear."

After dusk Dr. Durgapada Ghosh wanted to know how he was feeling. Swami Brahmananda replied, "The scriptures tell us to tolerate all kinds of suffering without even trying to mitigate them. This is my thinking now. Please try to understand."

At midnight he asked his sannyasi disciples to come and

sit close to him. He said to them very tenderly in a soothing voice, "My children, where are you? Come closer to me." After they had come closer, he said, "Have no fear my children!" He continued giving them hope and encouragement through comforting and loving words. Then he lovingly started saying, "My Vivek, my big brother Vivekananda! ... I know Baburam. ... I know the lotus feet of Sri Ramakrishna ..." etc.

He also asked Swami Saradananda to come close to him. Swami Saradananda had spent the whole day with Swami Brahmananda. He returned to the Udbodhan Ashrama only around dusk. On the previous day he had been by Swami Brahmananda's bedside from morning till late at night. At the dead of night Swami Brahmananda asked for Swami Saradananda. Hearing that, Swami Saradananda immediately left the Udbodhan Ashrama and came to the Balaram Mandir, accompanied by Sitapati (Swami Raghavananda) and Ishwar. Sitapati and Ishwar, the two sevaks of Swami Brahmananda, had contracted fever. That's why they had been sent to the Udbodhan Ashrama nearby. Seeing Swami Saradananda, Swami Brahmananda said, "Brother Sharat, you have come! My Brahman-consciousness is in jeopardy! You are a Knower of Brahman. Give me a little Brahma-jnana!"

He replied, "Brother, Thakur has already given you everything that can be achieved in spiritual life. Is there anything else left for you to achieve?"

Swami Brahmananda said, "I am almost there. There's only a thin screen between me and Brahman."

He wanted to drink a little lemonade. Then he smiled and said, "What's happening to me? I'm talking about Brahman and lemonade at the same time!" He continued, "The idea of 'Father in heaven' is also a beautiful concept. This too is an aspect of God."

Swami Saradananda requested him to drink a little lemonade and try to sleep. Swami Brahmananda said, "My mind is now in the domain of Brahman-consciousness (Brahmaloka). It doesn't want to come down. What will you do now? All right, pour the lemonade into Brahman!" He drank a little lemonade and kept on saying, "O, how wonderful is Brahman! Brahman is the ocean! I'm floating in it on the banyan leaf of faith. Om. Salutation to the supreme Brahman (Parabrahman). Salutation to Paramatman (the Supreme Self)!"

It seemed that the cooling and spiritually refreshing touch of the ocean of Brahman was having its impact on the hearts of the assembled monks as well. Everybody present there experienced great peace. Then, coming out of his indrawn mood, Swami Brahmananda blessed his disciples present there and instilled courage into their hearts with inspiring words.[84] At that time Ishwar was holding his hand and stroking it gently. The Swami asked, "Who are you?"

Swami Saradananda gave the reply. He said, "That's Ishwar."

Then very lovingly Swami Brahmananda said, "Ishwar, you needn't have any fear. You have served me so well!" After pausing for a little while, he said, "Our Krishna is not the Krishna of pain and suffering. Our Krishna is quite different." Then

---

84. The following day also he blessed many others. For example, holding
Amulya Maharaj's hand, he said lovingly, "Amulya, my dear son, I
made you suffer a lot. I made you move from one place to another.
But whatever I did, I did for your own good. I caused you pain,
but my pain was not any less than yours." He said to Sharvananda,
"Sharvananda, you are mine in this life as well as hereafter." To
Ambikananda he said, "Why should you fear? Liberation is assured
for you. Know that I'll always be with you!" He said to Nirvanananda,
"You've served me a lot. By my blessings you will attain Nirvana." He
said to all the others, "Don't forget God. Chant His holy name. You all
belong to Him."

he paused again and in a very sweet voice chanted a scriptural verse in salutation to God. Addressing Ishwar tenderly he said, "Try to love me a little!" [85]

Suddenly his mood changed. He went on muttering to himself, "Look, Krishna has come. Please decorate my feet with ankle-bells. I'll hold Krishna's hand and dance with Him with my ankle-bells jingling. I'm the cowherd boy of Vrindaban. I'm Krishna's friend and companion.

"My Krishna is not the Krishna of pain and suffering. He is Krishna—the darling of the devotees of Vrindaban." Then he quoted from an Upanishad: "He is the Light beyond all darkness." He continued saying, "Krishna is standing on a lotus. Alas, you don't have eyes to see Him! How beautiful He looks in His yellow robe!"

Then he said, "A young child is stroking my back with his little hands and saying, 'Come with me!' You all move away. I have to go now. Om Vishnu! Om Vishnu! Om Vishnu!" He continued saying, "The writing of the script of my life is now over. My role-playing in this divine drama also ends here." Then he chanted, "O Krishna! O Krishna!"

◊ ◊ ◊ ◊ ◊

Returning from the Balaram Mandir to the Udbodhan Ashrama Swami Saradananda said, "We won't be able to hold

---

85. Ishwar told Swami Brahmananda that he didn't want to stay in the Ramakrishna Order, because he didn't like anybody there except Swami Brahmananda. The Swami knew that Ishwar craved love and affection, and was still incapable of loving anyone without any expectation. In other words, he only wanted to *receive* love and affection from others. He hadn't yet learnt to *give* love and affection to anybody. It was mainly the Swami's love and affection toward him that made Ishwar stay in the Order for as long as he did. The Swami wanted to teach Ishwar that he should learn to *give* love to at least one person. That's why he said that to him.

SRI KRISHNA

Swami Brahmananda back here any longer. We heard him talking about his vision of Sri Krishna standing on a lotus. Once, in his absence, Thakur told us that Swami Brahmananda's life would end with this vision. But he asked us not to tell him about it."

On Monday, April 10, 1922, at 8:45 pm, Swami Brahmananda, the companion of Sri Krishna in Vrindaban and the manasa-putra of Sri Ramakrishna, departed from this world, leaving behind numerous grieving devotees and friends.

APPENDIX

Sri Pareshnath Gupta's Reminiscences Revealing Swami Brahmananda's Love and Affection for His Disciples

The following incidents happened in the Bhubaneswar Math in 1920:

Nirod, Dwijen, Amiya, Haripada and a few others came to Swami Brahmananda at the Bhubaneswar Math to be invested with brahmacharya. I was married and had come there for a visit. When those monks had their brahmacharya, I felt that I had deprived myself of that wonderful opportunity because I had married. The thought made me quite sad. Understanding my mental condition, Swami Brahmananda said, "You needn't worry. I'll shoulder the entire burden of your spiritual life." But due to my weak mind, it was hard for me to feel comforted by his words. That's why I kept on asking many questions. Without showing the slightest displeasure, he gave me the same assurance again.

The following morning I accompanied him during his walk. We walked a fairly long distance. While walking, he discussed so many things. I brought some water from a pool and gave that to him to wash his hands. As I was going to the pool to collect the water, he became worried lest I slip and fall into the pool. Out of his loving concern, he cautioned me a few times to be very careful.

When I was visiting the Math, he would often say, "Good foodstuff is pretty scarce here. I wonder what we can give you to eat. Alas, we haven't been able to give you any good food!"

Once, out of paternal affection, he held me in his arms. I used to feel so close to him that I wouldn't hide anything from him. The day I departed from there, he blessed me wholeheartedly. Those memories of my association with him are the most precious possession of my life.

◊◊◊◊◊

The following incidents took place in Madras in 1921: Ramlal Dada, Bankim Ghoroi and myself took the clay image of Mother Durga from Calcutta to Madras. Swami Brahmananda arrived in Madras from Bangalore the day after we arrived in Madras. Swami Sharvananda, Sri Ramu and I went to receive him at the railway station. Seeing me he smiled and said, "It is nice that you have come. Are you all right?"

One day he asked, "Don't you want to visit Bangalore? Go and visit it once. You have come this far, won't you go and visit it?" Then he told his sevak Sujji, "Give twenty rupees to Paresh for his train fare to go to Bangalore."

When the news of Lalit Chatterjee's death came, it made him grief-stricken. That evening he talked about Lalit Chatterjee a lot.

The day I went to take leave of him before starting for Calcutta he said, "Sharvananda told me that you brought the image of Mother Durga from Calcutta. Go to him. He will pay you your return fare."

◊◊◊◊◊

The following events took place in Belur Math. The morning after Swami Vivekananda's birthday, I went to Swami Brahmananda's room to salute him. As soon as he saw me he said, "I've been thinking of you. Where were you yesterday?"

254

I replied, ""Why, Maharaj, I came and saluted you yesterday!"

He said, "So many came and saluted; can I remember all of them?"

◊◊◊◊◊

I went to Belur Math for a visit in the afternoon of Dol Purnima. A public meeting was being held, but it ended shortly after my arrival.

Swami Brahmananda was then having a walk on the grounds of Belur Math with a few devotees. A little later he came walking to the open courtyard of the monastery building. Ramlal Dada was with him. The Swami wanted to sit on the bank of the river Ganga. So I brought a bench for him to sit on. After taking his seat, he said, "I've talked so much today that my throat is burning. They make me talk a lot! But no more talking now." The evening was descending on the Math. He took a little Ganga water in his hand and facing the Ganga, saluted God a few times.

A little later he went upstairs. Following him, we came up to the upstairs veranda. He said to his sevak Ishwar, "Some amritis (a Bengali sweetmeat) have come from Dacca. Give some to Hariprasanna". He asked Hariprasanna Maharaj (Swami Vijnanananda), "How many will you eat?"

He replied, "Give as many as you want!" After serving him and Ramlal Dada, Swami Brahmananda told me to distribute the remaining amritis to the rest of us.

◊◊◊◊◊

My last meeting with Swami Brahmananda was in Belur Math. One day I arrived in Belur Math around 4 o'clock in the afternoon. I saw Swami Brahmananda sitting downstairs on a bench. He was facing the Ganga. It was quite hot that day. Bowing low, I saluted him. After loving inquiries about me, he stroked my body with great love and affection. My mind became filled with great joy. Then he asked me to sit with him on the bench. After a while the veranda on which we were seated and the courtyard were washed with cold water. With great concern in his voice, he asked me not to walk barefooted on the wet floor saying, "Don't walk on the cold, wet floor. You will catch a cold."

A little later he decided to go for a walk and asked me to go and bring his cane. I ran and brought the cane from his room. When I gave it to him, he asked, "Are you doing well mentally? How is your spiritual practice?"

I replied, "Impure thoughts come to my mind. I don't know how to handle them!"

He said, "It's natural to have such thoughts at your age. Don't worry, everything will be all right in course of time."

Walking a little more, we came close to Swami Vivekananda Temple. Then I said, "Maharaj, I would like to ask you a question."

With curiosity in his eyes he said, "Tell me what it is."

I said, "What do you want your disciples to be like?"

He smiled and asked, "Why do you want to know this?"

I replied, "If I can hear from your own mouth what you expect me to be, I can wholeheartedly try to be that way."

He laughed and said, "All right, ask me again some other day, then I'll tell you. This is an inauspicious hour on Thursday.

APPENDIX

I'll go to Calcutta in a day or two. You ask me at that time." But alas, that opportunity never came. The following day I took leave of him and returned to Calcutta.

◊ ◊ ◊ ◊ ◊

Seven days later when he was in Calcutta, he started feeling unwell. I went to see him that morning. He had just returned from his morning walk and was rinsing his hands and face with water. Entering his room a little later I saluted him. With a smiling face, he blessed me and said, "I don't know why I haven't been feeling well lately." Then he said to me, "Paresh, go and sit outside, I've got to lie down now."

He asked Swami Bhumananda to shut the door of his room. In the evening I got the news that he had had an attack of cholera.

GLOSSARY

Abhaya Mudra: Traditional hand sign made to dispel fear in the hearts of others.

Abhisheka: Ritualistic bath for the image of the deity. Also called Mahâsnânam.

Acharya: A world-teacher.

Achine tree: A tree that is not recognizable.

Adhikarika Purushas: Persons endowed with extraordinary spiritual powers.

Advaita: Non-dualism.

Ajapa: Effortless chanting of the holy name by the mind.

Ajnana: Ignorance.

Alfanso tree: A kind of mango tree.

Amritis: A kind of Bengali sweetmeat.

Anartha: Disastrous or meaningless.

Anurag: Love and devotion.

Aparigraha: The practice of non-acceptance of gifts by spiritual aspirants.

Artha: Wealth—one of the four goals of human life.

Arati: Worship using the symbols of the five elements that constitute this world.

Aratrikam: Vespers in Hindu temples or shrines. The same as Arati.

Balushai: A kind of sweetmeat.

Baudidi: An endearing and respectful term used to address an elder brother's wife. It is a Bengali word that literally means "sister-in-law."

Begunis: Eggplant fries.

Beson Flour: Chickpea flour.

Bhandar: Storeroom.

GLOSSARY

Bhandara: A feast for monks.

Bhuto Bombai tree: A kind of mango tree.

Bidis: A kind of cigar.

Bol: Oral imitation of the sound of the drums.

Brahma-sangeet: Songs about Brahman.

Brahmachari: A novice who has taken the first vows of monastic life.

Brahmacharya: The first vows in monastic life.

Brahmavadini: A woman who is a knower of Brahman.

Brinjal: Eggplant.

Chamara: The yak tail used for fanning deities in Hindu temples.

Chapatis: A kind of thin bread made with wheat flour.

Charanamitra: Holy bath water of a deity.

Chhana: Doughy fresh cheese.

Chini: Sugar.

Chuddar: A wrapper made of either cotton, wool or silk.

Chum chums: Curds made into sweets soaked in syrup.

Darga: A tomb of a Muslim saint.

Darvesh: An all-renouncing monk.

Devi: Goddess.

Devi-shakti: A girl endowed with divine propensities.

Dharma: Religious duty. Also means one of the four goals of human life.

Dharmashala: A shelter (rest house) for pilgrims.

Dhoti: A long piece of cloth worn by men in India.

Dhuni Fire: A holy fire lit up for Hindu rituals.

Dhyana: Meditation.

Dhyanam: Meditation.

Diksha: Spiritual initiation.

Dhopwali: A woman singer.

Durgabari: A building used for the annual worship of the Divine Mother Durga.

Dvaita: Dualism or pluralism.

Ekka: A two-wheeled carriage drawn by a horse.

Ektara: A single-stringed musical instrument.

Gaur: The name of an Indian melody.

Ghee: Browned butter.

Gopal Goppa: A delicious rice and lentil dish invented by Swami Brahmananda. It is made of mung dal, rice, peas, potatoes, beets, carrots, green coriander leaves, khir and ghee.

Gopi: A dairy maid.

Gopuram: Ornate temple gate.

Havishya: A sacred meal of boiled rice, vegetables and browned butter.

Hekimi: Islamic system of medical treatment.

Hemp: A narcotic such as hashish.

Hubble-bubble: Water-pipe for smoking tobacco.

Ishta: Chosen deity.

Ishwarakotis: Souls who are born free.

Jagat: The world.

Japa: Chanting of the holy name of God, sometimes using a rosary to keep count.

Japa Mala: A rosary.

Jilebi: A kind of sweetmeat.

Jivakotis: Ordinary individuals who are not born spiritually illumined.

Jive-gaja: A kind of sweetmeat.

Jnana: True knowledge of God or the Divine Reality.

Jnani: One who has known God or the Divine Reality.

Kachauri: A kind of pastry made of wheat dough that is deep fried in ghee or any other edible oil.

GLOSSARY

Kala-ajar : A fever transmitted by sand flies.

Kalai Pulse: A kind of lentil.

Kalia: A rich fish dish.

Kalikirtan: Devotional singing on the Divine Mother Kali.

Kalo Jira: Black onion seeds.

Kalpataru: Wish-fulfilling tree.

Kama: Lust or sensual desire—one of the four goals of human life.

Khichuri: A dish made of rice and lentils.

Khir: Thickened milk. Also may mean a kind of rice pudding made of thickened milk, sugar and rice.

Kirtan: Devotional singing.

Krishna-lila: The divine play of Sri Krishna. It also means a kind of theatrical performance depicting the life of Sri Krishna.

Kulakundalini: The spiritual power that lies dormant in every person like a snake in hybernation.

Laddu: A kind of sweetmeat made of chickpea flour, sugar and ghee.

Ladykenny: A kind of Bengali sweetmeat.

Leela: The world of phenomena.

Lila: The world of phenomena. Also may mean the divine play.

Lord Narayana: Lord Vishnu.

Luchi: A kind of round and thin bread made of white flour which is then deep-fried in oil or butter.

Madar Tree: Coral tree.

Madhukari: Begging for food as traditional monks are expected to do.

Mahabhava: Supreme spiritual ecstasy. Only the divine incarnations have such spiritual ecstasy.

Maharaj: A word usually used to address a monk. It means "revered sir."

Mahasamadhi: Passing away or death of a saintly soul.

Mahasnanam: Ritualistic bath for the image of a deity.

Mahavira: The last great spiritual teacher of Jainism. It also means a great hero.

Malpoa: A kind of sweetmeat made of thickened, doughy milk first deep-fried in butter and then soaked in sweet syrup.

Manasa-putra: Mind-born child.

Mathur: A singing narrative on Sri Krishna's life in Mathura.

Mangalarati: Early morning arati.

Mind-born: Manasa Putra.

Moglai Tea: A special hot drink invented by Swami Brahmananda. Put a few pods of small cardamom, cloves and cinnamon sticks inside a small bag made of cheesecloth. Then put the bag into boiling milk. Otherwise boil the bag of spices in water for a while, and then add that water to the boiling milk. Prepare a decoction of tea leaves in a separate container and put into the boiling milk. Add Saffron and sugar at the end.

Moksha: Liberation, one of the four goals of human life.

Maulavi: A Muslim teacher or scholar.

Naga: Naked.

Nama-Ramayana: Singing of the life and glories of Sri Rama.

Nirakara Brahman: Formless God.

Nirguna Brahman: The Ultimate Divine Reality, devoid of attributes.

Nirvikalpa Samadhi: A state where the mind melts away in Nirguna Brahman (the Ultimate Divine Reality).

Nitya-muktas: Those who are born free or born with spiritual illumination attained in some past incarnation.

Nitya: The noumenon.

Ostad: Maestro.

Pakhoaj: A percussion instrument used to accompany North Indian vocal music.

Panchapradipa: Ceremonial oil lamp.

Pantuya: A delicious Bengali sweet made of fresh cheese.

Papadam: A kind of thin cake made of chickpea flour.

Parabrahman: The Ultimate Reality. Supreme Brahman.

Paramahangsa: A saint who can separate the Divine Reality from this world. Also, a class of Sannyasis.

Paramatman: The Supreme Self.

Payesh: Rice pudding.

Polau: A delicious rice dish made with butter and spices.

Prana: Vital energy.

Prarabdha karma: The effects of karma that have begun to take effect.

Prasad: Consecrated food.

Premashru: Tears of divine love.

Punjabi: A kind of shirt used in India.

Puri: A kind of round and flat bread made of whole wheat flour, which is then deep-fried in some edible oil.

Purnabhisheka: A kind of sannyasa according to Tantra.

Radhaballabhi: Similar to Puri. See Puri.

Ramanama-Sankirtanam: Singing of the holy name of Sri Rama.

Rabri: A sweet made with the crust of sweetened, thickened milk.

Râgi: Short-tempered.

Rajas: According to Sankhya philosophy, one of the three 'guna's consti-tuting Prakriti or Mother Nature. It is characterized by activity, the tendency to dominate over others, boastfulness, etc.

Rasagolla: A sweetmeat made out of little balls of fresh cheese boiled in syrup.

Rash-lila: A festival associated with the life of Sri Krishna.

Rui fish: Carp fish.

Rasagollas: See Rasagolla.

Roti: A kind of flat, round, unleavened bread

Sadhana: Spiritual practice.

REMINISCENCES OF SWAMI BRAHMANANDA

Sadhu: A monk. A sannyasi.

Saguna Brahman: God with attributes.

Saguna-nirakara Brahman: God without form, but endowed with attributes.

Sakara Brahman: God endowed with form.

Samadhi: The acme of mental concentration. In this state, the mind communes with God.

Samsara: The transient universe.

Samskaras: Inherent tendencies.

Sankirtanam: Devotional singing.

Sanatana Dharma: The perennial religion. Also called Hinduism.

Sandesh: A kind of sweetmeat made of fresh cheese and sugar.

Sannyasa: The final vows of monastic life.

Sannyasin: One who has taken the final vows of monastic life.

Sarang: A kind of classical Indian melody.

Sataranchas: Carpets made of cotton.

Satchidananda Brahman: Brahman who is Eternal Existence (Sat), Absolute Knowledge (Chit) and Infinite Bliss (Anandam).

Sattwa: According to Sankhya philosophy, one of the three gunas or the constituent parts of Prakriti or Mother Nature. It is characterized by the power to reveal, clarity in thinking, serenity, compassion, etc.

Sattva Guna: The same as Sattva.(See Sattva.)

Sattvika food: Food conducive to spiritual growth.

Sevak: An attendant.

Shakta: A worshipper of the Divine Mother.

Sharbat: A cold drink made of sugar, lemon juice, yoghurt, etc.

Shraddha: Respect.

Skanda-mool: A kind of edible root.

Sutra: Thread.

GLOSSARY

Sweet curd: Sweet yoghurt.

Tala: Rhythm in music.

Tamas: One of the three gunas. Characterized by darkness, inertia and confused thinking.

Tapasya: Spiritual austerities.

Tabla: A pair of North Indian drums played with both hands.

Telakucha leaves: A kind of tropical herb.

Tilak: Holy mark put by Hindus on the forehead or the nose to show sectarian affiliation.

Upa-devatas: Some deities of the lower level.

Upanayanam: According to Hindu tradition, a ceremony connected with the investiture of the Upavita (sacred thread).

Vaishnava: A follower of the doctrine of Vaishnavism, which is the path of devotion to Lord Vishnu or to one of Vishnu's avatars (incarnations) such as Sri Krishna, Sri Rama and Sri Chaitanya.

Vatsalya Bhava: The spiritual attitude of looking upon God as one's child.

Vijnani: A vijnani knows and experiences God more intimately than the jnanis, knowing that the divine absolute or noumenon (nitya) and the world of phenomena (leela) are only two aspects of the same Ultimate Divine Reality.

Vilwa trees: Wood apple trees.

Virat Bhoga: A devotional food-offering to the all pervading Divine Spirit manifested in the form of the universe.

Vishistadvaita: Qualified non-dualism.

Vrajagopi: A milkmaid companion and devotee of Sri Krishna.

Zamindar: A rich landlord, comparable to a baron in the West.